THE POET'S MYTH OF FERNÁN GONZÁLEZ

BY

JEAN PAUL KELLER

Scripta Humanistica

Library of Congress Cataloging-in-Publication Data

Keller, Jean Paul, 1912–
The poet's myth of Fernán González / by Jean Paul Keller.
  p. cm. -- (Scripta Humanistica : 81)
Includes bibliographical references.
ISBN 0-916379-87-6: $47.50
 1. Poema de Fernán González. I. Title II. Series: Scripta Humanistica (Series); 81.
PQ6420.P54K4 1991
861--dc20   90-22462
                                                              CIP

Publisher and Distributor:
SCRIPTA HUMANISTICA
Chairman of the Board:
Bruno M. Damiani

Publication, Editorial, and Sales Offices:
1383 Kersey Lane
Potomac, Maryland 20854 U.S.A.

© Jean Paul Keller, 1990
Library of Congress Catalog Card Number PQ6420.P54K4
International Standard Book Number 0-916379-87-6

Printed in the United States of America
Impreso en Los Estados Unidos de America

THE POET'S MYTH OF FERNÁN GONZÁLEZ

Scripta Humanistica

Directed by
BRUNO M. DAMIANI
The Catholic University of America

ADVISORY BOARD

Samuel G. Armistead
University of California
(Davis)

Juan Bautista Avalle-Arce
University of California
(Santa Barbara)

Theodore Beardsley
The Hispanic Society of
America

Giuseppe Bellini
Università di Milano

Giovanni Maria Bertini
Università di Torino

Heinrich Bihler
Universität Göttingen

Harold Cannon
National Endowment
for the Humanities

Michael G. Cooke
Yale University

Dante Della Terza
Harvard University

Frédéric Deloffre
Université de Paris-
Sorbonne

Hans Flasche
Universität Hamburg

Robert J. DiPietro
University of Delaware

John E. Keller
University of Kentucky

Richard Kinkade
University of Arizona

Myron I. Lichtblau
Syracuse University

Juan M. Lope Blanch
Universidad Nacional
Autónoma de México

Louis Mackey
University of Texas

Francesco Marchisano
Pontificia Commissione per la
Conservazione del Patrimonio
Artistico e Storico della
Chiesa. Città del Vaticano

Leland R. Phelps
Duke University

Martín de Riquer
Real Academia Española

John K. Walsh
University of California
(Berkeley)

To
BGK
who served as mid-wife
over the forty-four year
gestation and birth of this book.

Acknowledgements

When I told Professor George W. Umphrey in 1946 that I had finished reading the *Poema de Fernán González* he again proved what a consummate teacher he was by responding with a question: had I been able to decide whether the poem came from the *Primera crónica general* or vice versa. Without knowing it, I was hooked and this book is the fish he landed. I trust that it pays off my debt to him.

I wish to thank the American Council of Learned Societies for a grant it made to help me during a sabbatical leave in Spain in 1971.

I further wish to express my appreciation to the editors of the HISPANIC REVIEW and the NUEVA REVISTA DE FILOLOGIA HISPANICA for permission to use materials from articles which I wrote and they published.

Finally, my thanks to Miss Esther Keller and to Dr. Vulgamore, President of Albion College, who have made possible the publication of this book .

Albion, Michigan

Foreword

It has been said that every person accepts a set of beliefs, myths, concerning transcendent matters he cannot otherwise explain and that he lives his life within those beliefs, myths. The poet-monk who composed the POEMA DE FERNAN GONZALEZ was a deeply religious man who infused his work with his own beliefs and so created his own myth about the hero and his Castile . He thus satisfactorily explained to himself at least the world in which he lived.

TABLE OF CONTENTS

Page

Foreword

Chapter One	Introduction	1
Chapter Two	The Structure of the Poem	11
Chapter Three	The Poet's Gothic Spain	22
Chapter Four	The Mysterious Origin of Fernán González	42
Chapter Five	The Hunt and Prophecy Episode	54
Chapter Six	The Hero against Islam	65
Chapter Seven	The First Battle against Navarre	89
Chapter Eight	Cortes in Leon and Aftermath	107
Chapter Nine	The Last Three Battles	126
Chapter Ten	Inversion of the Prison Episodes	136
Chapter Eleven	Liberation	147
Afterword		160
General Bibliography		161

Chapter One

Introduction

The Poem

The *Poema de Fernán González (PFG)* is a thirteenth century epic composed some three centuries after the death of the hero. It contains legendary materials which had evolved far away from historical fact. It also contains anti- and extra- historical matter. It borrows from the verses of Gonzalo de Berceo, the *Bible,* the *Libro de Alexandre,* the *Cantar de Mío Cid,* the *Chanson de Roland,* a saint's life, from a scattering of histories in Latin and Arabic, as well as from local and Roman folklore, to say nothing of Provençal tradition. Some of these borrowings are used as surface decoration, others are incorporated into the structure of the poem. A hodgepodge? Well, yes. But one that is surprisingly well ordered, worked out, and filled with consciously controlled artistic details. Written about three centuries after the death of the hero, it has survived in a single incomplete manuscript, copied by two rather careless copiers, in the fifteenth century, according to C. Carroll Marden whose critical edition of the poem appeared in 1904.[1] Recently, John S. Geary identified a third hand in a small portion of the manuscript. The whole of the original poem is prosified in the *Primera crónica general (PCG).* Almost all scholars are agreed that it was composed by a monk attached to the monastery of San Pedro de Arlanza. which lies in the heart of the *alfoz de Lara* , the estate of the father of our famous hero. Fernán González, count, first of Lara, then of Burgos, and finally of all Castilla la Vieja, died in 970. The generally accepted date of composition of the poem, as established by Marden, is 1250-71, probably ca 1250.

The poem is written in the *cuaderna vía* or *mester de clerecía,* i.e., in stanzas of four verses, all of the same consonantal rhyme, of fourteen syllables, divided in the middle, and with stress on the sixth syllable of each half-verse. This rigid metric form had been extensively used by Gonzalo de Berceo, a monk of the monastery of San Millán de la Cogolla, Spain's first poet whose name is known, in the first half of the thirteenth century. Berceo had written numerous saints' lives and other religious verse. Our monk of Arlanza made bold to rewrite the juglaresque songs about the famous count of Castile in the *cuaderna vía,* a really surprising task that presented him with tremendous difficulties in adapting the free-flowing irregular, assonanted verse, for example, of the *Cantar de Mío Cid (CMC)* , to the rigid form used by Berceo.

The legends about the hero have been the subject of our poem, of plays, of novels, of polemic debates, over the course of more than four centuries. The *romances* about the hero are still alive today. In 1958 in Santillana del Mar I fell into conversation with two men who asked what I was doing in Spain. I told them that I was studying the poem and then recited the first two verses of the ballad:

"Buen conde Fernan Gonzalez, el rey envia por vos,
que vayades a las cortes que se hazian en Leon:
Without a pause or break in the rhythm one of the two continued with the next verse:
que si vos alla vays conde dar os ha buen galardon:"[2]
and I knew that the spirit of Fernán González was alive and that I was among friends.

Purpose and Scope of this Study

This study is intended to shed light on the work, on the poet and on his purposes, thinking, and craft, as well as on his learning and on the world in which he lived. It is not a study of history as such, but will necessarily touch on many historical matters. The balladry about FG all dates from after the poet's time and will not be considered. Some legalistic matters will be of importance and will be dealt with, knowing that there is all too often a wide disparity between the law and its application. Considerable material has been included in the text because it is pertinent to the discussion, sometimes because of the interest inherent in the material itself, or because it casts a sidelight on the subject. Several matters of speculation have been included in the hope that others may have access to information that will clear up the uncertainty. Some conflicting opinions have been left without an attempt to decide between them, leaving the matter for others to investigate. Finally, it is hoped that the date of composition can be shown to be 1280-85 instead of the "1250 o muy poco después" which has been accepted since 1904.

Studies on the Poem

From the time of Amador de los Ríos and Milá y Fontanals, in the last century, studies have been appearing. The latter listed what he considered to be the original juglaresque material of the poem. A series of articles by Georges Cirot from 1909-1930 in the *Bulletin hispanique* gave an impetus to the investigations motivated by Marden's critical edition of 1904 whose introduction dealt with the history, manuscript, date, language, sources, and other matters. Menéndez Pidal's review of it made numerous emendations and additions to Marden's work and was a help in itself to an understanding of the poem. Menéndez Pidal's own edition of the work in *Reliquias de la poesía épica española* in 1951 was followed by that of Alonso Zamora Vicente in the Clásicos Castellanos series in 1954, with illuminating introduction and notes. A non-critical edition of the poem with a lengthy and useful introduction had been published by Luciano Serrano earlier in 1943. At least eight more recent editions are listed in the bibliography of the facsimile transcription of John S. Geary, 1987. Of these, Zamora Vicente's edition is probably the most helpful and readily available. Its extensive notes must, however, be used with caution, because scholarship has advanced so much since its publication that some of his statements can no longer be accepted. To the names above must be added that of Fray Justo Pérez de Urbel whose writings about his personal hero, Fernán González (FG), extended over fifty years.

It was stated years ago by Milá y Fontanals that parts of the existing poem gave evidence of coming from a now vanished, juglaresque "canto escrito de Fernán González."[3] This viewpoint is commonly accepted today and has been dealt with in several of the studies consulted. It is probable too that there were numerous shorter *cantares* composed immediately after the events they celebrated in the life of our count of Castile and that some of these are now found in the *PFG*. In no other way could the verified given names of the hero's battle leaders have been retained to appear three centuries later in our poem. It was under similar circumstances that Ercilla in the sixteenth century wrote *La Araucana* about the conquest of Chile in which he took part, composing his verses at night after the day's fighting, by the light of the campfire, on any scraps of paper he was able to find. There must have been numerous such songs, composed right after the events in the life of Fernán González. Retained and retold repeatedly, they inevitably changed greatly with oral transmission. In some cases, *cantares* were combined. In others, songs about one man or event were retold with the exploit attributed to another. This probably happened in the case of our poem.

For years French scholars were reluctant to find, much less to admit, any Spanish influence on their *chansons de gestes*. Now they both see and admit. To a lesser degree, Spanish scholars were loathe to find French influence in Spanish materials. Now, however, both groups openly trace cross-cultural influences and borrowings. This inter-culturation could hardly be otherwise in view of the thousands of pilgrims who for centuries streamed along the roads of France into Spain and then westward on their way to Santiago de Compostela. They brought their songs with them, and took back those of Spain on their return home.

Menéndez Pidal was a lifelong adherent to the theory of Germanic origin of the *cantares*. Both the *Cantar de Mío Cid* and the *Poema de Fernán González* are Castilian in origin and it was long held that such songs were not to be found in other parts of Spain. Recently the other viewpoint has been heard, because Germanic custom was not restricted to Castile, but was ingrained in much of Christian Spain, and it would be unrealistic to hold otherwise. In her doctoral thesis, *The Hypothetical Epic Narrative Sources for the Catalan Chronicles of Jaume I, Desclot, and Muntaner*, 1976,[4] Beatrice Jorgensen Concheff quotes Henry J. Chaytor's *The Provençal Chanson de Geste, 1946,* [5] citing the merging of Provence and Catalonia, and the union of Catalonia and Aragon. If Romance epic narratives are of Germanic origin, he says, it would be unreasonable to hold that the northeast corner of Spain was left without epic narrative materials. Concheff reconstructs the content of a dozen *cantares* , taking her materials from the writers in the title of her thesis. The importance of Aragon will appear later in this study.

Another source of information about the *PFG* , increasingly available and recognized now is found in Arabic in the works of historians who wrote voluminously in the Middle Ages in distinction from the chroniclers in Christian Spain whose terse, laconic statements in Latin for centuries in all too many cases recorded little beyond the most important doings of the kings. Not until the *Crónica najerense,* ca 1160, (a recent study shows that it may have to be dated a bit later)[6] does any significant entry in these Latin accounts include material outside royal occurrences. And just as

Moorish histories exaggerate and extol Moorish victories over the Christians while commonly omitting all or most references to defeats, so also do the Latin writings often making victories of the Christians greater and minimizing their defeats or leaving them unmentioned. Since histories in both languages often incorporated marginal glosses into later texts, frequently with variations, it was not unusual for still later authors to give both versions of the same event as if there had been two happenings. This same process of duplication may have been at work in the *PFG*.

The poet was a man of his time. And he was also a monk who was educated and trained in the beliefs of the Church. It was inevitable that his poem should reflect the intellectual, cultural, and religious world in which he lived. He adapted juglaresque verses, pious legends, and much more to his poem, adding whatever needed, in such a way that we can see into the spiritual, cultural, religious, and historical world in which he lived.

Historical Background

In order to understand what Fernán González did in his lifetime, it is necessary to know something of the Spain into which he was born. [7] Ordoño II (913-923) was king of Leon at the beginning of the tenth century. Sancho Garcés, king of Navarre to the northeast, was married to a Toda, who was a redoubtable, ambitious, and consummate politician. To cement an alliance with Leon, Toda married her daughter Sancha to King Ordoño already fifty years old. At his death within the year, Toda married Sancha to Alvaro Harrameliz, count of Alava, to the south of Navarre. At Ordoño's death the crown passed to his sons, first to Fruela II, then to Alfonso IV, called *el monje*, because despondent over the death of his wife, he abdicated in favor of his brother Ramiro II and entered a monastery. After two years he left the cloister, rallied his supporters and retook the throne, only to be driven out by Ramiro and captured along with three sons. All four were blinded and shut up in the monastery, but a fourth son was left unharmed, (some say it was Fruela's son). More of him later.

Toda was still busy, and when the Galicia-born first wife of Ramiro II died, Toda married Elvira, another daughter, to the king of Leon. Then when Alvaro Harrameliz died, she married the twice-widowed Sancha to Fernán González, a promising young man. Lying between Leon and Navarre, Castile's geographic position was now enhanced with both those countries by the alliances Toda had effected and became increasingly important. Ramiro II found it expedient over a period of years to give help, favor, and tolerant treatment to his brother-in-law, and allowed him to expand and consolidate seven counties into one greatly enlarged Castile. However, in 943 Ramiro had to jail Fernán González, along with the latter's *consuegro*, Diego Muñoz, count of Saldaña, probably because those two had intentionally failed to support Ramiro in a war against the Moors who had invaded Leon. Released and restored to lands and position, the Castilian became even stronger when Ramiro married his older son Ordoño to Urraca, daughter of the count of Castile and Sancha. This son by Ramiro's first wife, the *gallega*, became Ordono III. His younger half-brother was Sancho, by Ramiro's second wife, the Navarrese princess Elvira. Toda wanted her grandson to rule Leon and allied with Fernán González in an unsuccessful attempt to oust Ordoño III from the throne. The latter then repudiated his wife, Urraca, who went back to Castile, to her parents but later was taken back by Ordoño. When he died after a reign of five years, Sancho, took the crown, much to Toda's satisfaction. He was proud, vain, and overbearing, according to Moorish historians, as well as so obese he could not ride a horse. Fernán González, his uncle, rallied disaffected Leonese nobles and with them forced Sancho I from the throne, replacing him with cousin Ordoño, the one who had not been blinded years before with *el monje* and his three sons. As Ordoño IV, this puppet-king soon found himself married to Urraca, widow of Ordoño III, and daughter of our count and Sancha. Sancho fled first to Navarre, then to Cordoba where Abderrahaman III, the Moorish king, had him treated by the royal physician for his obesity. Slimmed as in his early years, he went north with a Moorish army, strengthened by Navarrese forces from grandmother Toda and uncle King García Sánchez. The latter kept Fernán González busy on a second front and thus prevented his helping Ordoño IV who had to face Sancho I in Leon with only a few Leonese adherents to help him. Sancho, now on horseback as befitted a king, routed cousin Ordoño IV who fled northward and then south to Cordoba, without Urraca and maybe without their two sons. There he was well received and kept by Abderrhaman who refused to give him troops for an attempt to retake the throne of Leon.

While Sancho was defeating Ordoño with a Moorish army, in 960, García Sánchez and his Navarrese troops fought, captured, and jailed Fernán González, and held him in a prison near the border with Moorish territory for a year, resisting all Moorish efforts to make him turn the Castilian over to them. The Navarrese king finally released his prisoner and then married his daughter, princess Urraca, to the count whose first wife, Sancha, sister of García Sánchez, had died in 659. Sancho I, now restored to the throne, and his uncle, the count of Castile, reached a *modus vivendi* and lived in an uneasy truce or peace, with the latter virtually independent from Leon. The years until FG's death were marked by almost yearly incursions of the Moors into Castilian territory, with the count increasingly weaker due to well-advanced age. He finally died in 970, the same year as his brother-in-law, the king of Navarre. One final note, on the two families. Fernán González's daughter Urraca, widowed from Ordono III, and separated and probably divorced or widowed from Ordoño IV, again served as political pawn when she was married to Sancho Garcés II, son of García Sánchez.

During our hero's long military career, the Moorish king was Abderrahman III, a gifted military leader, and until 939 when he was defeated at Simancas by Ramiro II, he repeatedly made incursions into Christian territory. Throughout the poem, the Moorish leader is Almanzor, who in historical fact did not appear until after Fernán González was dead. This is another of the many anachronisms in the traditional materials current in the time of our poet who was no more concerned with the niceties of historical fact when it did not fit his purpose than were the *juglares* before him. In this case he may be excused, because the fame of Almanzor was so great that in the course of evolution of epic songs via oral transmission his name became almost a generic term for a great military leader. This is so true that we find it already in the *Chanson de Roland*, ca 1120,[8] with that meaning. He was a worthy successor to the equally outstanding Abderrahman III who waged so many campaigns against the Christians from the reign of Ordoño II until after the death of Ramiro II.

Axioms and Corollaries

Inherent in this study is the belief that there was a continuing life to *cantares* about the hero, some of them composed and sung shortly after the purported events they portrayed. Proper names of real men who are given as participating in the battle of Hacinas can also be found in documents of the period proving that there was a song composed about the battle, incorporating the names of those men while they were still alive or at least in the memory of participants in that combat. They were not written down in a list so that three centuries later our poet might consult it for his work. They prove the near contemporaneity of the event and a song about it, and that there was continuity over the centuries. Changes occurred as the audience changed, as more battles were fought in succeeding generations and were set down in new *cantares*. Clear, accurate details about one event became confused with those of another and gave way to new or reworked materials. At times these were combined with songs about other occurrences as the *juglares* plied their craft and kept the public interested by dressing up the old favorite materials in new guise. In his *Libro de buen amor,* ca 1340, Juan Ruiz told of the verse forms, songs, music, instruments, and dances which he had copied from the Moors. Ramón Menéndez Pidal has written about Moorish influences on the *cantares* and *canciones* of medieval Spain in his *Poesía árabe y poesía europea* (1941) and has shown their contribution to Spanish and other literatures, particularly in the 12th century. And his *Poesía juglaresca y juglares* (1942)[9] made clear how greatly Spanish life in courtly circles was influenced by both Provençal and French poets in the twelfth and thirteenth centuries. The *PFG* at one point shows these influences, absorbed and incorporated into its verses. As Menéndez Pidal observed, these was no *solución de continuidad* in the transmission of epic materials in medieval Spain.

It must be pointed out that what the poet omitted, what the *juglares* dropped or decided not to put into song is as indicative of their art and craft as what they included. Selection of materials is highly significant. There are many chapters in the *Primera crónica general (PCG)* which tell of exploits of our hero. Virtually the whole poem is prosified in that chronicle, which fortunately for us contains the few passages which are missing from the only extant manuscript of the work. The chronicle contains numerous chapters in which Fernán González appears, but which are not to be found in any episode of the poem. These historical matters, omitted from the poem, were clearly available to the poet, at least in the *Cronicon mundi, (Tudense)* 1236, of Lucas de Tuy, and the *De rebus hispaniae, (Toledano)* 1243, of Rodrigo de Toledo. The fact that they were not included by the monk of Arlanza is significant. Neither he nor the *juglares* were interested in matters that portrayed their hero in an unfavorable light, in which he called on others for help, or in which he may have been guilty of a treacherous or unworthy act. Since the materials were available to the poet, their omission shows that he exercised his right or duty as he selected only those which redounded to the advantage of his hero. It is probably fair to assume that there were songs that dealt with Ramiro II's coming to help Fernán González at the battle of Osma, as recorded in the *PCG*, a victory associated with the king and therefore not included in the

PFG. Neither do we find anything in the poem about Ramiro's jailing of the hero for not coming to aid his king in battle against the Moors, as recorded in the PCG. The poet chose not to include in his work this matter of a vassal failing to support his liege lord. Nor did he tell of the Castilians joining with Prince Sancho and the king of Navarre in an unsuccessful,and therefore less than glorious attempt to remove brother Ordoño III from the throne of Leon. The poet did not tell of how his hero later on unseated Sancho I and put Ordoño IV in his place. The latter was a pusillanimous individual who could not maintain himself in power and ignominiously fled to Cordoba where he cravenly begged for help in regaining his lost throne. Little wonder that the poet omitted this from his poem. He is very careful throughout to show his hero only in a favorable light. In so doing he was, of course, merely following the pattern of those who wrote poems about other heroes of the past. It could not be otherwise. "De mortuis nihil nisi bonum." Speaking only good of the dead applies as much to heroes of the epic as to others.

It is commonly accepted now that there was a final juglaresque version of the *cantares* about FG, designated as the *Cantar de Fernán González,* (hereafter *CFG)* on which the Arlantine based much of our poem. Avalle-Arce's work and that of Beverly West are clear demonstrations of the successive stages of development of the legends, showing how they grew and changed. The *PCG* which is much quoted in this study, was finished in 1289. The portions which deal with FG were based in great measure on the *Tudense* and the *Toledano* so that its major sources were available to and may have been used by our poet.

NOTE   Quotations are given as found in the sources, with their variant spellings and accents or lack thereof. Words and phrases in a foreign language are in italics, as is customary, unless they are repeated from a text, in which case they are enclosed in quotation marks. Geographical names are in English spelling unless diacritical marks are needed.

---

[1]   There apparently were other manuscripts of a poem or poems about FG. Gonzalo de Arredondo used one as a basis for his *Crónica del Conde FG,* 1514, which he says he took from a *Crónica de los rimos antiguos,* which Marden considered was the *clerecía* text he edited. Argote de Molina claimed to have a copy of a poem about the count "que yo tengo en mi museo." Fernando Colón, son of the Discoverer, also was said to have the MS of a poem about FG which began and ended: "en el nombre de Dios" and "beuamos vna bez," showing that it was not the text we have today. These manuscripts have all disappeared.

In 1986, José Hernando Pérez published a preliminary study, "Nuevos datos para el estudio del *PFG" Boletín de la Real Academia de la Historia* (BRAH)

(Madrid: 1986) pp. 135-52. He describes the text incised on a ceramic tile of fifteen verses of a *PFG*, transcribes them, discusses their context in our poem, and deals with linguistic matters.

[2] R. Menéndez Pidal, "Notas para el romancero de Fernán González," *Homenaje a Menéndez y Pelayo*, prólogo de D Juan Valera (Madrid: 1899), I, pp. 429-507.

[3] Manuel Milá y Fontanals, *De la poesía heroico-popular castellana*, ed. Riquer y Molas (Barcelona: 1959), Footnote 2, p. 259.

[4] Beatrice Jorgenson Concheff, *The Hypothetical Epic Narrative Sources for the Catalan Chronicles of Jaume I, Desclot, and Muntaner*, Ph.D. thesis, Univ. of Wisconsin, (Madison: 1976).

[5] Henry J. Chaytor, *The Provençal Chanson de Geste*, (London: Oxford Univ. Press, 1946), pp. 14-15.

[6] Georges Cirot, "Une chronique léonaise inédite," *Bulletin Hispanique*, 11, juillet-septembre, No. 3, (1909) pp. 259-282. This chronicle has been renamed *La crónica najerense*.
Derek Lomax has shown that it may have to be dated as of 1270 or later. See his article: "La fecha de la crónica leonesa " in *Anuario de estudios medievales*, (Barcelona: 1974-79) pp.405-6.

[7] The main works consulted for the history of these years are:
R. Menéndez Pidal, *Primera crónica general*, 2 vols. (Madrid: Gredos, 1955). Hereafter *PCG*.
Justo Pérez de Urbel, *Historia del condado de Castilla*, 3 vols. (Madrid: CSIC, 1945.) Hereafter *Historia*.
Cristina Grande Gallego, Margarita Cantera Montenegro, and Jesús Cantera Montenegro, "Orígenes de León y Castilla" in *Historia de León y Castilla*, coordinada por Enrique López Castellón. Vol. II (Reno: 1983).
Manuel Marquez Sterling, *Fernán González, First Count of Castile: The Man and the Legend*. (Univ. of Mississippi: Romance Monographs, 1980).
Justiano Rodríguez, *Ramiro II, Rey de León*, (Madrid: CSIC, 1972).

[8] *Chanson de Roland*, vs. 849, 909, 1275. It is used with the meaning of a Moorish military leader, spelled *almaçor* in the MS text.

[9] R. Menéndez Pidal, *Poesía árabe y poesía europea*. 4th ed. (Madrid, Espasa Calpe, 1955), pp. 19-55.
----------------------, *Poesía juglaresca y juglares*, 4th ed. (Madrid, Espasa Calpe, 1956.)

Chapter Two

The Structure of the *Poema de Fernán González*

Any discussion of the *PFG* must consider the plan which the poet followed and must clarify some of the matters which resulted from it. "The key to his procedure lies in the number three which has almost a magic fascination for him and which orders his work throughout. In no other work of Spanish literature does it exert a more important influence than in the *PFG* on structure, details, and method of composition."[1] That view has been only slightly modified since it was written some forty years ago. Scholars have agreed and disagreed with portions of that article. Another study on composition of the poem, by Joaquín G. Casalduero, divides it into only two portions, while agreeing with most of the article of 1957. [2] It is hoped that greater detail of statement in this chapter will clarify parts of the original statement.

The poem starts, most fittingly, since it was composed by a monk, with what was virtually a traditional invocation to the Holy Trinity, borrowed almost directly from Gonzalo de Berceo,[3] himself a monk of the monastery of San Millán de la Cogolla, which lay about thirty miles from the hero's home. Here the poet sets the tone for his pious and patriotic story of the man who fought for the honor and glory of God and Castile. (By the time of the poet Castile was no longer a county but rather a kingdom. In any case it was the *patria chica* of both the poet and his hero.) Then after a brief introduction, comes the first main section, twenty-three per cent of the whole poem, which summarizes the history of Spain from the time of the Gothic kings to the advent of FG. The second main section, fifty-three percent, deals with the military victories which establish the hero's supremacy over the Moslems/Moors and the Kingdom of Navarre. The third main section, which begins with the first mention of King Sancho I of Leon (mistakenly called Sancho Ordonnez instead of Sancho Ramírez because oral tradition had lost sight of the fact that he succeeded his brother Ordonno III, not his father Ramiro II), is devoted principally to the struggle whereby FG freed his Castile from subservience to Leon. The ending of the poem and a few portions within the text have been lost, but are considered to be preserved in the prose of the *Primera crónica general.* [4]

Each of the three main sections subdivides into three parts.

I   Spain before FG
    A   Gothic kings
    B   Conquest by Moslems
    C   Reconquest to advent of FG
II Establishment of hero's supremacy over Moslems and Navarre
    A   First battle against Moslems
    B   First battle against Navarre
    C   Second battle against Moslems
III Liberation of Castile from Leon
    A   Cortes in Leon with sale of horse and hawk; capture and imprisonment of FG in Navarrese jail; release by and marriage to Sancha
    B   Second battle against Navarre with capture and imprisonment of García Sánchez and release through intervention of Sancha;   third battle against Moslems; third battle against Navarre
    C   Cortes in Leon, imprisonment, release by Sancha; negociations over debt;   liberation of Castile from Leon

One may well object to the above outline on the grounds that, as Aristotle observed, everything has a beginning, middle, and end, and can be divided into three parts. Let us look, therefore, at one of the above portions, II A, slightly expanded, and see whether it was mere chance that produced the structure as outlined above.

    II   Establishment of hero's supremacy over Moslems and Navarre
        A   First battle against Moslems
            1   Events leading to battle
                a   Capture of Carazo by FG, anger of Almanzor, approach of Moorish army
                b   Discussion of Castilians as to whether to fight
                c   Hunt and prophecy episode
            2   Battle of Lara
                a   Rider and horse engulfed by chasm
                b   Fighting up to Almanzor's tent
                c   Anger and flight of Almanzor
            3   Events after battle
                a   Pursuit
                b   Collection of booty from battlefield

c Gifts to San Pedro de Arlanza

From this sub-analysis it is clear that the tripartite construction of the primary and secondary divisions of the poem is continued into the tertiary and quaternary divisions as well, and some of the latter even one stage beyond that point. Most, if not all, of the A, B, and C headings of the main outline can be divided in like manner, as a glance at any part of III will show. This regularity of construction can hardly be ascribed to mere chance. The poet first assembled the available materials and after studying them chose those which would let him form his outline by threes. He then composed his verses, borrowing and adapting from materials he had heard or read whatever he needed to fill out his pre-established plan.

Let us now look at the number three used as a surface decoration. FG is said to be one of three brothers, which was not true. There were three hermits in the chapel discovered by FG on his boar hunt. Of the three, one would have been enough for only one, Pelayo, speaks. He foretells, among other things, difficulties within three days. To encourage his men to fight in the first battle against the Moslems, the hero said that the enemy was not worth three beans, that thirty wolves (the Castilians) would kill thirty thousand sheep (the enemy). [5] In this battle, our hero faced the foe with three hundred horsemen. The second battle against Almanzor's forces was also full of the number three. The hero divided his army into three parts of three, six, and six thousand men respectively. They attacked from three quarters, and would not have fled if the thirty thousand enemy troops had been three times as many. The battle lasted three days and pursuit ended on the third day, and FG completed a threesome of kings killed. There were three battles against Navarre of which the last is merely a filler, with no apparent purpose other than to complete another threesome.

The above paragraph gives fifteen occurrences, and there are more, of the number three out of the thirty-three to be found in the poem. Any of them could be changed, even those which are connected with the time sequences of the battle which have been worked into the structure. To understand the importance of the threes, one must consider them in the light of the use of other numbers. A check of the poem shows that eighteen different numbers are used seventy-three times in situations that are significant.[6] Of these, thirty-one, as just stated, involve threes, which is eight times the four occurrences to be expected if the number three were not given more weight than any other. Of the others which are not three, thirty-one can be explained on the basis of sources the poet was following, on set phraseology, or on symbolic use.[7] Only eleven times does the poet use numbers without an apparent reason and even some of those might be explained. Since three is used eight times as often as might be expected if it were not constantly on the poet's mind, it is hard to deny its importance.[8]

If the influence of the number three now be admitted, in view of the evidence given above as to structure and incidental detail, it opens to us the possibility of using it as a criterion with which to test the poem in several ways. If an episode runs counter to historical fact and it is one of a set of three like or parallel events, we may well ask why the monk of Arlanza used it. Did he find it in some Latin chronicle, in the *CFG* or another juglaresque work, in some other poem ascribed to some other man, or elsewhere? It must not be forgotten that the Arlantine was working under the influence of, but not shackled by, Gonzalo de Berceo who had written "Al non escribimos si non lo que leemos," and therefore we may hope to find a source for the extra-historical matter in question. Conversely, if we find a number, not the magic three, we may ask why it was used. We start with the lost ending of the poem which is found in the prose of the *PCG*.

As seen from the outline, III C is the last third of the third main section, of which the final portion is missing from the manuscript. The *PCG* supplies the content of the lost portion. It gives us the third meeting of FG and King Sancho I of Leon, the third imprisonment in the poem, and the third release effected by Sancha. Finally, in the freeing of Castile, it brings to a glorious close a series of three successful struggles against the Moslems, Navarre, and Leon. When viewed in this light there can be little doubt that the lost portion was a part of the poet's original plan. Ordinarily, the ficticious freeing of Castile from Leon, attested to in the *Crónica najerense*, ca 1160, is considered as proof that the lost ending was part of the poet's plan.[9] The above threes give supporting structural evidence as well.

Let us now consider the prophecy made by the hermit Pelayo for it is the key to several matters in the poem. First, as already pointed out, the three hermits could be reduced to one, for only Pelayo speaks. Second, he foretold that the hero would 1) win great victories over Almanzor, retake much land, and shed the blood of kings, 2) would be jailed twice, and 3) would be in difficulties before the third day. This is a three part prophecy with the first made up of three parts. We ask why the poet had Pelayo foretell two jailings instead of three. The *PCG* tells of three, but one must be cast out for two reasons: it is merely a retelling of the first, transposed twenty years and three kings later (as will be shown in a subsequent chapter) and it brought no glory to the hero because he had failed in his duty as a loyal vassal. Our poet had another jailing in mind, ficticious to be sure, which would bring honor and prestige to his hero, which would fill out the threesome of jailings, and which indeed is in the

PFG. It was the historians of the *PCG* (Chap 717) who felt free to add, as it were, fact to fancy in telling of a jailing of FG by his king, Ramiro II. It must have irked the Arlantine poet, however, to depart from his pattern of working by threes, for he fought against the compulsion and devised a way out. If the hero was to be jailed only twice, then let someone elso be jailed so as to have another set of three like occurrences. He therefore composed FG's second battle against King García Sánchez in which the latter was defeated and captured, held in jail for twelve or thirteen months, and finally released through the intervention of Sancha, wife of the hero. Chronicles of the period record no such battle or misadventure of the Navarrese king. Furthermore, this time the poet changes his regular pattern in recounting battles. Five times he states specifically where the fight took place. This time he states merely that it was "a cabo del condado" avoiding the danger of having his statement questioned by anyone who knew the real history of Navarre. Because of the lack of corroboration in reliable chronicles and because of the apparently intentional vagueness of his changed pattern we can ascribe this battle and jailing to the poet or to his borrowing from juglaresque materials. Furthermore, and most important, it is artistically of merit for it balances the treacherous capture and jailing of FG by his brother-in-law with a contrasting, honorable victory over the latter in battle, and thus provides a suitable vengeance that restores the lustre of the count.

The first battle against Navarre as the poet gives it to us is non-historical because of the death at the hands of FG of King Sancho Garcés, father of the king of the preceeding paragraph, at the hands of FG.[10] The Navarrese ruler had abdicated in 924 in favor of his son García Sánchez and died two years later before FG came into prominence. The poem says that it took place at the Era Degollada which is a part of Valpirre, scene also of the third battle of FG against Navarre. Local tradition still points out the "piedra del conde' which connects the valley with our hero.[11] The count's name, apparently, was associated with that of the Era Degollada as well as with that of Valpirre, and both toponymics were used in telling about the hero. Our poet needed three battles against Navarre and used both names, one of them twice, as scenes of conflicts in his work. It is certain that FG and his Navarrese in-laws did fight more than once, but these three battles are all suspect as told by the poet. It is equally true that our monk of Arlanza used whatever juglaresque materials suited his needs. As historical reality faded into legend through oral transmission it may have given us here a duplication of one battle told again in different guise.

Why did he say that FG had killed the Navarre king? The battle was to be one of three against Navarre in the poem. The death of King Sancho added to the deaths of two Moorish kings slain by our hero made another three.¹² In his *Historia del condado de Castilla,* Fray Justo Pérez de Urbel posits that it was the son Sancho of García Sánchez and not the father Sancho who was slain by FG in this battle.¹³ He may be right, but this would make it necessary for us to believe that a young, inexperienced Prince Sancho led his troops against his battle-hardened uncle while his father and grandmother Toda were away in Cordoba seeking troops in support of Sancho I, whom FG had deposed. Toda was determined to drive out Ordono IV and restore her grandson Sancho to the throne. Furthermore, Pérez's position would make it a prince rather than a king who was killed here. This would destroy an important set of three kings slain by the hero. The *juglares* probably put in the deaths of the two Moorish kings, but that of Sancho Garcés was almost certainly added by the Arlantine.

In the poem's third battle against the Navarrese García Sánchez invades and ravages Castilian territory to avenge the affront his honor suffers in his jailing by FG. The poet by now seems almost tired of battles of Castile against Navarre and rushes through this one hurriedly. In mid-battle, apparently through no fault of the poet, the manuscript breaks off with the verses:
Quiso Dios al buen conde esta graçia fazer,
que moros nin cristianos non lo podian vencer. (752ab)
The *PCG* (Chap 716) brings this battle to a close saying "Et fue allí el rey Don Garçia uençudo con todo su poder," which is not historically true. To this the *Cl344* , in what is almost certainly a later addition, adds that FG killed the king. If the traditional juglaresque materials of the *CFG* carried this latter ending, our poet omitted it probably to avoid the death of a fourth king at the hands of our hero.

We now come to the three battles against the Moslems.¹⁴ Here we are at as much of a loss as before, as it is not clear, from what Christian and Arab chroniclers say, just how many times our hero did fight the 'Infidels" either as a loyal vassal at the side of his king or single-handed against them. It may well be that he faced them three times as the poem tells us with only his Castilians to help him, possibly at Lara, Hacinas, and in the Tierra de Campos as the poet says. Historical records give no support for these encounters. They are not a total loss, however, for in connection with these battles against the Moslems, according to our poet, there were three occurrences which must be ascribed to supernatural forces. The first was the opening up of a chasm which engulfed a rider and his steed and then closed over them, striking dismay into the Castilians. FG managed to use the disaster to encourage his men. The second was the appearance of a "flaming serpent" in the sky, which filled the Castilians with dread. Again the hero used the horrendous omen to encourage his men. The third was the appearance of Santiago and his heavenly host just in time to turn the tide of battle and save the

Christians from defeat. All three of these, which must be termed miracles, were in connection with fighting the Moslems. It is true that there is one for an encounter with Navarre, where Christian is arrayed against Christian, but this is to show God's displeasure over the treachery by which FG was captured, not a battle.[15] Our poet-monk used these supernatural signs to work out part of his purpose of showing the hero as God's chosen instrument working with Him against Islam.

There is another matter connected with the battles against the Moslem foe. In the *Cantar de Mío Cid (CMC)*, Ruy Díaz divided his troops into two parts of which the second was to attack from another side after the main force had joined battle with the enemy.[16] Menéndez Pidal quotes from an Arabic history the statement that the Moslems believed this second group was the vanguard of a supporting army and therefore withdrew, leaving victory to the Cid.[17] In the *PFG* there is a fairly elaborate account of the strategy and preparation for the second battle against the Moors, but because of the number three it must be cast out in its entirety. The poem says that San Millán appeared to the hero in a dream and ordered him to divide his forces into three parts and to attack from three quarters. The divisions were to be of three, six, and six thousand men respectively. The battle lasted three days and pursuit ended on the third day. It seems to have been based mainly on accounts of the victory of King Ramiro II of Leon at Simancas, in which FG and the king of Navarre aided the Leonese. The whole episode in our poem was designed to reestablish the connection of the poet's monastery of San Pedro de Arlanza with the hero and to destroy that of the rival monastery of San Millán de la Cogolla, as will be shown in Chapter Five.

We turn now to consider the poem as a whole and to clarify the relationship between the several sections. The first with a summary of Spanish history prior to the appearance of the hero shows the slow development of Gothic Spain which was abruptly ended by the treachery of count Julian and the conquest by the Moors. Note well the rise, treachery, and fall. This was followed by the slow process of the Reconquest in which both Leon, and Navarre became strong enough to be a threat to the unorganized area that was to become FG's Castilla Vieja, the future heart of the nation. With the appearance of our hero, in the second section we have his three great military victories and the rise of Castile. When he attended "cortes" in Leon at the start of the third section he quickly settled problems others were unable to resolve. Immediately afterwards he was lured into an ambush by the offer of marriage to Sancha, was captured, and imprisoned. Rise, treachery, and fall. Again FG struggled upwards in a series of military encounters and the poet closes this portion with the statement that neither Christian nor Moslem had ever defeated the hero. Then again at *cortes*, falsely and unjustly accused by his liege lord, Sancho I of Leon, of rebellion against the Crown, he was seized and imprisoned once more. Rise, treachery or false accusation, and fall. Finally, in the missing ending of the poem, which we have in the prose of the *PCG*, the inevitable rise, as he wins his lifelong struggle to make Castile strong enough to be free and Sancho I grants independence to Castile in exchange for cancellation of his debt to FG. The cycle has occurred three times. The first is related rather briefly, the second at length, and the third almost hurriedly. Because of the change of pace, with each succeeding cycle, the reader may not be aware of the recurrence of the theme. Moreover, the episodes of the cycles do not correspond to the main divisions of the poem, so the reader is further thrown off his guard.

The *CMC* also is made up of three sections, with three themes; undeserved suffering, glorious achievements, and justification. The themes of the *PFG* can be given those same headings, although they do not occur in that order. One of the reasons for the far higher artistic quality of the *PMC* is that the poet was not laboring under a preconceived plan as complicated as that which shackled the poet of the *PFG*. Nor were his variable meter and assonantal rhyme as restricting as the mono-rhymed, Alexandrine quatrains used by the poet of Arlanza.   In the *PFG* we probably have the first example in Spanish literature of a work that suffers from too complex a poetic art. It is a reminder that simplicity is a prime element of artistic success.

It is easy to see now the reasons for the anti- and extra-historical portions of the poem. It is also clear why the poet had to borrow from such disparate sources as those mentioned in the Introduction of this study: there simply weren't enough threes in current legends, enough threes of similar episodes about the hero to fill out the framework of his plan. It should be a matter for admiration that he carried out as well as he did that task of selecting, adapting, adding "de su propia cosecha" and fitting together the many pieces that make up the completed poem.

---

[1] See J.P.Keller, "The Structure of the *Poema de Fernán González,"*   *Hispanic Review*,   XXV, No. 4 (1957),   p. 235.   Portions of this article are used here through courtesy of the editors of the   *Hispanic Review.*

[2] Joaquín G. Casalduero, "Sobre la composión del *Poema de Fernán González,"* *Anuario de estudios medievales,* 5 (1968),   pp.181-206.

[3] Gonzalo de Berceo, *"Vida de Santo Domingo,"* *BAE*, LVII, Madrid (1952), p. 39. See also note 1, p. 1 of the Zamora Vicente edition of the *PFG*,   Clásicos castellanos, (Madrid: 1946). All references to the *PFG* in this book will be to this edition.

⁴ The lost ending of the poem is in the *PCG*, ed, R. Menéndez Pidal, (Madrid, Gredos, 1955) II Chaps 717-720. In the two portions missing within the poem. Marden numbers the first as stanzas 5l9c-523, the second as 701c-712. They concern the hero's encouraging his troops and the start of the third day of battle, Sancha's intervention to secure the release of her father from jail, and the summons of FG by Sancho I who was then besieged by the Moors.

⁵ *PFG* , p. 66, stanza 222 and note to stanza. Janer's edition of the poem reads: "Yrien tres lobos a treinta mil oveias," whereas the *PCG* gives: "mas pueden tres leones que x mill ouieas, et matarien xxx lobos a xxx mil corderos."

⁶ Not included in the count are: indefinite articles (some of which may really stand for the numeral one); contrasts of uno-otro, cada uno, a primera campana (early in the morning), numerals repeated in reference to the same matter when they have been counted at its first occurrence.

⁷ Sources given or recognizable: çient fermosas donzellas (104b); com diz la escrytura syete fueron (134b); Librest a los tres ninnos de los fuegos ardientes (109a); saquest a Daniel de entre dos leones (108b), etc.
Set phraseology: ocho dias-una semana; çient annos-un siglo.
Symbolic: the poet uses ten or a multiple for quantities noticeably larger than those from one to nine. Big amounts are shown by multiples of one hundred and enormous ones by thousands.

⁸ The best single volume consulted on the subject is *Medieval Number Symbolism by Vincent Foster Hopper* (New York: 1938), from which most of the following has been taken.
In universal folklore, one is unity, two is diversity, three is "all" in that it is the first number with a beginning, middle and end. It is the "best" as it is the final element of good, better, best. It is holy as it represents the Trinity and the triad. Four is the number of Earth. Ten is completeness, perfection, finality. In folkloric literature the three attempts, the three guesses, three suitors, three wishes, etc. are almost universally found.

The Old Testament contains many examples of the use of the number three: the triple blessing of God in Genesis 1; Ezequiel names three men of special sanctity-Noah, Daniel, and Job; the Lord calls Samuel three times; Elijah restores life to the dead child by stretching himself on it three times. From the New Testament come the three Magi and their three gifts, Peter's threefold denial, the three days between Christ's death and resurrection, the three figures of the Transfiguration; the three disciples at Gethsemane are awakened three times, Christ is tempted three ways, Christ appears three times after his resurrection.

The Book of Revelation is full of cabalistic symbolism. Its complex system of concealed meaning is intelligible only to those who know this art which Jewish writers had carried to a high level, and which has been much studied by Christian scholars. In the seventh century St. Isidore wrote: "other numbers appear in the Holy Scriptures whose nature none but the experts in this art can wisely declare the meaning of...Take number from all things and all things perish. Take calculation from the world and all is enveloped in dark ignorance, nor can he who does not know the way to reckon be distinguished from the rest of the animals" (*Etym.*, III, 4, 4). In fact Isidore devoted a whole book to the subject: *Liber numerorum qui in sanctis scripturis occurrunt.* Given the influence of Isidore in the Church in Spain in the centuries which followed him, it is not difficult to understand that number symbolism was extremely important. In the thirteenth century Albertus Magnus discussed the three methods and times of the adoration of God, the three attributes of God, the three dimensions of space, and the three dimensions of time. The number three, he concludes, is in all things and "signifies the trinity of natural phenomena." St . Thomas Aquinas, contemporary of our poet of Arlanza and of Albertus, wrote that "The Creator is threefold: Father, Son, and Holy Ghost The creature also is threefold and its triplicity is specifically related to the Trinity...." St. Thomas quoted *Job* ii. 8-9 as authority for the three dimensions of God. "Furthermore, by His rising on the third day, the perfection of the number three is commended, which is the number of everything as having beginning, middle and end" *(Summa Theologica,* tr. English Dominican Fathers, III qu. 53, art. 2). Theologians never grew weary of dilating on the Sublime Mystery of the Trinity, One in Essence but three in Persons.

St. Thomas' *Sermon for the Feast of St. Martin* is an excellent example of the influence of the number three on the structure of another work which is divided into three parts, each of which is in turn divided into three sub-parts. Many of the questions which St. Thomas argues in his *Summa Theologica* are divided into Antithesis, Thesis, and Synthesis.

Beverly West in her *Epic, Folk, and Christian Traditions in the Poema de Fernán González* , (Madrid: Porrua Turanzas, 1983) pp. 128-30, seems to argue that the number three was so important in folklore, found in so many aspects of daily life that our poet used it without being able to help himself. She says: (The number three) "reflects not a conscious, deliberated effort of elaborate poetic structure and ornamentation, but the most basic, naive, and uncontaminated law of folk narrative." We agree as to its pervasiveness, (see reference to Folklore above in this note) but insist that out poet was so deliberate in what he was doing throughout his work that his use of this number in his poem is conscious and intentional. He was not swept away by an "uncontaminated law of folk narrative." He merely followed his training as a monk and the accumulated experience of story tellers almost everywhere.

[9] Georges Cirot, *"La chronique léonaise ," Bulletin Hispanique,* XIII, No. 4 (1911). "...ferdinandum gundisalbiz qui castellanos de subiugo legionensis dominationis dicitur extrasisse."
p. 429.

[10] Concerning the first battle against Navarre, Luciano Serrano says:"Imaginamos que el hecho referido por el Poema se indentifica con la muerte del rey García de Navarra en los campos de Atapuerca a manos de Fernando I de Castilla, el cual tenía con el conde igualdad de nombre, Fernando, y una mujer que se llamaba Sancha, lo mismo que la de Fernán González" See *PFG,* ed. Luciano Serrano (Madrid: 1943), p.23.

[11] *PFG,* note to verse 308d, p. 92.

[12] For the deaths of the Moorish kings, see stanzas 491 and 538 and the accompanying text of the *PCG* at the foot of the pages.

[13] Justo Pérez de Urbel, *Historia ,* II, pp. 551-556. He bases his hypothesis on verse 288d: "feziste te amigo de los pueblos paganos." He takes issue with my opinion above

in his "Glosas histórico-críticas al *PFG*," Boletín de la Institución Fernán González. 48, No. 175,1970. (Burgos) 231-265. See pp. 237-8.

14 The taking of the fortress of Carazo by FG is not to be counted as his first battle against the Moslems. Zamora Vicente's heading for the episode is, correctly, "Conquista de Carazo," as it was a siege. The poem itself says: "movio se con sus gentes Carazo fue çercar." (19lc) Thus it was not a "lid, batalla campal" as are the other six encounters against Moslems and Navarrese.

15 This supernatural event occurs when García Sánchez captures FG through treachery. When the latter surrenders, the altar of the little church is split from top to bottom. This is a sign from Heaven showing God's anger at the capture of His champion, like the rending of the veil of the Temple in Jerusalem at the moment Christ expired on the cross.

16 *Poema de Mío Cid,* ed. R. Menéndez Pidal, (Madrid, Clásicos castellanos, 1940), vs. 1227-1246. In his three volume study of the poem Menéndez Pidal changes the title to *Cantar de Mio Cid.*

17 R. Menéndez Pidal, "Cuestiones de método histórico. 3) Mio Cid el de Valencia" in *Castilla la tradición, el idioma.* (Buenos Aires: 1945). p. 156.

Chapter Three

The Poet's Gothic Spain

"En el nombre del Padre que fizo toda cosa," (l,a)

    In the Introduction to his edition of the poem Luciano Serrano gives what he sees as the "Tesis o idea madre del poema."
La idea latente, pero fundamental del Poema y que sin duda fue su inspiradora, se reduce a la siguiente: Después de la invasión musulmana, el imperio visigodo de España continuó en Castilla primitiva, y por ende, también su legítima soberanía sobre toda España. En la conquista mora, Castilla la Vieja fué el único territorio de toda España que no ocuparon los árabes; por esa misma razón, Castilla es heredera nata del honor, poderío y derecho dominativo del imperio godo-español. Castilla ha sido también la fuerza vital e impulsora que ha ido reconquistando el territorio de la España visigoda. Cual sea la grandeza y honra de esta restauración aparece claro de la exposición de cómo se fundó el imperio godo y cómo se deshizo por la cimitarra de los agarenos, que el Poema describe en su primera parte.[1]
It is this view of the Goths that the poet takes up as soon as he has introduced his work.
    As a good churchman, our poet-monk of San Pedro de Arlanza, the Arlantine, invoked the Holy Trinity as he started his work. In so doing, he was following the example of Gonzalo de Berceo, a monk from the rival monastery of San Millán de la Cogolla, who fives times had started with an invocation to the Trinity or the Virgin. Our poet writes:
    En el nonbre del padre que fizo toda cosa,
  del que quiso nasçer de la Virgen preçiosa,
  e del Spiritu Santo que ygual dellos posa,
  del conde de Castiella quiero fer una prosa. (I)
He takes this almost word for word from the start of Berceo's *Vida de Santo Domingo*, varying only in the last line by naming the count instead of the "*santo confesor.*" Then he assures us that the Lord will show him what he must write: he will tell of things past, how the land was won "de mar a mar,"[2] was lost, how the people lived in straightened circumstances

suffering hunger, cold, bitterness, slowly winning back parts of the loss until FG came upon the scene. When Rodrigo became king, the enemy conquered them because Mohammed preached his message and Christian Spain forgot the death of Christ. They had suffered much: saints, virgins, kings, high prelates died for their faith and went to their reward. In this statement of what is to come in the poem, the fervent, devout churchman sounds what will be keynotes throughout the poem: the hand of the Lord is constantly active in controlling mankind's destiny, and He will give rewards according to what mankind deserves. At this point, the Arlantine returns to his written source :

-commo el escrito diz, assy lo fablamos
en los rreyes primeros que godos los llamamos. (l4cd)

Christ sent them, "de partes de oriente," these Goths, " del linax de Magog," not yet Christians, but clearly in the mind of the poet chosen by God to carry out His purposes. It is obvious that he knew the ancient folkloric tales about Magog, because he says that their ""linax" came from the East, where Indo-European peoples did in fact have their origin.³ They moved westward, and devastated " toda tierra de Roma," taking prisoners, killing, advancing as far as Spain where they settled, gave up their idols and asked for instruction in the Christian religion:

Rescibyeron los godos el agua a bautysmo
fueron luz e estrella de tod el cristianismo,
alçaron cristiandat baxaron paganismo,
el cond Ferran Gonçalez fyzo aquesto mismo. (23)

thus characterizing the hero as the successor of the Goths who had been chosen by God even before they had become Christians. The count too was "luz e estrella" of all Christendom.

Much has been written about the sources of the poet for this history of the Goths. Marden's Introduction ascribes a lot of it to the *Continuatio Hispaniae* or *Epitoma Imperatorum* .⁴ Others have agreed or differed. Rosa Lida de Malkiel pointed certain errors in Marden's explanation.⁵ Menéndez Pidal said that much had come from the *Tudense*. ⁶ Most recently and reliably, Lindley Cintra has demonstrated that the "escrytura" referred to is almost certainly the *Cronicón villarense* or *Liber Regum* which its editor Serrano y Sanz had dated as of the first years of the thirteenth century, early enough for our poet and for "juglares" before him to have used in their works. Lindley Cintra shows parallels.⁷

Liber regum

Al tiempo que los godos passaron mar estonz se movie Mafomat de Meca e fo predicant en Arabia e convertie grant gent en so lei. (BAE, VI p. 207.)

The equivalent in the *PFG* is:
> Esto fizo Mafomat, el de la mala creençia,
> ...
> ca preico por su boca mucha mala sentençia
> Desque ovo Mafomat a todos predicados
> avian esas gentes los cueres demudados
> ...
> e la muerte de Cristo avyan la olvidado   (7-8)

Lindley Cintra says that the eulogy of the faithfulness of the Christians to the "lei de Cristo" must be an addition by the poet himself who informs us at that point that he is going back to his source material, "commo el escryto lo diz." He shows that this must be the *Liber regum* which says:
> Et en esta sazon andavan los godos en España. Estos godos foron del lignage de Gog e Magog e foron paganos. E movieronse doltras flum de Danubium e passaron mar e venieron gastando por por tierra de Roma. Et era apostoli en Roma el Papa Aldebrando. Et uenieron estos godos en España e estidieron hi CCCLXXXLLL annos, e muitos dellos tornaronse a la fe de Xps.
> (BAE, VI, P 207.)

The poem gives this as:
> Venieron estos godos de parte d'oriente,
> Cristo los enbio est pueblo descreyente,
> del linax de Magog vino aqueste gente
> conquirieron el mundo, esto sin fallimiente.
>
> Non fueron estos godos de comienzo cristianos,
> nin de judios d'Egito, nin de lei de paganos,
> antes fueron gentiles unos pueblos loçanos
> eran por en batallas pueblos muy venturados.
>
> Toda tierra de Roma venieronla avastando,
> a los unos predicando, a los otros matando,
> ...
> Passaron a España con el su gran poder,
> ...
> era en este tiempo el papa Alexandrer. (15-18)

Lindley Cintra notes that there was no Pope Alexander at this time, but that the *Liber Regum* names an Aldebrando. This name would fit the rhyme -ando- of the previous stanza and he asks whether it isn't necessary to put verse 18d into the defective stanza 17 which lacks two verses, and change the pope to Aldebrando. It seems sensible to do so. It is easy to see how much our poet followed his source material, what he omitted and added. The effect of his contribution is a gloss that vivifies and makes more dramatic the account he gives us. The details he adds, though imaginative, are true to life.

By this time, another purpose of the Arlantine poet is becoming clear: to show that the course of Spain's history was under the guiding and controlling hand of God, the "Cryador", or of His Christ. He does this repeatedly and clearly as the work develops. God's decision to have the Goths, before they were Christians, move westward across southern Europe, taking Rome, all of Spain and part of "Afrryca e Turonnia" (Touraine in France), was deliberate on God's part, in His omniscience. Then they asked for instructions in Christianity and received "el agua a bautysmo." The words "pueblo muy escogido" in 24c , and "pueblo escogido" in 28b show Spain as a new "chosen people" of God who controlled their destiny, even to the point of using Mafomat and the Devil to work out His purposes. The Goths led Spain onward, undergoing suffering, hardships, hunger, and oppression for their religion. When they forgot it,
> e la muerte de Cristo avyan la olvidado (8 d),

Christian Spain fell in a way that could only be a deliberate act of God to punish his people and bring them back to Him.

It is probable that in showing Spain's history here as being according to God's purposes, the poet has remembered a portion of the history of the children of Israel, as told in the Book of *Judges* in the *Bible*. In several almost parallel passages, we read that "the children of Israel did that which was evil in the sight of Jevohah...and He delivered them into the hands of their enemies...(*Judges* Chap 2:ll-l4), ...and He sold them into the hands of... (Chap 3:7-8; Chap 4: l-2; Chap 6:l). Three of these passages accuse the Israelites of whoring, allied to the charge of seduction traditionally leveled against King Witiza and to the seduction by King Rodrigo of whom the poet says only :
> por culpa en que era non le era Dyos amigo (35d)

It was not according to the Arlantine's purposes to show this leader of Christian Spain in a poor light, so he barely mentions Rodrigo's fault in Spain's downfall, which is a parallel to that of the children of Israel as cited above. It is quite probable that the Arlantine monk, knowing the book of *Judges*, chose to show the parallel in a way that would let him use the version that blamed Rodrigo, which was the most dramatic, most stirring, and probably the best liked of the juglaresque forms of the legend.

The poem next states:
> Quando los rreyes godos de este mundo passaron,
> Fueron a los çielos, grrand rreynos eredaron;
> Alçaron luego rrey los pueblos que quedaron,
> Com diz la escrytura don Çindus le llamaron. (25)

The poet here, continuing to put on the best face possible in presenting the royal line as a legitimate continuer of Gothic rule, says that don Çyndus became king by popular election. The truth is quite different. The *PCG* (Chap 504) tells us that "tomo Cindasuindo el reyno por fuerça e fizose rey de Espanna" at the death of King Thoas. It says that the latter was removed from the throne because he was ineffective and that he then took orders as a cleric, but that "esto no podrie estar nin es cosa de creer." The law forbidding the throne to anyone who had killed the king or engaged in removing him from the throne (of which Cyndus was guilty) was, of course, originally instituted to cut down the rather appalling number of rulers in those years who lost their throne or their life through violence of some type. The best-known example of this is King Sancho II who was murdered outside the walls of Zamora by Bellido Dolfos, at the instigation of Sancho's brother who became King Alfonso VI, but only after the Cid made him swear three times that he had nothing to do with Sancho's death *(PCG* Chap 845). (J.J.Victorio Martínez says of this: "Todo esto le hace pensar que la célebre Jura de Santa Gadea es pura invención." [8]

Vanva/Bamba

The poet omits the reign of Çyndus' son Rescesvinto and gives us Vanva, a good ruler "chosen by God" about whom legends early developed. The poem says:
    dio los pastor muy bueno luego el Cryador (27c)
a ruler as good or better than Çyndus. That Vanva was well known to the people who listened to the *juglares* is shown by: "commo avedes oydo." (28a) The poet then tells his public:
    venia de los godos, pueblo [muy] escogido; (28b)
Here the manuscript does not carry the "muy" which is regularly inserted today by editors. The correct reading, therefore, is "chosen people" which the poet keeps in our mind. Vanva was, in fact, one of the best of the Gothic rulers. He had been elected in spite of his efforts to avoid the responsiblity. There are several versions of his story which tell of his being forced to accept the throne, under threat of death, a sort of *lèse majesté* before the *majesté* was reached. We have here another case of the "reluctant ruler" theme, best known from the case of the Roman general Cincinnatus, who was plowing with his oxen when a delegation came to him and begged him to come to Rome, assume the leadership of troops, and put down a rebellion that threatened the city. Cincinnatus accepted his responsibility, left his oxen and plow in the field, put down the rebellion and then returned to his interrupted plowing. Another of the legends that accumulated about Vanva is that after some ten years of rule, his rivals gave him a potion that put him into a deep sleep, during

which they tonsured him. It was against Gothic custom to allow the throne to any tonsured person, by which they had originally meant a churchman. Vanva though not a cleric was nevertheless forced from the throne and retired to a monastery where he ended his days.

Stanza 3l, which says:
Partyo las tierras, ayunto los bispados,
....
estableçidos fueron lugares sennalados,
Commo fuessen los terminos a ellos sojuzgados. (3I acd)

may be a reflection of his reorganization of the bishoprics of Spain, a measure which brought recognition and acceptance of the authority of the king over the churchmen of the country. (The annointing of kings, initiated at the Fourth Council of Toledo in 633, lent an aura of legitimacy and the Church's blessing to the monarchs rather than really increasing the power of the Church over the Crown.) Vanva promulgated a law to force both the clergy and the high nobles to accept the authority of the king in cases where a royal summons for purposes of defense called on all within a hundred mile radius to come with supporting troops, under penalty of confiscation of property and exile. This is in the *Fuero Juzgo* where we find [9]:

Libro IX Titol II Ley VIII   De los que no van en la hueste en el día ó en el tiempo establecido.
...tod omne que recibe su mandado, o que lo sabe por qual manera quier, ó en que logar deve seer la hueste, manteniente se vaya pora la hueste e non por fincar en su casa dalli adelante ...omne de grant guisa como rico omne pierda todo quanto ha é sea echado de tierra y el rey faga de sus cosas lo que quisiere.
Libro IX Titol II Ley IX
...Y esta pena mandamos que ayan los obispos, é los sacerdotes, é los diáconos, é los otros clérigos que non an dignidad, que sean penados segund como dice en la ley de suso.

This and other limits and checks to the freedom of action of both upper classes brought a measure of relief to the common people and made them look upon Vanva as their benefactor. This law was changed shortly after Ervigio succeeded Vanva. The nobles were then required to come with only one tenth of their vassals and the clergy was exempted. Nevertheless, Vanva was remembered as having done much for the people, he was a "pastor muy bueno."

Another story about him was that he insisted that he not be called king until he had been anointed in the church of Santa María in Toledo, at which time the bishops and nobles signed an oath of fealty to him. He was also famous for putting down a rebellion led by a nobleman, Paulus, who had earlier sworn to be his vassal. This military action even extended north of the Pyrenees, covering a considerable area of what is now southern France. (*PCG* Chap 513-523)

It is strange that the poet omits any reference to the annointing of Vanva, in view of the fact that he is so concerned about showing the legitimacy of the Gothic rule in Spain. He does, however, point out that "dio les pastor muy bueno luego el Cryador." (27 c), showing that it was God's will that Vanva be king.

The Arlantine ends his story of this ruler saying that matters were in a such a good state, that the Devil couldn't stand it and the king died from poison. The final verse of the stanza is a prayer:

en parayso sea tan buen rrey heredado. (32 d)

which undoubtedly was echoed by all those who heard or read the Arlantine's work.

Again it must be pointed out that our poet cares little for the niceties of historical accuracy. We have just seen how he ascribes much of the history of Spain to the will of God. He now omits the reign of King Ervigio and tells us that Egyca was the king who followed Vanva, that he was "malo provado" (33d), and that he died after two years, when the truth is that he ruled some ten. Egyca was followed by Vautiçanos (Witiza) and he by Rodrigo who, as we have seen, "no era de Dyos amigo." At this point the poet inserts three stanzas devoted to a "Golden Age" of Spain: the churches well provided for, tithes and first fruits regularly paid, the people rooted in the faith, living from their labor, the "grandes potestades" not robbing their people but acting as "leales sennores," all living from their rightful income (37-39) Matters were so good that it bothered the Devil and the "gozo que avya en llanto fue tornado" (40 d). Here again we have God's servant, the Devil, at work. Mankind is never in control over his affairs.

Conquista

la cavtyva d'Espanna era mal quebrantada (74d)

The next section of the poem deals with the invasion by the Moors and the downfall of Christian Spain. It is clear that the poet is thoroughly familiar with the current legends of the Conquest for he combines several of them. He starts with the version favored by the Christians of the common people, the *mozárabes*, who, for the most part, at first had lived in uneasy peace with their conquerors. They of course preferred the version that cast the blame for the downfall of Christian Spain on traitors and on the Moors. In their most dramatic form, however, the legends involved King Rodrigo, so the poet used that version in the major portion of this episode. The *PCG* account is quite different (Chaps 549-557), from our poem. It tells of the whoring and other excesses of Witiza, with the consequent weakening of his government, much like the situations summed up in "And the children of Israel did that which was evil in the sight of Jehovah." It makes Witiza the one who orders Spain's weapons destroyed; it tells of three separate invasions by the Moors over a year's time, in the first two of which Julian, the "conde don Yllan" of the poem, is suborned by Muça, leader of the army of King Ulid. It says that Rodrigo seduced Julian's daughter (or maybe his wife) while the count was in Ceuta collecting tribute. For revenge, the latter accepted Muça's proposal and led Moorish troops into Spain, and did so again the next year. Then Muça himself conquered Rodrigo whose army had been deprived of its weapons through the actions of Witiza. Moreover, Rodrigo had against him the two sons of Witiza. Angry and jealous of him for his having been preferred over them to succeed their father, they held back their troops in the battle led by Muça, ensuring the defeat of the Christians. In this we have a combining of the legendary elements preferred by both the anti-Witizanos and by the anti-Rodriguistas.

To all of this, over five centuries later, the poet presents as good a face as possible, not wanting to blame either Rodrigo or his army. He says:
> Fyjos de Vautiçanos non devyeran nasçer,
> que esos começaron traiçion a fazer,
> volvyo lo el diablo e metyo su poder,
> esto fue el comienço de Espanna perder (41)

So, with treachery and the Devil doing God's work against them, it is no wonder that the Christians were defeated.

The poet now turns to count Julian and the version of the legend that was developed among the upper class of Christians, the anti-Rodriguistas, who were living as important officials working for the controlling Moors. Their version blames Rodrigo for Spain's downfall. The poem tells of Julian's anger as the cause of his treachery.
> Fyzo le la grrand ira traiçion volver,
> fablo con Vusarvan que avya grrand poder,
> dixo commo podie a cristianos confonder,
> no s' podrya nulla guisa Espanna defender. (43)

There is in the poem no reference to the seducing of Julian's daughter or wife, merely that his "grrand ira" caused his treachery. The *PCG* (Chap 554) made the accusation of the seduction by Rodrigo, but the poet omits this entirely, glossing over this unsavory detail to which he had earlier alluded with his "por la culpa en que era non le era Dyos amigo," a very attenuated reproach to Rodrigo. The poem's ensuing account of Julian's plotting with Vusarvan, the tribute he brought back, (with the humorous "Is it straw or wheat, what you brought back?"), the advice to turn swords into plowshares, the spears into pruning hooks, and the war horses into plow horses, is from the best known version of the legend. It fits the purposes of our poet to use it and he does so.

The disarming of Spain was ascribed to Witiza in the *PCG* (Chap 55l), and to Rodrigo by the *Tudense*.[10] The defeat of the Christians was attributed to their having passed one hundred fifty years without war, and to their being "lassos et flacos ca dos annos avien passados en gran pestilencias de fambre et mortandad et la gracia de Dios avie se arredrado e alongado dellos..." (Chap 557). Who can expect them to win against what has been ordained by God, or reproach them for being overcome? Even the *PCG* here puts the best face possible on the downfall.

At the start of this section the poet says:
  era de mala guisa la rueda trastornada, (74 c),
which is a reference to the wheel of Fate, a delightfully pagan *cliché* in a Christian poem. The verse:
  ca fue de los profetas esto profetizado, (77 d)
has been shown to be a reference to spurious prophecies in Arabic histories written after the events.[11] The monk's Christian viewpoint is again affirmed by:
  Era la cosa puesta e de Dios otorgada,
  que seyan los d'Espanna metydos a espada, (80 ab).
Just before these last two verses the poet calls the Christian forces the "cruzados." This cannot be considered an anachronism even though the First Crusade was not preached until 1095, because Christian Spain considered that its crusade to retake the lost territory had begun even before Pelayo and Covadonga in 717. The poem's account of the conquest itself combines the second and third battles of the *PCG* at Gibraltar, Seville, and Sangonera into one into one engagement at the latter place, tells of the disappearance of Rodrigo, and ends with the legendary discovery of his supposed tomb in Vyseo.[12]

The follow-up, the "Llanto de España", is the traditional telling of the suffering of the conquered: churches desecrated, their treasures stolen, and Christians slaughtered. The story that some of them were eaten was spread to strike fear into the survivors. Mothers and babes-in-arms were said to have been killed, just as in stories told in every war by conquered peoples everywhere. The important thing to note is that these stanzas, 90-97, telling of Spain after its downfall, contrast vividly with and balance the Golden Age passage about an idyllic peaceful Spain just before the conquest . The poet sounds two notes that will be repeated later in the poem:
  diera nos Dios Espanna, guardar la non sopimos,
  en grrand cuyta somos, nos byen lo meresçimos,

por nuestro mal sentydo en grrand yerro caymos. (98bcd)
in which he shows that he believes that we all receive our just deserts.
The charge of not holding what had been won for them by their forefathers
is repeated three stanzas later in:
lo que otros ganaron emos todo perdido (l0l b).
Even stronger is the idea that we deserve what we receive, this time
expressed by the poet almost as a condemnation from God.
Nos a Dios falesçiendo a nos el falesçido. (l00a)
How could such a disaster as the total collapse of Gothic Spain occur?
The answer is clear and inevitable as the reader or audience knows by this
time:
"Diera Dios essas oras grrand poder al pecado (l0la).
This "pecado" is, of course, the Devil, the instrument sent by God to effect
His will. The passage corresponds to the *Bible'* s statement: "and He
delivered them into the hands of the spoilers and sold them into the hands
of... and He strengthened the hands of Moab against them." (*Judges,* Chaps
2,3,4,6)   Clearly from Gonzalo de Berceo, as   Marden pointed out, are
stanzas l05c-l08, taken from the *Loores de nuestra sennora* (9l-92).[13]
This whole passage is a prayer in which Christians ask God to help them
as He had helped eleven people or groups named in the *Bible* who had been
saved by the hand of God. The Arlantine ends with:
"Somos mucho errados e contra ty pecamos,
pero cristianos somos e la tu ley guardamos;
el tu nombre tenemos, por tuyos nos llamamos,
tu merçed atendemos, otrra non esperamos. (ll3),
asking that He now succor them as He had helped those named in the
stanzas borrowed from Berceo, in terms that express a total and almost
abject dependence on the mercy of God.

It might be well at this time to draw the parallel with the story of
Abraham and the children of Israel who in the Biblical account were
chosen by God to be His people, His "pueblo escogido." He led them through
many regions for many years until their fighting won them the land they
considered to be theirs as promised to them by Jehovah *(Genesis* Chap
l2). Later they forgot the laws which He had set out for them, and then,
having been punished for their sins by Him, they returned to the prescribed
ways. Finally they were defeated, taken captive, and led into exile in
Babylonia, from which they later returned to the land which the Lord their
God had given them. In similar fashion:
Venieron estos godos de partes d'oriente,
Cristo los enbyo... (l5ab),
and were directed by God,
"Dios los quiso guiar..." (l9d)

through their wanderings for many years until they reached Spain, the land which they chose over all those which they had conquered. The poet calls them "pueblo muy escojydo" (24c) and " pueblo escojydo" (28b). Vanva, their king, was chosen by God:
dio les pastor muy bueno luego el Cryador (27c),
just as he had given Saul to the children of Israel to be their king, who was annointed by the prophet Samuel with Jehovah's blessing *(I Samuel Chaps 9:15-17, 10:1).* The Goths likewise adopted the custom of annointing their rulers, some of whom like Vanva felt that they were not really kings unless and until they had been annointed. Finally, because of the lax moral standards of Witiza and his government, they too "did that which was evil in the sight of Jehovah" and the Gothic kingdom fell to the Moorish invaders (*PCG* Chaps 549-50). While they were not led into captivity, they languished for years under the heel of the oppressor. Although the poet does not directly state it, he makes the parallel abundantly clear. History has repeated itself, as is its wont, and Christian Spain has undergone what all too many countries have experienced in their turn in the normal course of human events. In one major respect, however, like that of the children of Israel, it is different from the fate of most peoples who have fallen, because Israel and Christian Spain rose again. It is this rise that forms the next portion of the poem. And very personal from his monk's point of view is the fact that our poet ascribes it all, from the coming of the Goths, through their downfall and subsequent rise, to the will of God.

It must be admitted that there is no way to prove that our poet intended to liken the Goths to the children of Israel. The accumulation of details, however, continues throughout this portion of the work: the poet has repeatedly ascribed events to the hand of God, of Christ, or of the Devil acting at God's will; he has twice repeated "pueblo escojydo" in connection with the Christian Spaniards; he presents clearly the story of the wanderings of the Goths from the East to Spain as a parallel to those of the children of Israel as both take posession of the land to which God has guided them The fall of each and their captivity, real in one case and figurative in the other under the heel of the oppressor, is the same. This may well be nothing but coincidence, but if so, it is astounding. And as the reader will see it is an example of a frequently used device of our poet: to present evidence and leave it to the reader to draw the conclusion in order to avoid laboring the obvious.

Reconquista

Pelayo

> Dyxo les por el angel que Pelayo buscasen   (II5 a)

After the lament over Spain's plight the poet continues:
> Duraron en tal vyda al Cryador rrogando,
> de llorar de sus ojos nunca se escapando,
> syenpre dias e noches su cuyta rrecontando,
> oyo les Jesu Cristo a quien seien llamando.
> Dyxo les por el angel que Pelayo buscassen,
> que'l alçassen por rrey e que a el catassen,   (II4-II5a)

When they found Pelayo they had difficulty in persuading him to accept the responsibility for the kingdom:
> ovolo rresçebyr *pero non de su grado*
> Rresçibyo el rreynado mas*a muy grrand amidos.*   (II6d, II7a, emphasis added).

This reiteration of reluctance shows either that there was a body of legend about Pelayo and his attitude about accepting the crown, or that the poet added this detail on his own. Louis Chalon has traced the real history of the period and found that Pelayo was far from reticent to accept the position. [14] Son of a high nobleman, duke Favila with royal blood, Pelayo was sent to Cordoba either as emissary or hostage. He escaped northward, and blocked the marriage of his sister to Muniza, Moorish governor of the Asturias, in 7I7, six years after the Conquest began. Rallying men around him, he led a continuing resistance to the Moors. From the *Crónica de Alfonso III* and Moslem sources, it seems that a small detachment of Moors found Pelayo and his men in a grotto consecrated to Santa María (Cova Domenica > Covadonga) and was annihilated. Militarily unimportant to the Moors, this battle was of enormous spiritual value to the Christians, for it proved they had the aid of their God who "turned back arrows and spears in their flight so that they wounded the Moors" who feared that "les avya el Cryador grrand sanna" (I20d). (We note that Gonzalo de Berceo transferred this bit of folklore in his *Vida de San Millán* to the battle of Simancas, which shows how carelessly he observed his own stricture of "Al non escribimos si non lo que leemos."). But in spite of this and other victories, the poet says, the Christians never lost their fear of Almanzor.

The poem now says that Vauilla succeeded his father Pelayo on the throne, but died after little more than a year. His sister (Ermesinda) married Alfonso (I, el Católico), "sennor" (duke) of Cantabria. Taking advantage of a civil war among the Moors, which the poet omits so as not to detract from the accomplishments of Alfonso, the poet tells of his victories and names many but not all of the cities he took back back from the enemy. He was followed by his son Fabya who ruled only a short time (his name was really Fruela and he ruled for eleven years). Again we

cannot tell whether the poet was following popular sources here or whether he was adding this portion from his own inventiveness. Next the poem tells us of Alfonso II, el Casto 791-842, omitting Aurelio, Silo, Mauregato and Vermudo, four weak kings who brought no glory to the Christians and were therefore left out by our poet and probably by the *juglares* before him (768-791). It was under Aurelio or Mauregato that the tribute of the "cien doncellas" began. Vermudo, recognizing his own weakness and inability to control the country, abdicated in favor of his nephew Alfonso (who should have come to the throne in 783, but was pushed aside by Mauregato). Chronicles tell us that Alfonso did build the church of San Salvador in Oviedo, as the poet says in l26d.[15] At this point Chalon's article becomes particularly pertinent, for he again details closely the action of the poem and compares it with historical fact. The *PFG* says that Charlemagne sent word that he was coming to Spain, "pora gela ganar" (l27d), and Alfonso answered that he refused to pay tribute, as he would be considered "torpe" for doing so, that he preferred matters as they were, that the French wouldn't be able to boast of subjugating Spain. Then comes the verse "que mas la querian ellos en cinco annos ganar." (l29d), which Menéndez Pidal concluded reflects the beginning verses of the *Chanson de Roland* :[16]
> "Charles li Reis, nostre emperedre magnes,
> set anz tuz pleins at estet en Espaigne:
> Tres qu' en la mer cunquist la tere altaigne."

We note that here our poet shortens the seven years to five, thus disparaging Charlemagne by making him start home two years earlier, wishing he had been able to win in Spain. Our poem continues, telling that after consulting with his "pueblo famado" Charlemagne was advised to come in force to Spain. He assembled his whole army and set out for Castile.

Bernardo del Carpio

Chalon continues with the strangest part of this account. Bernardo del Carpio learned that the French were coming, that they were arriving at Fuente Rrabya and sent his army, including Alfonso's men, to that seaport where he kept the French from landing:
> e dessi enbyo los al puerto de la mar,
> ovol' todas sus gentes el rrey casto a dar,
> "non dexo a ese puerto al rrey Carlos ribar." (l33bcd)

In the battle many French were killed, including seven of the twelve peers. Charlemagne withdrew to Marsylla/Marseilles, regrouped and returned to Spain through the Pyreneen "puertos" of Gitarea (Cize, Cizère) and Aspa.

version, in his words, is "simplista y torpe"[19] and makes Bernardo militarily active for over seventy years:

...las batallas juglarescas de Bernardo contra los moros, propias de la gesta hispanizada, las fue identificando con las batallas cronísticas del reinado de Alfonso III el Mayor.[20]

These versions were all in existence in time for the Arlantine to use whatever portions he wished, and we have just seen what he did with the materials available. With such a rich but jumbled body of legend to pick from, it is not hard to see why the poet made errors: the twelve peers killed at Aspa when seven of them had already been disposed of at Fuente Rrabya, the second expedition leading to battles at both Gitarea/Roncesvalles and Aspa, and the latter occurring on Charlemagne's entry into Spain instead of on his withdrawal from Zaragoza. Another error for which the poet cannot be blamed lies in the fact that Roncesvalles took place in 778, well before the start of Alfonso II's reign. The truth is that the battle occurred during Charlemagne's retreat from Zaragoza and opposed the French rear-guard not to the troops of Alfonso II but to Basques from the region of Pamplona, aided possibly by Moors. And Charlemagne had come to Spain to weaken the Moorish King Abderrahman I, not as the poem says "pora se la ganar." Chalon concludes his article pointing out what our poet contributed on his own: the doubling of the battles fought at the "puertos" (probably because of the double meaning: seaport, mountain pass) of Aspa and Roncesvalles, and the "castilianization" of the troops who defeated the French, because at Roncesvalles it was probably Basques, not Castilians, who opposed Charlemagne's rear guard under the command of Roland.[21]

The poet has been reproached for having Bernardo ask the Moorish king for permission to go into battle, because it was wrong for a Christian to ally himself with Mohammedans against Christian, or to even admit the rule of the Moors over Christians (in spite of the fact that the Cid had fought as a mercenary for the king of Zaragoza for five years). This request made to a Moorish king to lead the action is the only point in the poem where the poet fails to maintain the superiority of the Spaniards and, more particularly, of the Castilians. It must be remembered that in the poet's day, three centuries after the Cid, the situation had changed greatly with the virtual completion of the Reconquest. All we can add is that the effect of doubling the battle is to make Bernardo more impressive with a second victory. The other change turns Basques into Castilians and further glorifies the latter, which would not have been the case if the poet had been historically accurate and opposed Basque troops to the French, a detail that had been lost to legend.

Elogio de España

Again Bernardo and his men went to meet the French, by way of Zaragoza where Bernardo kissed the hand of Moorish King Marsil and asked for permission to lead the front line of battle with his troops. Surprised at such a dangerous request, Marsil granted permission. It is ludicrous to read that Bernard again fought the twelve peers when, according to the poet himself, he had already killed seven of them (l4ld), clear evidence that this is an amalgam of two or more accounts. Once more the "espannones" won:

vençieron essas oras a frrançeses rrefez
byen fue essa mas negra que la primera vez. (l43cd)

What is to be made of all this? Menéndez Pidal wrote that:

La leyenda de Bernardo no nace como las demás leyendas españolas, a raíz de un suceso histórico, sino como necesaria réplica a la epopeya francesa, que durante los siglos XI y XII venía gozando en España de un éxito creciente...El Carlomagno liberador de España por los juglares franceses de aquende y allende el Pireneo, despertó pronto indignación en muchos españoles que veían en ello un atentado a la empresa nacional de la reconquista, y esta reacción nacional tomó cuerpo en la contraleyenda de Bernardo." [17] (Note the French *jongleurs* at work on both sides of the Pyrenees.)

The legends of Bernardo developing in France and Spain fed on each other, growing considerably more to the south of the Pyrenees, with a whole *romancero* and several plays about him. In mid-XIII century an amalgam was made of the two now almost independent versions, and parts of both were incorporated into the *PFG*. In the fused legends Bernardo is the son of count Sancho and doña Timbor, sister of Charlemagne who goes on pilgrimage. Alfonso discovers the love affair and angrily imprisons Sancho with a vow to keep him there for life, "de por vida." Charlemagne adopts Bernardo and rears him as his son in his court until Bernardo opposes the emperor's plan to invade Spain. Bernardo drives his uncle back at Fuente Rrabya, killing seven of the twelve peers, without Moorish help and then again at Aspa, this time allied with Marsil, the Moorish king, killing all twelve peers. Charlemagne recognizes and honors Bernardo who fights for him in the expedition against Zaragoza and then remains in Spain instead of going to France with the emperor. The rest of the combined legend, as it developed in Spain, deals with Bernardo's attempt to free his father from prison, succeeding only after the latter's death. As Menéndez Pidal said, this departure from the French version, which was a "cantar principalmente hazañoso," made it a "valioso drama de amor castigado y piedad filial perseguida," but as such it no longer has any relation to the Bernardo story of the *PFG*.[18] The *Tudense*

Zamora Vicente gives the heading "Elogio de España" to a fourteen stanza passage devoted to praising Spain which comes next and which closes the section on the Goths. As he says, it is a literary commonplace. [22] Menéndez Pidal showed that some of it comes from the *Tudense*, while agreeing with Marden that part of it was from San Isidoro's *De laude Hispaniae*. Part of it was original with our poet. It is a paean of praise, an exultation to which our poet predictably adds in order to exalt his Castile.Vyeja. A count shows that he names twenty-eight or so matters to be proud of. The list in the *PCG* (Chap 558) from the *Tudense* is longer, while that in Isidore's *History of the Goths* is slightly shorter. Our poet's version is stylistically pedestrian, until he tells of his Castile, while those of the other two are highly lyrical. Isidore said Spain was "rich in foster-sons, opulent in leaders and blessed in producing them," a feeling echoed by our poet. The *PCG* does not mention leaders as such, but does say:

> Espanna es sobre todos engennosa, atrevuda, mucho esforçada
> en lid, ligera en afan, leal al sennor, afincada en el estudio,
> palaciana en la palabra, cumplida de todo bien.

Some of this applies as much to the common man as to the high born. Isidore began with:

> Of all lands which stretch from the West to India, you are the
> most beautiful, oh Spain, sacred and ever blessed mother of
> leaders and of nations.

and ends with:

> ...Thus rightly did golden Rome, the head of nations, once
> desire you, ...the most flourishing nation of the Goths after
> many victories present amid royal insignia and abundant
> wealth, secure in the felicity of empire.[23]

The Arlantine lets his feelings show only in stanzas l55-l57.

> Com ella es mejor de las sus vezindades,
> assy sodes mejores quantos aqui morades,
> omnes sodes sesudos, mesura heredades,
> desto por tod el mundo muy grrand preçio ganades.
>
> Pero de toda Spanna Castyella es mejor,
> Por que fue de los otros el comienço mayor,
> guardando e temiendo syempre a su sennor.
> quiso acreçentar la assy el Cryador.
>
> Aun Castyella Vyeja, al mi entendimiento,
> mejor es que lo hal por que fue el çimiento,
> ca conquieron mucho, maguer poco convento,
> byen lo podedes ver en el acabamiento. (l55-l57)

Here his pride shows as he tells of their being "sesudos", of the "mesura" which comes to them from their ancestors, qualities for which the Cid and Fernán González are famous. Then he bursts forth in exultation in naming his own Castyella Vyeja as best of all, for it serves as the foundation for the whole country. Concluding with:
> byen lo podedes ver en el acabamiento,

he shows that he intends his poem to make clear by the way it ends that Castyella Vyeja is the best. Looking ahead to the close of the work, we find in its lost ending, as prosified in the *PCG*, that the poet's "patria chica" has indeed won its freedom from Leon, and that it is no longer a vassal state.

Another other matter in our poet's "Loor de Espanna," as it is also known, but not found in the *PCG* or in Isidore, is the "apostol honrrado, fyjo de Zebedeo, Santyago llamado," patron saint of Spain (l52cd). The Arlantine makes a very strong point of God's having honored Spain in this way above all other nations, particularly over England and France. Here his pride shines bright. While those two countries may have "aceyte," it is not in the same measure as that of Spain, and they have no Santyago at all. Our poet's deep feelings for the Church and its position is clear in his pious respect for the "santos muertos por su sennor," the "virgenes santas," and the "mucho buen confessor" (l52-l54). He lets his deep devotion to the Church and those who made it great show in his extolling of its role in Spain. It is interesting to note that the poet has said that England and France are supplied with "aceyte." For parts of France this may have been true, but not so for England where there never has been an olive-oil industry.

Again the intrusion of the poet who now tells us that he is going to change the subject as he is afraid of erring were he to continue extolling its role in Spain and Castile. He says he will instead return to King Alfonso (el Casto), whose death then led to extreme trouble in the land. Control and protection from Leon failed, due to the weak king who followed Alfonso, leaving Castile virtually helpless:

> Eran en muy grran coyta los espannones,
> duraron muy grrand tienpo todos desavenidos
> commo omnes syn sennor, tristes e doloridos,
> dizien: "Mas nos valdrrya nunca seer nasçidos." (l60)

We see here the close of the Gothic period in Spain, the end of an era, with the Christians still suffering under the Moors. In the next we begin a new epoch as Castile takes its fate into its own hands, inaugurating a glorious future.

Before starting the consideration of what FG and his Castilians did it will be well to look back at what he has just done in this first portion of his poem. This will allow us to understand better what is to come. As seen he makes important use of Berceo's work, adapting it to his purposes, fitting it to his needs. Not only will Berceo's verses be used to tell part of the story of Castile and its leader, but it will also allow the Arlantine to exact a measure of revenge or justice against a rival monastery. Historical writings have been put to use in portions of this first section of our poem, but this has been done in a manner that reflects the poet's own religious training and beliefs. His considerable knowledge of Christian Spain's past, preserved in historical works by outstanding writers whose names are still illustrious today, forms the framework of this introduction to the hero. To this must be added what was already legendary in his time in the juglaresque traditions about former rulers and leaders including material from Arabic and French sources.[24] Where tradition would reflect adversely on the poet's presentation of Christian Spain, it has been dropped or changed so as to attenuate the unfavorable picture it would otherwise give. All this is done to show the guiding hand of the Christians' God whose purposes are being worked out. It matters little that historical fact may be set aside, but is is all important that the Creator be made all-powerful. Our poet-monk had his convictions and told his story and his truth in such a way as to shape what was and in many cases is popularly still believed today.

---

[1] *PFG,* ed. Luciano Serrano, (Madrid: 1943), p. 39.

[2] When Cartagena was taken in 1243 and Cádiz in 1253 this "de mar a mar" was reached. Juan Victorio believes that the *PFG* was composed in praise of Fernando III, who died in 1252 after adding vast areas to Christian Spain, as had our Fernán González of legend. The military conquests of the second Fernando had cost enomous sums and had thus reduced the monies previously given to the Church. Victorio believes the monk of Arlanza hoped to secure gifts for his monastery by flattering the king with his veiled comparison of the king to the count. See Juan Victorio, ed. *PFG,* Madrid: Cátedra, 1981. pp. 27-8.

[3] In Biblical folklore, with which our poet was familiar, Japhet, youngest of Noah's three sons, from whom all mankind is descended, was father of the Indo-European race. Magog was the son of Japhet.

[4] *PFG,* ed. C. Carroll Marden, pp. xxxiii-iv.

[5] Rosa Lida de Malkiel, "Notas para el texto del *Alexandre* y para las fuentes del *Fernán González,"* Revista de filología hispánica, VII (1945). pp.47-51.

[6] R. Menéndez Pidal, "Reseña de *'El Poema de Fernán González,'* " ed. Marden," *Archiv für das Studien der Neureren Sprachen ,* CXIV (1905), pp. 243-257. (Hereafter *Reseña*)

7 L.F. Lindley-Cintra, "*O Liber Regum*, fonte comum do *Poema de Fernán González* e do *Laberinto* de Juan de Mena," *Boletim de Filologia* , (Lisboa: 1952), pp. 289-315. M. Serrano y Sanz, "Cronicón villarense (Liber regum)," *Boletín de la Real Academia Española*, VI, (Madrid), pp. 192-220, and VIII, pp. 367-382.

8 J.J.Victorio Martínez, "Nota sobre la épica medieval española: el motivo de la rebeldía," *Revue belge de philologie et d'histoire*, L (1972), pp. 777-92.

9 *Fuero Juzgo en latin y castellano cotejado comn los mas antiguos y preciosos códices* por la Real Academia Española. (Madrid, Ibarra, 1815).

10 R Menéndez Pidal, *Reliquias*, p. 13.

11 See footnote to 77d on p. 22 of *PFG*. Zamora Vicente quotes Dozy *(Recherches,* I, p. 30.) to the effect that the Conquest had been prophesied in Egypt by Arab historians. Juan Victorio, in his edition of the *PFG*, p. 60, says that the prophecies were invented later on in both Christian and Arab literature.

12 See Zamora Vicente's footnote to 84b.

13 See Marden, p. xxxii. He attributes our poem's 107-108 to Berceo's "Loores de nuestra sennora," 91-92 and 129d.

14 Louis Chalon, "L'histoire de la monarchie asturienne, de Pelayo à Alphonse II le Chaste dans le *PFG", Marche Romane Hommage des romanistes liêgeois á la mémoire de Ramón Menéndez Pidal.* XX-1 1970 Cahiers de l'A.R.U.Lg. pp. 61-67.This is a brief but very discerning study of the history of the years concerned and of the legends that developed about them. Chalon also points out several errors that have been made in previous studies.

15 See Zamora Vicente's note to 126d.

16 See Marden, p. 172. Menéndez Pidal concurs with Marden's opinion. *(Reseña,* p. 246.)

17 R. Menéndez Pidal, *Romanceros del Rey Rodrigo, y de Bernardo del Carpio,* ed. y estudios a cargo de R. Lapesa, D. Catalán, A. Galmés, J. Caso, (Madrid: Gredos, 1957), p. 143.

18 ibid. p. 147.

19 R. Menéndez Pidal, *Romanceros,* p. 150.

20 Chalons, p. 67.

21 Chalons, p. 67.

22 See Zamora Vicente"s footnotes p. 44.

23 Isidore of Seville, *History of the Goths, Vandals, and Suevi,* trans. Guido Donini and Gordon B. Ford Jr. , 2nd rev. ed. (Leiden: EJ Brill, 1970), pp.1-2.

[24] See Antonio García Gallo, "El carácter germánico de la épica y el derecho en la edad media española." *Anuario de la historia del derecho español.* XXV,1955, pp. 583-680. While the whole study is significant, section III, pp. 63-90, EL FOLKLORE JURIDICO EN CASTILLA, is particularly pertinent to our poem, discussing in detail the Horse and Hawk material, which will be considered in our Chapter Eight.

Chapter Four

The Mysterious Origin of Fernán González[1]

"Ovo nombre Fernando esse conde primero," (l73a)

In the Scandinavian formula for the mythical hero, the story begins with his lineage. Whether or not our poet knew that he was following a time-honored way of starting an epic poem, he used the old pattern and gave us the ancestry of FG, preceeding it with an introduction, as he regularly did with his episodes. While Castile was suffering from lack of control and protection:

Todos castellanos en uno s'acordaron
dos omnes de grran guisa por alcaldes alçaron,
los pueblos castellanos por ellos se guiaron,
que non poseyeron rrey grrand tiempo duraron. (l62)

Much has been written about the " jueces" of the chronicles whom the poem calls "alcaldes." The *PCG* (Chap 678) says that Fruela, the king under whom intolerable conditions started:

fue malo; e luego que regno mato sin culpa II fijos de un omne onrrado a que dezien Olmondo, e echo de tierra a otro so hermano daquellos dos que avie nombre Fruminio e era obispo de Leon. En aquel anno otrossi alçaron contra ell los altos omnes de Bardulia, que es una tierra que dizen Castiella Uieja cal non querien aver por so rey...e otrossi que recibien ellos muchos tuertos e hontas quando yuan a juizio a la corte de Leon, et por que se veyen apremiados otrossi de los uezinos de arredor que les fazien muchos males et muchas soberuias. Onde ouieron so conseio et so acuerdo los omnes buenos. et fizieron desi dos juyzes que escogieron entressi.

The tumult in which they lived led the Castilians to take matters into their own hands to solve their own problems themselves, acting with self-reliance, independence, and resourcefulness, proving that they had sufficient self-respect to refuse to live any longer under such conditions of injustice. As did the children of Israel, they chose "alcaldes," traditionally called *jueces*, judges, to exercise governing, fiscal, military and judicial powers.[2]

The *PCG's* words, reflecting the treatment Castilians felt they received in courts of law in Leon, find echoes of various kinds. Probably the best-known is the folkloric tale of FG's burning the books of the *Fuero*

Juzgo, the Visigothic code of law by which Leon and its vassal territories were ruled.³ In an area less densely populated than others, Castile was far from the courts of law in Leon, and it was expensive, time consuming, and often dangerous for Castilians to make the trip to the courts where more often than not they were discriminated against. They preferred to follow their unwritten customs rather than the provisions of the *Fuero Juzgo* which all too often were foreign to their own ways.

The poet uses the matter of the "jueces" to introduce don Nunno and don Layno from whom came both of Castile's legendary heroes, Fernán González and the Cid. Menéndez Pidal and Pérez de Urbel have both written about the lineage of FG, in widely differing accounts, both plausible and both inconclusive.⁴ On two matters they do agree: that our hero's mother was high-placed either by birth or by marriage, and that she was called not merely" cometisa," countess , but rather "cometissima" in Latin documents of the day, showing the great respect accorded her in her lifetime. The lineage of our hero as given in the poem is faulty, as might be expected, because details of the origins of any hero are not written down until well after he has achieved renown through his actions. And so it was with the count of Castile. In historical fact, about sixty years passed from the time of the "jueces" to the uncertain date of the birth of FG, early in the tenth century. The poet used existing legends to give us three generations to fill these years, which is acceptable: Don Nunno Rrasura, the "juez", was father of Gonçalo Nunnez whose three sons were Diego Gonçalez, Rodrigo, and Fernando, our hero (l64-l69). One writer has suggested that the three brothers really represented three generations, but this would give an unacceptable five generations for sixty years. Furthermore, the use of the number three is immediately suspect and in addition documents of the time tell us that FG had only one brother, Ramiro. The truth of the matter will never be known, but that didn't bother the *juglares* who invented their own facts when necessary. Our poet followed theirs or devised his own.

He tells us that at the advent of FG Castile was only a "pequenno rryncon" stretching from the Montes d'Oca to Fitero, and that Carazo was in Moorish hands The latter is false as that fortress had been retaken, in all likelihood by our hero's father, a few years earlier. The boundary markers, the "mojones," were much further apart than the verses indicate. In order to impress on his audience and readers how much FG did in enlarging Castile, he says that it was then a single "alcaldía." In the count's lifetime, as the public knew, FG extended it to include a total of seven counties, no small achievement. The pride of the poet shows clearly in the last stanza before he introduces his hero:

   Varones castellanos, este fue su cuydado:
   de llegar su sennor al mas alto estado.

> D'un alcaldia pobre fizeron la condado,
> tornaron la despues cabeça de rreynado.   (l72)

Castilians had elected the "jueces" and it was Castilians who supported FG and with him changed their *patria chica* from "alcaldia" into "condado" and then into "rreynado." The poet here clearly presages Castile's becoming a kingdom. From his vantage point three centuries later, he knew what had happened and foretells Castile's future status. It is important to note here that the stanza begins "Varones castellanos..." for he is intent on praising his Castile and it was not only his hero, but also the men of his home region who made possible what FG accomplished. A cooperative venture, it would have been impossible without them, and he took time to point it out. Repeatedly, in democratic fashion, the poet has his hero take his men into his confidence in the decision making process before important events.

Up to this point the poet has drawn his materials from mainly from Latin chronicles, although he uses popular tradition in telling of Vanva, Pelayo, Bernardo, and Rodrigo. It is at the first appearance of FG that the *Primera crónica general* (Chap 684) in its prose picks up the story of the poem, adding to it with material from the royal histories of Ramiro II and the three kings who followed him. As usual, the poet put into his verses only that which redounded to the glory and prestige of FG, omitting what would cast greater honor on the king, or show the Castilian as a vassal reluctant to carry out his duties, treacherous, or asking for help. Who was this Fernando, this "Fredernandus Gundisalbiz" of Latin documents? Pérez de Urbel said he was "el héroe que hizo a Castilla," while Claudio Sánchez Albornoz said, to the contrary, that "Castilla más bien hizo a Fernán González."[5] Lucas de Tuy in his chronicle of 1236 characterized him as a trouble maker. The man, however, was a hero to the Castilians of his time and later, and to the *juglares* who for three hundred years and more sang his deeds and virtues in the *cantares* that the public so loved, and which continued and expanded in the *romances* which are still alive today.

What is possibly the earliest record of the origins of the hero comes in the *Crónica najerense*, ca ll60, which says that Nunno Belchidiz begat Nunno Rrasura, who begat Gonzalo Nunnez, who begat Fernán González.[6] This same genealogy is in the *Liber regum (Crónica villarense)*, some fifty years later. Like others in the *Crónica najerense* it is already folkloric in nature and suspect, which we know because here it does not give FG's father his correct name.

It is known that FG's parents, Gonzalo Fernández and Munniadonna, in 912 made a gift of land to the monastery of San Pedro de Arlanza which lay about five or six miles from don Gonzalo's feudal estate, the *alfoz de Lara*, a gift confirmed by their son, FG, and his wife Sancha, and

reconfirmed years later by their grandson.[7] Gonzalo Fernández disappeared early and nothing certain is known of his end. Our Fernando's mother, on the other hand, the "cometissima," lived until 935, and throughout her lifetime ruled along with her son. The poem, however, tells nothing about his parents, because epic poets sing of their heroes and what they do, not what the parents did. In this case the Arlantine or those he followed even went so far as to attribute to FG the taking of the fortress of Carazo from the Moors, thus robbing his father, who had won the castle, of any place in tradition. When our poet took up FG's story, using materials current in his day, he knew that he needed to supply a beginning which would effectively introduce the young FG. He did not depend solely on his imagination for he was still influenced by the "al non escribimos si non lo que leemos" of Berceo. He chose from numerous models one that he adapted so as to present his hero as a boy living in wretched condition, in order to increase the contrast with the heights of prestige, wealth , and power to which he later rose. The poet tells us:
> dezir vos he del conde qual fue su cryazon,
> furtol' vn pobrezyello que labraua carbon,
> tovol' en la montanna vna grrand sazon. (l76)

With no explanation other than that he "furtol," we learn that a man who converted wood into charcoal stole the boy and reared him in the mountains for a long time.[8] From poverty to eventual eminence! The poet makes repeated use of striking contrasts, and often relies on his audience or readers to supply the second part of the comparison as must be done in this case, for the public knew what FG did in his lifetime. Audience participation is always a good stratagem for an entertainer.

In the Introduction to his critical edition of the PFG, Marden says that nowhere outside the poem does he find another mention of the "pobreziello que labraua carbon."[9] This gives rise to two questions: Where did the poet get the idea for a mysterious origin, and where did he get his charcoal burner? We shall answer those two questions presently, but there are other matters that enter the picture.

> Quanto podia el amo ganar de su mester,
> todo al buen cryado daua muy volunter,
> de qual linax venia faziagelo entender,
> avya cuando lo oya el moço grrand plazer.
>
> Quando yva el moço las cosas entendiendo,
> oyo com' a Castyella moros iban corriendo,
> "Valasme dixo, Cristo, yo a ti me encomiendo,
> en coyta es Castyella, segunt que yo entiendo. (l77-l78)

Some have wondered why the boy was reared in the mountains. Pérez de Urbel suggests that in a time of great danger from almost yearly incursions by the Moors it would have been only good sense to have the boy grow up in some inaccessible spot where he would be safe.[10] This would agree with later versions of FG's origin. And it is also true is that any charcoal- burner had to live in the forested mountains where he would have a plentiful supply of wood at hand. We can be sure, from the terms "amo" and "criado" (l77b), that the boy worked for his living, that the man was tutor to the boy, and that they shared the fruits of their labor. Far more important is what the "amo" taught his charge as to who he was, what his duties and responsibilities were, and most of all, the oppression under which Castile was living. Again the poet alerts the public as to what will be coming: the plight of Castile and the boy's duty in the matter. Then comes the first of the prayers of FG, and they will be heard repeatedly throughout the poem:

    Ualasme, dixo, Cristo, yo a ty me encomiendo,
      en coyta es Castyella segunt que yo entiendo, (l78cd).

The first statement the poet has FG make is this prayer for help by a young man who entrusts himself unreservedly to Christ. He continues, saying that it is time to leave the mountains and meet the world and its ways which are strange to him. He adds that when his brother Rodrigo died, Castilians lost one who was a mortal enemy to the Moors, (after FG's lineage has been given, this is the poem's only reference to any family the hero had, and this is about a brother who had existed only in legend, who had been given as one of the three supposed brothers) (l67b). Finally, summing up his own situation, FG says that he would never be worth "a fig" if he didn't get out of there (l8ld). Again the contrast of what he was then and, unstated, what the public knew he became and did, considerably more than "un fygo."

    When the young FG was old enough, the "pobrezyello" left the mountains with his charge and "vynos pora poblado." The news reached the whole county and young and old "avyan con el plazer" and accepted him as their lord, whereupon the young man again prayed: "Sennor, Rrey de los Rreyes" and told of the troubles of Castile assailed by the Moors And then said, most significantly, presaging what will soon be coming:

    yazemos catyvos de todos los d'Espanna,
    los sennores ser syervos tengo lo por fazanna. (l87cd)

This is his way of proclaiming to both Christians and Moors that it will be his great accomplishment to reverse the positions of oppressor and oppressed. It is also significant of the attitude of the poet and the public for whom he was writing that he had the people of Castile recognize and accept FG as their liege lord without waiting for the king of Leon to appoint him to the position. Castilians had elected their "jueces" without asking permission, and now they chose their own count themselves as they took this most important symbolic step with their new leader to what will be independence. The prayer ends with the stanza:

> Sennor, esta merced te querria pedir,
> seyendo tu vassallo, no me quieras fallir;
> Sennor contygo cuedo atanto conquerir
> porque aya Castyella de premia a salir. (l89)

This is the fourth statement in the last six stanzas of the life-long goal of the hero who is presented as a pious, devout, determined servant of the Lord. FG had previously stated that it was high time for the wheel of fortune to turn for Castile's betterment (l79b), a pagan figure of speech in a Christian prayer which is used twice more in the poem, with no embarassment to the poet. The other matter here which appears throughout the work is the *quid pro quo* attitude that if FG does his Lord's work, he expects his Lord to return the favor.

Very different is the first apearance of the hero in the *PCG* (Chap 684). Here he is presented as a grown man and experienced warrior when:

> ouieron so conseio los ricos omnes et los otros caualleros de Castiella de alçar por conde a FG, fijo de Gonzalo Nunnez (the old identification as in the matter of the "jueces") ca era a essa sazon grand cualleros, et de tomarle por sennor ca le amavan mucho et preciavanle todos. Et non azian en ello sin guisa ca ell era muy verdadero en su palabra, et en juizio, et buen caualleros en armas, et muy esforçado (echoes of Saint Isidore"s list of virtues), et gano mucha tierra de moros, assi como lo diremos adelant, et ensancho Castiella quanto el mas pudo.

Thus in its prose version, the PCG too tells its readers what to expect, luring them on, taking its lead from the poem, and implying conquests of land that almost certainly never occurred.

If the *PCG* says nothing about the boyhood of our hero, the *Cl344* does tell us of his early years:

> ...fue criado en la montanna e criolo vn cavallero bueno, que era ya viejo de edad e non pudo husar armas como complía; e el cavallero era muy sesudo e muy de buenas maneras, e así como el era muy bueno, ansí mostró al conde FG todo aquello que le conplía de fazer, para onbre como el que despues fue. E quando legó a los diez y seys años fue atan grande e atan valiente que adura fallarian en toda la tierra onbre de su edad o de mayor que tan bien oviere cuerpo e mañas.[11]

On the death of his father, the Castilian leaders came to the mountains to get him and brought him to Burgos with his "amo" whom he later rewarded. What is more, the Castilians made him count, which his father and grandfathers had not been.

Comparing the *PFG* with the *PCG* we see significant differences: the dropping of the "pobreziello" who had kidnapped the boy, knowing who he was, and thefore keeping a proper respect for him, and teaching him what he would need to know. He is instead, in the *PCG*, a "cauallero," no longer able to bear arms but still able to instruct in their use. We are not told how the boy came into his care. The *Crónica del conde Fernán González*, ca 1520, by Gonzalo de Arredondo, follows the account of the *C1344*, but adds that the boy's father gave him over into the care of "montañeses para que lo guardasen y sirviesen como a su persona mesma," and that the tutor's name was Martín González, whose descendants won great fame in the struggle against the Moors.[12] It is easy to see that the slow but steady accumulation of details about the origins of FG has followed the regular pattern of legend and folklore.

These several accounts have no confirmation in early Latin documents. Let us now see where the poet may have found the diverse elements which he integrated into his telling of the *mocedades* of FG, keeping in mind Berceo's "al non escribimos si non lo que leemos." As Beverly West points out (and we add that it was whether or not the poet knew he was following a long-used pattern) the poet's account of the early years of the hero meets five of the nine criteria that Lord Raglan set up for the entrance of the hero. Those missing are due to the fact that Raglan based his list on the Greek myths in which the hero is "son of a god," a feature impossible in this work by our poet-monk in Christian Spain. Our poem also coincides with six of the ten points in Jan DeVries' list of the hero of tradition. It is, moreover, so close to the hero of Heroic Scandinavian Family Saga, as given by Lord Raglan, that it will be enlightening to show this whole list.

    Prologue: Hero's pedigree: in brief the principal facts of his ancestors.
    First Act: Birth and upbringing of the hero; youthful exploits; rise and progress of the family feud.
    Second Act: Hero leaves home, kills and defeats enemies and becomes a principle leader.
    Third Act: Hero home again. Guiltless, is involved in feuds with powerful, unscrupulous neighbors and is killed fighting against enormous odds.
    Epilogue: Hero's death avenged.[13]

Although the birth is omitted, the poet does give us FG's descendance from the "jueces", the rearing of the boy, and his first military exploits. All of Act Two is found in our poem, as are the first two parts of Act III. The Epilogue is not needed because our hero is not killed. There is a real family feud with several family-by-marriage entanglements in the poem's conflicts, with the powerful, untrustworthy royal families of both Navarre and Leon. The poet planned to end his work, with the liberation of Castile, so the death and the vengeance for it are missing. As stated above, Marden says in his Introduction that outside the poem he found no mention that "el Conde fuese hurtado y criado por un pobreziello que labraua carbon." This is probably because the poet seems to have supplied this detail "de su propia cosecha," that it was not part of the legends of his day, so we look for a source, and find one in a most improbable place. There was a copy of the *Libro de Alexandre* in the library of the monastery of Santo Domingo de Silos, less than ten miles from San Pedro de Arlanza, so our poet undoubtedly had read that work.[14] He must also have read the *Crónica troyana*, which Menéndez Pidal dated as of ca l270.[15] He was undoubtedly familiar with the current hagiographic writings of Spain and of nearby France, and he planned to use one of them in his poem. Beverly West points out the coincidence of the *PCG* with some of the materials of the *lais* of Marie de France and of other Brittany materials.[16] Most important for the Arlantine were of course the works of the *juglares* whose livelihood depended on getting and keeping the attention of a public that lived in a period of wars, treachery, violence, and slavery for captured enemy, in a Castile that because of its nature was destined to become the vital center of all Spain. Thoroughly imbued with juglaresque materials of Spain, our poet-monk also knew much of those of France which were brought in by the entourages of numerous Spanish kings or their French-born wives. In addition there were thousands of pilgrims who yearly for over two centuries flowed across northern Spain along the "camino de Santiago" a scant twenty-five miles north of his monastery, bringing with them an enormous amount of French epic and other materials. Menéndez Pidal has told of the poets, *jongleurs*, entertainers of all kinds whom Spanish kings, including Alfonso el Sabio, a contemporary of our poet, maintained in their courts.[17] So, with the widely diverse background of what he had read and heard he had much to choose from. It must be noted first of all that one of the common-places of folkloric literature is the theme of the hero who appears unannounced out of nowhere. FG is one more of a growing list that included Paris, Moses, Romulus and Remus, and King Arthur, and which would soon make room for the illustrious Amadís de Gaula. In the *Libro de Alexandre* (hereafter L de A), (*BAE*, t.57, p. l57, stanzas 323-335) we find the theme of the mysterious origin of the young Paris (who had first been called Alexander). His mother Hecuba, about to give birth, dreamed of flames issuing from her vitals. This was interpreted to mean that the child she was about to bear would cause the destruction of the city To save it she ordered that the child be killed as soon as it was born, but her ladies-in-waiting were so taken by the beauty of the baby that they saved it and turned it over to to the care of shepherds to rear. When the boy was able, he "vinos pora poblado," was recognized by his father Priam and accepted with great joy as son and rightful heir.

There are five points of coincidence here with our poem: the two boys are I) reared, by 2) rural people, 3) both return "pora poblado," 4) both are received "con alegría" and 5) are recognized as lord or heir to the throne. Although we have no proof, it is almost certain that in view of his numerous borrowings from the *Alexandre* our poet knew of this use of the theme of mysterious origin and adapted it here. Alan Deyermond in his "Una nota sobre el *PFG* " in *Hispanófila* , 1960 pp.35-37, pointed out a closer, more immediate possible source for this *L de A* parallel.[18] He said that in the *Liber regum*, ca 1211, fifty years after the *Crónica najerense* had proved that there was an already well-advanced juglaresque legend of FG, we find the account of García Ennequez who was killed by the Moors. At the same time his wife Urraca was struck with a lance, and from her wound a son was born alive. A rich man from the mountain took the baby and reared it as best he could, naming him Sancho Garcés. When the boy was grown, he was "omne muit esforçado e muit franc" and attracted to himself all the "fillos dalgo" he found nearby and gave them "quanto que podia auer." They named him Sancho Abarca and raised him to king. (The folkloric nature of this account is obvious from the second name given to the man. Legend here couldn't decide whether he was Sancho Garcés I or Sancho Garcés II, showing that even pious stories underwent the process of evolution into folklore.) Deyermond says that as our poet has just been following the *Liber regum* it is fair to assume that he continues to do so here, and that he adds the detail of the boy being reared in the mountains. The acceptance by "ricos omnes," is closer to the poem's "avyan chycos e grrandes todos con el plazer" than is Alexander's being welcomed by King Priam his fatherin the*LdeA*. (We add that there is one difference in the change from the *LR* 's "daua les quanto que podia auer." In the poem this is reversed into:

    Quanto podia el amo ganar de su mester,
   todo al buen cryado dava muy volonter, (l77ab))

From the fact that the *LR* contains the salient features of the account in our poem, Deyermond concludes that evolving folklore had affected not only Castilian materials but also those of Aragon from which the García Ennequez-Urraca story was taken. This bit of legend, seriously recorded, had undoubtedly developed from the story of the birth of Julius Caesar who was born the same way, as commemorated in the term "caesarian section."

As previously stated, Marden said that outside the poem he had found no mention that the Count was "hurtado y criado por un pobrezyello que labraua carbon." Where then did our poet get the idea for having the boy kidnapped by a "carbonero"? In the next chapter there will be a discussion of the poet's use of the hagiographic legend of Saint Eustace as part of the "Hunt and Prophecy" episode. The life of this saint, well known in the Middle Ages, had been translated from Latin. Some French manuscripts, differing in several details from the Latin version, show changes which are also found in the Castilian translation of the fourteenth century. The variants of one of the French translations, contained in manuscript A, coincide with the aforementioned Castilian translation.[19] We conclude that it was this version of manuscript A which circulated in Spain. Our poet, who was planning to use the Eustace story in his poem for the hunt and prophecy, also used it here for the detail of the charcoal burner in presenting the young FG. Where the Latin says that the sons of Saint Eustace were saved by "pastores et aratores, " manuscript A of the French (which is the one that coincides with the Spanish version) says "car li bovier " and "pastors," but A here has the word "charbonnier crossed out and replaced by "car li bovier." The poet took from a manuscript of the A filiation of the legend of Eustace this detail of the charcoal burner. He avoided the difficulty of explaining how the boy came into the control of the "pobrezyello" by saying merely that "furtol."

A final question arises. The *Cl344* and the *Crónica de Arredondo* agree with our poem in that the young boy was reared in the mountains. Did they find this in already existing tradition or was it added by our poet after a long evolution that had already produced the *CFG*? It seems more likely that, coming from the life of St. Eustace, this was added by the Arlantine. It is well-known that the early years of epic heroes are the product of later telling, invented to satisfy the interest of the public in learning more about their already established favorites. What is not given in trustworthy documents (and who keeps a record of a hero's boyhood before he is a hero?) must needs be invented later. Thus the accounts of the exploits of many of the best-known epic protagonists are early fiction which is the pretending, the "fictionem" or feigning of reality. Historical truth mattered little to the public which never tired of hearing of more and new accomplishments of its heroes.

It is also known that the reworking of Spanish epics in prose or verse often added new materials. The *Cl344* , sixty years after the *PFG*, does so with its rendering of FG's story, adding two whole new chapters of materials not found in the poem, nor contained in the *PCG* of 1289, showing that they were of later composition. These contain the episode of the "vistas de Carrión" in which King Sancho I is splattered with water and sand by FG's horse. The chronicler added this passage to his *Cl344*, dropping entirely the attitude of respect and obedience of the count to his liege lord, the king, which are always clear and sustained throughout our poem, thus destroying one of the prime purposes of our poet. Another reworking, as we have seen, eliminated the contrast between the lowly conditions in which we first meet the boy with his "pobrezyello", and the glorious heights which FG finally reached. By substituting "cauallero" in place of the poem's "carbonero" the rearing of FG is placed on a higher level, but the loss of the poet's intended contrast changed the tone and significance intended by the Arlantine. So we see that in order to exalt the accomplishments of his hero, our poet adorned his tale with the telling of the early years by the use of fictional elements which he borrowed from legends, folklore and hagiography. Young FG, probably in intentional imitation of the *L de A* rather than through implausible chance coincidence with it or merely following a now vanished juglaresque tradition, is reared in the mountains as is Paris in the *L de A*. He is cared for, as in the French manuscript A of the Eustace story, by a "charbonnier/carbonero" who rears him to take his rightful place when the time has come.

---

[1] A major portion of this chapter appeared originally in 1956. See: J.P.Keller, "El misterioso origen de Fernán González," *Nueva Revista de Filología Hispaníca,* X (1956) No.1, pp.41-4.

[2] José Orlandis, *Historia de España La España Visigótica,* (Madrid: Gredos, 1977), p. 221.

[3] R Menéndez Pidal, *Reliquias,* p. 33.

[4] R. Menéndez Pidal, "Fernán González, su juventud y su genealogía," *BRAH,* 134, (1954), pp. 335-358.
Pérez de Urbel, "Fernán González: su juventud y su linaje," *Homenaje a Johannes Vincke,* (Madrid, CSIC, 1962-3), I, pp. 1-26.

[5] Pérez de Urbel, *Fernán González, el héroe que hizo a Castilla,* (Buenos Aires, Espasa Calpe, 1952). The sub-title is enough to show the nature of the whole book.
C. Sánchez Albornoz, "Observaciones a la 'Historia de Castilla' " de Pérez de Urbel" *Cuadernos de la historia de España,* XI, (1949), p. 149.

[6] Georges Cirot, op. cit. pp. 428-9. See also:
M. Serrano y Sanz,. "Cronicón villarense (Liber Regum)," *BRAH,* VI, (1919), p. 209.

[7] Pérez de Urbel, *Historia,* I, pp. 351-2.

[8] J. Corominas, *Diccionario crítico-etimológico de la lengua castellana* , 4 vols. (Berna: Editorial Francke, 1954.) Corominas gives a family of words of which the pertinent ones follow: carbón--Materia que resulta de la combustión incompleta de la leña, carbonear--Hacer carbón de leña, carbonero--El que hace o vende carbón.

[9] Marden, p. 175.

[10] Pérez de Urbel, *Historia,* I, p. 356.

[11] Marden, pp. 174-5. See also:
R. Menéndez Pidal, *Reliquias de la poesía épica española,* (Madrid, Espasa Calpe,1951), p. 156.

[12] Marden, loc. cit.

[13] Beverly West, op. cit. pp. 26-33. West compares the *PFG* with Lord Raglan's pattern of the Hero of Tradition and finds that it meets ten of the twenty-two items, which she considers a good score in view of the fact that four of the birth items and the eight of the death rite are missing because of the circumstances of the poem and its lack of the death rite.

[14] Pérez de Urbel, "Glosas histórico-críticas al 'Poema de Fernán González' p. 265. See also Zamora Vicente's *PFG,* note to pp. xiv-xv concerning RMP's *Reseña,* and the influence of the *LdeA* in *Anuario,* CXIV, pp. 243-56.

[15] E. Correa Calderón, "Reminiscencias homéricas en el "Poema de Fernán González" Estudios dedicados D Ramón Menéndez Pidal, IV. (Madrid: CSIC, 1953) p. 388.

[16] West, op. cit. pp. 52-53.

[17] R. Menéndez Pidal, *Poesía juglaresca y juglares,* (Madrid:, Espasa Calpe, 4th ed. 1956). p. 132. Other references are scattered throughout the book.

[18] Alan Deyermond, "Una nota sobre el 'Poema de Fernán González" *Hispanófila,* VIII, pp. 35-7.

[19] *Vie de Saint Eustace,* ed. Jessie Murray, (Paris: Classiques Français du moyen âge, 1929), t. 60, p. 61.

Chapter Five

The Hunt and Prophecy Episode[1]

"Vera a do envian los pueblos so aver" *(Vida de San Millan 1d)*

Our poet has just introduced his hero who with the Lord's help is determined to free Castile from its "premia," oppression. There follows a brief account of the siege of Carazo which leads into the battle of Lara. This is immediately preceeded by an important episode which relies principally on the same Eustace story of manuscript A that was the start of the rearing of the young FG. The Arlantine had two objectives here: to show the count as the chosen instrument of the Lord who directed the hero's steps, and to even the score with Gonzalo de Berceo of the monastery of San Millán de la Cogolla, some thirty kilometers from the *alfoz de Lara*. By so doing he would destroy the connection that Berceo had established between the count and that monastery and reestablish the ties of the count with his own of San Pedro de Arlanza. Berceo's poem, *Vida de San Millán* (hereafter VSM), must have rankled in the heart of our poet for it was an outright distortion of fact for La Cogolla's monetary gain and to Arlanza's loss. Berceo admits his purpose in his first two stanzas:

> Qui la vida quisiera de San Millan saber
> E de la su historia bien çertano seer,
> Meta mientes en esto que yo quiero leer,
> Verá a do envían los pueblos so aver.
>
> Secundo mia creençia que pese al pecado,
> En cabo quando fuere leydo el dictado,
> Aprendrá tales cosas de que será pagado,
> De dar las tres meaias non li será pesado. (l-2)

(This and the next seven quotations in verse are all from the *Vida de San Millan,* hereafter *VSM*.)[2]

The final verse of each stanza is the one to be noted. "He'll see where people send their money" and "He won't be burdened by giving his three "meaias," (a copper coin).

The first three quarters of Berceo's *VSM* are an "ordinary" saint's life much like the others he composed. The last quarter, however, is an outright plea for money for his monastery, that people again pay the annual "tres meaias" that supposedly had been promised to the monastery by FG and his Castilians. What were these "votos de San Millán?" The answer comes in two parts. The *PCG* (Chap 629) tells us that in 822, King Ramiro I of Leon, (843-850) received a demand from the Moorish ruler that tribute be paid: fifty virgins, "las mas fijas dalgo," to be married to Moors, and fifty more, from "el pueblo", for the Moors "con que ouiessen entre si sus solazes et sus deleytes." Ramiro refused to make the payments which had started under either Aurelio or Mauregato, and the Moorish army invaded to force the Christians to hand over the maidens. The king had a dream in which Santiago appeared to him and promised that God would help him win the coming battle, and that he, Santiago, would appear, "veer medes cras andar y en la lid en un cauallo blanco con una senna blanca, et grand espada relucient en la mano." He said that many Christians would die, that for them "esta apareiada la gloria de Dios et la su folganza que siempre durará." (This is esentially the same promise for which Moslems have gladly died while fighting "for the faith.") Ramiro of course won this battle of Clavijo because Santiago did appear and helped them. (*PCG* Chap 629). A little more than a century later, Ramiro II (927-950) won a tremendous battle against King Abderrahmán III at Simancas. An enormous amount of booty was won, King Abenhaia was taken prisoner, and Abderrahmán barely escaped alive to Cordoba. The battle was preceeded by a solar eclipse, "escurecio el sol et duro quanto podrie ser una ora." (*PCG* Chap 693). In this battle Ramiro was supported by his two brothers-in-law: our count and King García Sánchez of Navarre. In thanks for his victory Ramiro promised, for himself and his people, to give an annual "tres pepiones" (a coin of silver and copper) to the church in Compostela. These "votos de Santiago" were paid for years, if not centuries. Then in about 1200, a "privilegio" was found in a chest in the monastery of San Millán de la Cogolla which told of similar "votos de San Millán" promised by FG and his people of an annual "tres meaias" (a coin of copper to the saint. That this was designed solely for monetary gain, and that it was paid for a time is shown by Berceo who wrote:

"Oid me dixo el cuende, amigos e ermanos:
Fizieron leoneses commo bonos cristianos.
...
Querria que fiziessemos otra promision:
Mandar a San Millán nos atal furción,
Qual manda al apostol el rey de Leon.
...
Respondieronli todos: sennor de muy buen grado. (427c-43ld)

Our count then vowed that if God helped them win, he would draw up the formal papers embodying the promise. After the victory:

Pusieron e iuraron de dar todas sazones,
A Sant Millan cada casa de dar tres pepiones. (461cd)

We do not know how long these "votos" were paid, but enthusiasm dwindled with the years and finally Berceo decided to rekindle the religious zeal and thus restore the annual giving. In his poem he wrote:

Amigos e sennores entenderlo podedes,
Que a estos dos santos en debda iazedes:
Deste seet seguros que bien vos fallaredes
Si bien lis enviaredes este que lis devedes . (4)

After study of the documents of the monastery, Luciano Serrano wrote in 1930 that: "Se forjó el diploma por fines económicos."[3] Brian Dutton concurred with him on the spurious nature of the "votos" in his article "Gonzalo de Berceo and the Cantares de Gesta," 1961. In his last footnote Dutton wrote:

"My provisional conclusions are that while fully aware that it was a forgery, Berceo gave the document a Romance form as an act of propaganda with economic motives. Hence his lack of respect for the original, in contrast to his reverent fidelity to the *Vita Beati Aemiliani* of San Braulio."

Earlier in the same article Dutton quoted the *VSM* saying that God gave Castile a great leader, FG, because the kings were so sinful that:

el regno de Castiella tornara en condado. (*VSM* 395d)

The idea that it had once been a kingdom "would almost certainly originate with some epic *juglar* reflecting the Castilian nationalism which abounds in the FG story." The idea of a Castilian monarchy was related to Visigothic legitimacy. After adding some linguistic evidence Dutton suggests that there may have been an early copy of the FG legend in the monastery archive of San Millán. "...such seems to be indicated to Fray Martín Martínez in his *Apologia por San Millán de la Cogolla, Patrón de España* " (Haro, 1632) According to an old parchment in the archive, in the drawer of the "votos" one reads that Santiago and San Millán appeared with many armed knights with crosses on their chests against Almanzor in the battle of Azinas. This is repeated in the history of Fray Gerónimo de Castro de Castrillo. What is important, he says, is that this account is closer to the *PFG* than the *Privilegium* which names Abderrahman and doesn't name the battlefield. There are no knights with crosses on their chests, only two horsemen...seen before the battle starts, and Berceo mentions only these knights. After a few more details Dutton says: "we may see the interplay of juglaresque variants, and *refundiciones, clerecía* winnowing and Berceo's own object of exalting San Millán." He quotes one more verse from Berceo"s poem.

En tierras de Carazo, si oyestes cantar, (187a)

which proves that the poet expected his public to have heard a *cantar* about the taking of the fortress, which further strengthens his belief that there was a current legend about the count which was circulated by *juglares* of the area. 4

One of the interesting aspects interest in the "privilegio" today lies in the knowledge it gives of the economic life of Castile in the early thirteenth century. Many towns are listed with the contribution each is expected to make: money, wheat, wine, wax, leather, cloth, cheese, ironware, cattle, etc. These are incorporated into Berceo's verses, along with the boundaries of the area concerned, the purported authorization of the Pope, and excommunication for those who do not pay. (462-474)

Berceo apparently combined the two victories of Ramiros I and II for he tells of the shame of the LX (sic) virgins and of the sorrow of the "Rey celestial," of God's displeasure as shown by the solar eclipse ("de prima a terçia el sol non paresçio"), flames from heaven, stars flying to and fro in the sky, and then the verse: "ca lo al apos esto todo fue juglaria" (384d), which Dutton understands to mean that all the rest of the legend is juglaresque fiction. The "lo al apos esto" tells of towns far and wide that were burned, "Encendiendo las villas, quemando los ravales, ...burgos et villas cabdales..." (388bc) from Sahagún to Burgos and beyond.

God's mercy finally ended the destruction and He gave FG to help the people. Then Abderrahman approached with his army, King Ramiro II made his "votos" in return for the saint's help in battle, and FG followed suit. In the battle at a crucial point, Berceo inserts the appearance of Santiago, assisted of course by San Millán:

>Vieron dues personas fermosas e lucientes,
>Mucho eran mas blancas que las nieves luçientes.
>Vinieron en dos caballos plus blancos que cristal,
>Armas quales non vio omne mortal,
>El uno tenie croza, mitra pontifical,
>El otro una cruz, omne non vio tal. (437cd-438)

Then he identifies the two heavenly apparitions:

>El que tenia la mitra e la croza en mano,
>Essi fue el apostol de Sant Iuan ermano,
>El que la cruz tenie e el capiello plano,
>Esse fue Sant Millan el varon cogollano. (447)

After the Christians' victory, Ramiro and FG confirmed their promises in the name of their people. Berceo detailed the expected contribution of each community or group of households, as did his source, adding several stanzas in a plea that these "votos" again be loyally paid in recompense for the services of the two saints. Only thus would the monks of la Cogolla have "pan e vino, temporales templados," and would no longer be "de tristicia menguados." (479cd) It is clear that by Berceo's time the historical details had entered legend and evolved well away from fact. In the *PCG* account (Chap. 693), the Moorish king was given as Abderrahman, and the celestial portent was an hour-long eclipse of the sun. In the *VSM*, the battle occurred in the Campo de Toro (456c), not at Simancas, the king was Almanzor, the eclipse lasted two hours and was repeated five days later, flames appeared in the sky, stars moved around colliding with each other, and a burning wind from the west set fire to many towns killing animals and people. (We are happy to note that Berceo recognized and rejected at least some of the juglaresque elements.) Santiago with "mitra e croza" and San Millán with a cross appeared on their white horses and helped the Christians defeat the Moors.

Dutton's discussion lets us see what changes were made by our poet. In the *PFG* account, FG had two dreams instead of one, the eclipse became the flaming serpent, Santiago appeared on a white horse with a heavenly host, but San Millán failed to come to help. Almanzor was the Moorish king, the battle occurred at Hacinas, and there was no mention of Ramiro. As can be seen there was a real variation in the two versions, which shows both the popularity of the theme, and how little it mattered to either poet to adhere to his source. Both men gave their public what they, the poets, wanted.

Why did the Arlantine feel so strongly, resent so acutely what Berceo had written? Arlanza lies less than ten kilometers from the hero's home at Lara. Significant gifts had been given to the monastery by FG's parents, including money for the construction of buildings. Our hero himself with his wife Sancha had made other gifts. Five times in all the family had favored San Pedro de Arlanza with their generosity, and, even more, our count and his wife had both been laid to rest within the monastery walls at his instructions. In spite of FG's gifts to San Millán,[5] Arlanza's monks had good reason to consider their establishment to be the count's spiritual home and their reputed founder Pelayo to be FG's "santo patrono." Suddenly in the thirteenth century the Cogollanos produced a document that purportedly showed that the hero of Castile had promised to make annual gifts to la Cogolla thus undoubtedly diminishing the income of Arlanza and clearly destroying at least the luster of Arlanza's connections to the count. Then Gonzalo de Berceo renewed and exacerbated the damage with his poem about his founding saint. And even worse was the other result: it was made to appear that San Millán was the saint of the count's preference. Resentful of the spurious "votos," angered at the blatant attempt at money-grabbing, by the move to "steal" their count, determined to right the multiple wrongs, the Arlantine felt that he had to reestablish the ties of his establishment to FG, and he found a way to do so.

It may be well to note that our poet, in what he says here about his hero and will be saying repeatedly about him throughout the hunt and prohpecy episode, mentions no "lienda, dictado, escryto, or escrytura." We find no "commo avedes oydo" or other similar phrase such as he has used before to let the public know that they are familiar with what he is going to say. What he offers here in this episode is from a less known source that he feels they are not familiar with. He did, however, rely on his readings for the framework of what he put into verse at this point. Let us see now how he went about his task. He started with certain basic facts about his man and his monastery. FG was a famous warrior who had made gifts to Arlanza, which had begun as a tiny chapel in a cave high up on the river's bank. He had won great triumphs, had been imprisoned, shorn of and restored to power, won great battles. With these facts in mind our poet cast around to find a story he could adapt to his needs and he decided that the Eustace legend suited his purposes.

The French *Vie de Saint Eustace*[6] was known early enough in Spain for him to use. Manuscript A, with its "charbonnier" (*PFG* "carbonero") tells us that l) at the start, its hero Placidus was 2) a famous warrior. One day 3) he left his companions and 4) went hunting. 5) He followed a huge stag which led him to 6) a high rock so steep he could not climb it. A glowing cross appeared between the stag's horns 7) and the voice of Christ told him he must be baptized, and 8) promised to foretell the future if he returned 9) the next day. Placidus went home and that night was baptized with his whole family by the bishop who 10) asked to be remembered when Placidus, now Eustace, came into his glory. The next morning, in the same place the voice of Christ spoke again and 11) prophesied trials and triumphs plus final restoration to honor. Such is the introduction to the adventures of the saint. How did our poet adapt it to his work?

He sets the stage by telling of FG's conquest of the fortress of Carazo, which was ficticious because it had been taken from the Moors at the end of the ninth century or early in the tenth, probably by FG's father when the count was a small boy or possibly not yet born, a minor detail for the *juglares* or our poet. Almanzor, the Moorish king, enraged at the effrontery of the young Castilian upstart, marches northward with his army to avenge the loss. The count convinces his men that they should fight. With this as an introduction we are ready for our episode. FG leaves his men to go hunting, follows a boar that leads him to a "peña" so steep he has to dismount, chases the quarry on foot up the hillside to a cave where it takes shelter at the foot of an altar. Seeing that he is in a holy place, FG asks forgiveness for desecrating the chapel, meets Pelayo, one of the three hermits there, who promises to foretell the future the next day. Sharing the rude hospitality, the count sleeps well and In the morning Pelayo tells him that"

"Fago te, el buen conde, de tanto sabydor,
que quier la tu faziendo guiar el Cryador,
vençras tod el poder del moro Almanzor." (236bcd)

The hermit prophesies trials and triumphs for the hero, says that he will take back much land, will shed the blood of kings, will be imprisoned twice, will win the coming battle against Almanzor, thus establishing FG as the chosen instrument of the Lord. At another time and in another place, in a more formal setting, this would have been accompanied by a laying on of hands in blessing and consecration to the appointed task. Pelayo also says that before the third day there will be a "fuerte sygno" that will terrify FG's men. He will have to restore their courage, tell them that they are afraid like women, and anything else he may think of. He then adds a plea that the count not forget the hermitage after the coming victory because the three hermits are so poor they will have to give their habitation over to the serpents if no help comes to them. FG promises to give his "quinto" from the spoils of the battle to the hermitage, to construct a building that will shelter "mas de ciento," and will give instructions that he is to be buried there. The count then goes back to his men and tells them where he has been, and what the monk Pelayo prophesied.

Note the parallels to the Eustace story. l) At the start, 2) a famous warrior, 3) left his men 4) to go hunting. He 5) pursued his quarry, 6) to a "peña" too steep to climb except on foot. He met 7) not Christ but a servant of the Lord who 8) promised to foretell the future 9) the next day. l0) The prophecy concerned trials and triumphs. There was ll) a request to be remembered. These eleven points common to both stories and falling in the same order, except for one, are too numerous and too similar to be considered mere coincidence. The poet saw the possibilities of the Eustace materials and adapted them to his needs. This portion of the *PFG* involving a saint's life, like that of the hero's origin, is undoubtedly the addition of our poet of Arlanza. He moved the request to be remembered to its position after the prophecy, and dropped the trip home for baptism. He altered details as required: combining the voice of Christ and the bishop into Pelayo who thus became the count's protective patron saint, to be forever connected with the hero, and changed the high rock into the "peña" to fit the local terrain. He turned the request to be remembered after coming into his glory to a plea to be remembered after the coming victory which was guaranteed by Pelayo on behalf of his Master.

On completing this episode, the poet had restored the connection to the monastery of San Pedro de Arlanza, but he had not yet finished his task. There remained the severing of the ties to San Millán de la Cogolla. He deferred this portion to a later episode, the battle of Hacinas, but it will be dealt with now. In it the saint of la Cogolla was supposed to come to the aid of the Castilians just as Berceo said he had come to the aid of King Ramiro II at Simancas. In Berceo's poem, San Millán had promised in a vision that he and Santiago would help win the fight. When

the Christians were hard pressed, two strangers who could be only the two saints, appeared in the fray. Moorish arrows speeding from Moorish bows reversed their flight and killed Moors unnerving the others and allowing the tide of battle to turn in favor of Ramiro's army. (This detail was borrowed by Berceo from the legend of Pelayo, hero of Covadonga as will be remembered.) In the *PFG* by the monk of Arlanza, FG dreamed before the battle of Hacinas that the hermit Pelayo appeared to him and promised, under authorization from Christ to come with Santiago and a heavenly host to help the Castilians win the battle. In a second dream, San Millán appeared to FG and promised that he would come with Santiago to help the Christians. He further stated as in the *VSM:*
"Entrrante de la lid ver m'as vesyblemiente (413b),
and that victory would fall to FG on the third day. Then when the count and his men were on the point of defeat, Santiago, but not San Millán, did indeed come with a heavenly host and turned the imminent loss into victory. Our poet omits all mention here of San Millán.

The Arlantine has been criticized for carelessness in this omission after telling FG that San Millán would be there "vesyblemiente." There can be nothing further from the truth than this charge of carelessness. All mention of that saint was left cut so as to prove that he had nothing to do with the victory of the Castilians, and if, as Berceo's *VSM* had stated, the saint said he would appear, he was not to be trusted. In our poet's account, San Millán's promise in the dream is given just as in Berceo's poem. His failure to appear "vesyblemiente" is heightened by the lack of any mention of an appearance, contrasting harshly with that saint's fulfilling his promise in Berceo's poem. It would be hard to discredit San Millán any more than is done here by simply ignoring him. He has proved to be untrustworthy and is not worth mentioning again. In the *PFG* , the earlier promise of Pelayo was put into the story to let the public know the "real" explanation of the victory. It was he who said he would bring Santiago and the heavenly host, under authorization from Christ, and he did so, whereas an unreliable San Millán, on his own authority, had promised to be there with Santiago and, predictably, had failed to keep his word. With this our Arlantine poet completed his task of destroying the connection of the saint of la Cogolla to our hero and restoring the ties that bound FG to Pelayo, his real patron saint, and to the monastery at Arlanza. It would be hard to alter, add, and omit more effectively than our poet has done here to disparage the untrustworthy Cogollano. And it should also be pointed out that he has again used the stylistic ploy of omitting the second half of a comparison or contrast, leaving it to the public to supply the missing element. San Millán just "vanishes" and is not heard from again.

In the introduction to his edition of the poem, Luciano Serrano cast doubt on attributing the *PFG* to a monk from Arlanza.[7] He cited the fact that before the battle of Lara, Almanzor was said to be "cerca Lara" when he was at Muñó, "más de cuarenta kilometros" away. This can be countered by pointing out that Almanzor had started out from Cordoba, summoning his troops from "toda Almeria." (387b). The *PCG* (Chap 688) says:

> vinieronse pora ell assi como a perdon, muchos caballeros almohades et turcos et alaraves... et todo el poder de los moros dell Andaluzia.

This means that he started north gathering troops along the way. By the time he reached Muñó, a day's march away, he would naturally be considered to be "cerca Lara," nearing his goal. Serrano also objected to the poet's placing the hermits' cave high up on the river bank when the ruins of the monastery buildings are at river level. These two geographical discrepancies prove, he said, that the poet did not know either the area or the terrain around Arlanza and that the poet was not from the monastery there. Pérez de Urbel countered this by pointing out that Muñó is about twenty-five kilometers away and that there is, in fact, a cave high above the river, which must have been the hermitage where FG met the hermit Pelayo.[8] Thus both of Serrano's objections can be disregarded. There can be little doubt that the poet was indeed a monk from San Pedro de Arlanza.

It is amusing to note that our poet was no more scrupulous than Berceo who set aside the truth in the fabrication of the "votos de San Millán." If these are ficticious, so also are the buildings which our poet says were paid for out of FG's "quinto" from the battle of Lara.

Beverly West's study of the folklore in the *PFG* showed that it contained five of the nine points listed by Lord Raglan for the Birth of the hero, all four points of the Initiation Tests, but only one, the "holy sepulcher," of the last nine, because the death of the hero is not in our poem. At this point her treatment of the Separation and Return is pertinent and illuminating. She says that "in almost all hero tales there is a pattern in which the hero ventures forth at the start of his career into a strange world where he encounters supernatural beings who offer prohecies or aid. He then faces many dangers and near-death experiences before returning victorious." In our poem we have FG leaving his men, following the boar, a very dangerous animal, into the cave/hermitage where Pelayo prophesies his future: battles, overcoming kings, imprisonments, victories, entirely consistent with the folkloric pattern. West likens FG's entrance into the cave as a birth and his leaving as the rebirth, corresponding to the folkloric feature of the death and rebirth of the king.[9] For her, the main contribution of our poet is the

Christianization of the legend. This can be added to what has been shown above to be the heart of the total episode.

West also discusses an equally close parallel between the Eustace elements of the episode in the *PFG* and the tale of *Guigemar* by Marie de France, listing the points of similarity as was done above.[10] She also quotes Alan Deyermond's *Epic Poetry and the Clergy* in which he tells the foundation legend of a church in Palencia. The protagonist, Sancho Garcés, el Mayor, chases a boar into a cave where there is an altar. He tries to kill the quarry but his arm is paralyzed. Recognizing his sacrilege, he promises to build a church there and his arm is restored. (Marden had told of this legend in his note to 226-231.) Thus there are three similar accounts of the hunt, boar, and cave/altar. As stated in the previous chapter, in the preparation of the article "The Hunt and Prophecy Episode in the *Poema de Fernán González* ", in 1955, it was necessary to choose between the three possibilities and the inescapable choice was for the Eustace source because of the more than merely astounding "charbonnier-carbonero" coincidence. It had to have come from the manuscript A filiation. Later Pérez de Urbel wrote that there was a copy of the *Vida de San Eustaquio* in the monastery of Santo Domingo de Silos at the time of our poet,[11] confirming the conclusion that the poet had used the legend of Saint Eustace. The interesting thing here is that there should have been parallel stories in the "matière de Bretagne," in a Latin saint's life, and in the purported story of an early king of Spain. The influence of folklore is really astonishingly pervasive.

---

[1] A major portion of this chapter appeared under the title "The Hunt and Prophecy Episode in the "Poema de Fernán González" in the *Hispanic Review*, XXIII, No. 4 (1955) pp. 251-58.

[2] Gonzalo de Berceo, "Vida de San Millán" *BAE*, 57, (Madrid: 1952), pp. 65-79.

[3] Luciano Serrano, QSB, *Cartulario de San Millán de la Cogolla*, (Madrid: 1930) p. xxix.

[4] Brian Dutton, "Gonzalo de Berceo and the Cantares de Gesta," *Bulletin of Hispanic Studies*, XXXVIII, (1961) pp. 197-205.

[5] Pérez de Urbel, *Historia*, III, Documents 116 and 148 concern gifts to Arlanza. Documents 154, 161, 187, 188, 220, 221, and 227 concern gifts to San Millán de la Cogolla.

[6] *Vie de Saint Eustace,* ed. Jessie Murray, ed. cit., pp. 35-37. On p. vi, the editor states: "D'autre part, la déclinaison et la conjugaison y sont conservées à un état assez ancien qu'on ne puisse placer cette composition plus tard que la première moitié du XIII siècle."

[7] Luciano Serrano, *PFG*, pp. 44-45.

[8] Pérez de Urbel, *Historia*, I, p. 418, note 2, discusses the sites and some of the early history of the monastery of San Pedro de Arlanza. He says that: "La descripción (in the poem) es una de exactitud impresionante. La eremita de San Pelayo, el monasterio primitivo, se halla, efectivamente, sobre una roca, adonde es imposible llegar a caballo. Y es esta eremita el monasterio al cual se refiere, no el monasterio de abajo, construido casi al nivel del río."

[9] West, op.cit. pp. 26-31.

[10] West, op. cit. pp. 52-53.

[11] Pérez de Urbel, "Glosas," p. 265. : "por esa época había en en Silos un ejemplar del poema de Alexandre, que se menciona con el número de 47 del catálogo con estas palabras: "Alexandre de la orcias de plata (silver corner guards). Otra observación del mayor interés. En Silos se conserva un manuscrito del siglo XIII escrito poco antes de 1254, y que se intitula 'Flores Sanctorum. En él encontramos ya la pasión de San Eustaquio...y aquí tenemos una explicación de cómo el monje de Arlanza pudo conocer la leyenda de San Eustaquio." Pérez de Urbel may have found the above evidence of the *Alexandre* in Mario Férotin's *Histoire de l'abbaye de Silos*, (Paris: 1897), pp. 262-3. "Un moine du XIIIe siècle a inséré (fol.16) un catalogue des manuscrits de Silos qui formaient à cet époque un ensemble d'environs cent cinquante volumes... #47 *Alexandre;* orcias de plata (c.a.d. dont la reliure a des coins d'argent).

Chapter Six

The Hero Against Islam

alzaron cristiandat baxaron paganismo
el cond Ferran Gonzalez fyzo aquesto mismo." (23cd)

Of Things Military

In all the legendary baggage that grew up about FG in the centuries following his death, the two most important areas were those of his military prowess with victories over Moors and Navarre, and his freeing of Castile from subservience to Leon. Soon after coming to power, ca 931-2, he began his career as a soldier, the leader of his Castilian fighters in wars against "enemies of the faith" and also against Christians. This last was a matter for which he never forgave the Navarrese who fought him for their own gain instead of standing with him against Islam their common foe. There were great reaches of land and cities southward to the Duero River to be taken or retaken: San Esteban de Gormaz, Osma, Roa, and others. For a time they were almost yearly subjected to assaults by the Moors, who more than once took and razed them. They were then retaken and refortified by the Christians. Life was dangerous, hard, full of uncertainties. In order to resettle the areas won back from the Moors, the kings of Leon offered land to any who were willing to occupy it and put it to use, to bring it into the life of the kingdom. This freedom to migrate, this absence of compulsion to stay where they were born and the opportunities offered them in Castile led hundreds if not thousands to move into Castilian regions. The settlers had to be courageous, willing to risk not only their lives, but also those of their families, as well as their property, all of which were constantly under the threat of invasion. They had almost to live with the plow in one hand and a sword in the other. No wonder that Castilians, who had come from several areas of Christian Spain, were of a hardiness and independence of spirit that was proved by the very fact of their being there. In no other area were rewards commensurate with the hard work and risks inherent in the life they had voluntarily chosen for themselves and their families. FG repeatedly expressed his determination to relieve his Castile from the "coyta/cuita," and the "premia," in which it lived. His people, recognized his ability, his concern, and his leadership, and were willing to follow him because they knew that his cause was also their own. So much was this true that a great body of verse grew up about him and continued growing for several centuries after he was gone. A reflection of this is found in Pérez de Urbel's *Historia*.

> La toma de Lara, el sitio de Muñó, un encuentro con el fabuloso rey Acefali (misunderstood from the Arabic word (*aceifa*, army)[1], las batallas de Hacinas y Cascajares, el avance hasta el Duero...son hechos legendarios introducidos casi todos por primera vez...por la disparatada *Crónica de Arredondo*. De hecho, cuando FG empezó a gobernar el condado, hacía más de veinte años que todo este territorio era tierra de Castilla. Pero si él no ensanchó en gran manera los dominios cristianos, puede decirse que los robusteció, los unificó y los defendió, en un tiempo en que conservar era más difícil que anteriormente conquistar. [2]

In 932 Ramiro II and his Leonese army, with the aid of FG and his Castilians took Madrid on their way to an unsuccessful attempt to wrest Toledo from the Moors. *(PCG* Chap. 686). In 933 a warning reached FG that Abderrahman III was approaching and he sent word of the coming invasion to Ramiro who came to help him at Osma. The next year another invasion made the Christians retire into their castles and wait until the enemy had gone on by. The Castilian leader later accompanied his king on an expedition to Zaragoza. None of these military actions is mentioned in the poem, but all are in the chronicles, some in that of Sampiro as early as the start of the eleventh century.[3] As a general rule, if it redounded to the honor of FG it may be in the poem. If it increased the fame of the king, it is in the chronicles.

To show the count's growing stature as a leader we again quote from Pérez de Urbel:

> en un códice de los Morales de San Gregorio que se guardaba en la iglesia mayor de Toledo: "En la era de 971 (933ad), segundo de los idus de abril, vino el rey Ramiro contra los moros con el conde Fernán González." Para el copista mozárabe, el conde de Castilla tenía ya una grandeza que no se eclipsaba ni ante la dignidad real. 'Con motivo de esta campaña -dice Lucas de Tuy - los castellanos reconocieron sus derechos al rey Ramiro, mas no sin conseguir de él la concesión de ciertos privilegios.'

This last really means that FG forced his king to grant these privileges in return for the military aid that the Castilians under their count gave to Leon in this campaign. Thus Lucas de Tuy as chronicler writing with a definite bias against FG and for Ramiro, acknowledged the growing the importance Castile had gained under its new count in both military and political areas in less than two years. The fact that he was the brother-in-law of the king was an advantage that FG did not hesitate to use.

Through a combination of military skill and strength, through a wily shrewdness, with a politician's bold playing one force off against another, blessed with family ties through marriage into the royal house of Navarre and connected thereby with that of Leon, our count slowly, steadily, with few reverses, built up his ever more pervasive influence in Castile and beyond.[4]

In the preceeding chapter it was shown that the poet was insistent on demonstrating that his hero was successor to the Goths who under the guidance of God had made their way into Hispania, the foremost of Roman colonies. He established, as it were, the legitimacy of Gothic rule, set forth the judgement of God in the conquest by the Moors, and then introduced his hero in a way that showed him as the choice of the "Sennor" to lead Christian Spain to free his nation from domination by the Moors. FG was figuratively consecrated or annointed by Pelayo on authorization from Christ. The hermit's prophecy foretold a glorious future in which, though beset by hardships, FG was to be the champion of God. It is with the hero as military conqueror that this and the next chapter will be concerned. They will deal with his first two battles against the Moors, and then with his first against the Navarrese.

Our poem deals with a succession of events that lead eventually to the independence of Castile, that is, the struggles against the Moors, Navarre, and finally Leon. There are: a siege and three "batallas" or "batallas campales" against the "descreyentes," those enemies of the Faith, in which FG is characterized as as the champion of God, fighting to uphold his "Sennor," suffering for Him, doing His pleasure. There are three battles against the Navarrese king who is always the aggressor who has wronged our hero, engagements in which our count seeks justice to avenge "tuertos," or merely defends himself. And finally at the very end of the poem there is an incursion into the territory of King Sancho I, in which the Castilian acts justifiably, to warn the king that it is time to end a grievance of long standing. In every case, the poet shows us an FG who acts honorably. He could not do otherwise.[5]

Before discussing the several battles recounted in the poem it will be well to look at "the state of the military art" in the poet's day. This can most easily be done by considering the article "Reminiscencias homéricas en el *Poema de Fernán González,* " 1953, by E. Correa Calderón[6] who discusses similarities and differences between our poem, the *Libro de Alexandre* which Berceo claimed to have written, and the *Historia troyana,* which Menéndez Pidal dated as of ca 1270.[7] Correa Calderón accepts Marden' "1250 o muy poco después" for the *PFG.* and writes of what for him can therefore be only similarities between the *Troyana* and the *PFG.* If, however, the composition of our poem can be set at ca 1280, as will be attempted in the next chapter, then the *Troyana* may really have had a significant influence on our poet and his work. Correa Calderon's demonstration is clear and pertinent, tells much about epic poetry itself, and deserves attention for its own sake. Moreover, it serves as a basis for showing more adequately later in this chapter how our poet dealt with classical materials by the way he borrowed, adapted, and integrated parts of the epic tradition into his work.

Scholars, both before and after Marden and Menéndez Pidal, have abundantly shown that our poet repeatedly borrowed from the *Alexandre*. Luciano Serrano and Pérez de Urbel both tell of a listing of books in the library of the monastery of Santo Domingo de Silos, about five or six miles from Arlanza, which contains the *Alexandre* (with "orejas de plata," silver corner guards). This means that it was readily available to our poet. While Correa Calderón's article deals mainly with the *PFG* and the *Troyana*, it says that the *Alexandre* echoes the spirit of the Greek *Iliad*, whereas European epics are more factual, realistic, and prosaic, more "razonables, verosímiles." The *Alexandre* names many classical figures whereas the *PFG* names only Alexander himself and draws on only one "libro caballeresco," the *Crónica de Turpín,* from which it gets its list of the twelve peers of France. The *PFG* seems to be "en violenta reacción contra el poema que imita. There is an "alarde de mitología" in the *Alexandre* as against the "devoción religiosa reiterada" in the *PFG,* the a "sumisión a lo clásico" in the *Alexandre* / "exaltación de lo nacional" in the *PFG,* "exótica geografía" in the *Alexandre* / "mundo circunstante y vital de todos los días" in the *PFG* which presents "verdad cotidiana y humana de un caudillo de tamaño natural cuyos hechos y aventuras en ningún caso exceden el límite de lo posible." The classicism of the *PFG* is only that of an "influencia evaporada y tenue."

Comparing the *PFG* and the *Historia troyana* he finds that both poems deal primarily with the military exploits of the heroes. A section on the materials of warfare states that arms and armor were essentially the same in both ages, except that the Greeks had war chariots which were lacking in Spain. Fighting was therefore essentially the same in both poems: on foot or horse, with sword and lance, spear and arrow, streams of blood, running the enemy through or splitting his skull, leaders seeking each other out for face-to -face combat. He says that there is less of the supernatural in the *PFG* . This seems strange in view of three miracles with the battles against the Moors: the opening up of a chasm which engulfs rider and steed before closing over them, the flaming serpent that strikes terror into the Christian troops before the battle of Hacinas, and the appearance of Santiago and his heavenly host to save the Christians during that combat. This hardly seems less, particularly if we add the dream sequences before Hacinas. He is correct in saying that there is little exaggeration in our poem, other than the enormous numbers of enemy who cover hills and valleys and die by the thousands.

In the *Iliad*, Agamemnon has a "sueño divino" which tells him that Zeus is interested in and watching over him, orders him to call up his men, arm his archers, and instructs him as to how to order his forces for battle. This dream is similar in content and purpose to that of our hero in which Pelayo gives encouragement and advice and tells him that Christ had authorized him to say that the Christians would beat Almanzor. It is furthered and supported by the following dream in which San Millán gives instructions on how to arrange the troops. In both poems the armies eat, drink, and sleep before battle. Both give names of leaders who exhort their men to greater effort, both show the same attitudes towards fear, bravery, and death. Epithets are sharp and graphic in both, and in both the leaders are called lions. Because he believed the *Troyana* was written after the *PFG*, Correa Calderón called attention to what for him could be only "similarities," concluding that the points of coincidence might well be due to the very nature of epic poetry. As will be shown, our poem is almost certainly not to be dated before 1275 and probably 1280-85, so that Correa Calderón was probably more correct than he believed in his comparisons.

In a summarizing paragraph, he restates the parallels between the two poems: the intervention of the gods or saints in the struggles of men, the scenes of the dream sequences of Agamemnon and FG, the enumeration of the combatants and their enemies, the realistic notes which refer to the daily life of the heroes and their men, the similarity of the harangues, the idea of death as an unvoidable fact, the feeling concerning honor and future glory, the horror of slavery, the realism of battle scenes, and the likening of the heroes to "leones bravos, hambrientos." For him, these can be only similarities, because of the accepted dates of the two works.

It must be remembered that our poet was reworking *cantares* that were current in his day, from the repertory of the *tradición juglaresca*. This had been developed over centuries to a fine art, adapted continually by each succeeding generation of *juglares* to fit the changing tastes of the public and the purposes of the singers at the time of their performances. Their livelihood depended on how well they satisfied their public and therefore a knowledge and practice of the fine points found universally in techniques of composition and presentation were transmitted from previous ages along with materials of the poems or the songs themselves. In Menéndez Pidal's terms, there was no "solución de continuidad" in the oral and written transmission in Spain of the songs of military feats.

In our poem, only in the battle of Hacinas does the poet really spend time on the fighting itself. This is as it should be, for the *juglares* knew that they could not hold the attention of their public by dwelling overly long on a blow-by-blow description of the action as the hero defeated one opponent after another. As in any sports story today, the writer focuses his account on the highlights in the action, on the dramatic moments of confrontation, and on the few decisive acts that determine the outcome. What is done by the common soldiers is not in the poem because the public is not interested in them. In the introduction to Hacinas we are told that Almanzor summoned his troops from Morroco and all Africa, and then "turcos, e alarabes, almohades, and benimerines" ("aves marinos" in the poem through exigencies of rhyme and possibly the carelessness of the copyist) (381-384). Another matter of Greek tradition found in the introduction to the battle of Hacinas is that of the the names of the leaders of the several divisions of FG's army and of the standard bearer. [8] These detailings are possibly in imitation of the *Troyana*, because that poem showed that it was proper epic form to list such matters. The action dwells almost exclusively on what FG does: encouraging his men, seeking out and killing enemy kings, wounding and being himself wounded and unhorsed and thus thrust into dire straits before his Castilians are finally able to rally round and save him.

One matter of interest connected with the battles is that FG armed knight two of his nephews (450ab), and then, shortly after that, another twenty men(459b). According to Correa Calderón (*Reminiscencias*), it is found as well in the *Alexandre* in which five hundred are armed knight by their leader before a battle. It is no surprise to find the custom recorded in a poem, about Castile and it does point up the importance attached by the public still in the poet's day to the rise in rank.

One of the prime ingredients in the art of telling a story is the use of suspense, and the *juglares* and our poet availed themselves of it. In our poem, one of the ways the listener's or reader's attention is caught and held is by the use of elaborate introductions to the battles. These provide the desired delay of the account of the fighting whose outcome, of course, was already known to the public because they knew that their hero had died an old man. The introductions also provide the situations leading up to the fighting, the size of the forces involved, the seriousness of the "premia" in which the hero finds himself, and the psychological motivation of the Castilian and Moorish forces as FG and Almanzor rouse their men to do battle. It is with the latter purpose that the next portion of the discussion will deal.

Speeches

In a technique foreshadowing that in which Juan Manuel's Conde Lucanor's asks Patronio for advice, FG calls his leaders together before the first battle and asks them whether to fight.[9] It has already been pointed out that it was the practise for the Gothic leaders, in assembly to consult together and then elect a king by popular choice (unless a would-be ruler had removed the previous king and put himself on the throne by force). The newly elected king was then, if possible, annointed by the bishop in the church of Santa María in Toledo. This democratic practice of asking the advice of leaders is inherent also in the assemblies in which FG asks for counsel. The format is much the same throughout, but the content changes with the situation. First comes the statement of the problem, then one of the leaders speaks against fighting, after which FG responds with arguments of such length that they are virtually speeches, and they end with his decision to fight. The first of these discussions preceeds the battle of Lara just before FG leaves to go boar hunting.

The first military engagement of FG against the Moors is really an introduction to the first battle. Zamora Vicente entitles this the "Conquista de Carazo," because it is a siege, not a "batalla campal" or "lid" as the final engagement against the Moors is called by the poet. Using it solely as an introduction he gives only two stanzas to the military action, a victory for the Castilians. This fortress, which lay mid-way between the count's home at Lara and Silos, a few kilometers to the southwest, was a lofty peak standing up in the valley as a sentinel visible from afar. Berceo had mentioned it in his *VSM*. (Stanza 187). As already stated, it had been taken back by the Christians before FG's time. Undoubtedly recorded in a song by the *juglares* the event was easily attributed to our hero's prowess, without objection on the part of the public which delighted in hearing about their favorites and didn't mind the inconsequential alteration of a mere change in the main character. The victory of the Castilians at Carazo in our poem infuriated Almanzor in Cordoba, and thus serves as a motivating introduction to the battle of Lara. Angered, affronted, "maltraydo" by our count, the Moorish leader summoned his forces from far and wide, from " toda el Almeria." Serrano said that:

> en el siglo XIII los moros más cercanos de Castilla eran los de la provincia de Almería con Albacete, puesto que Murcia, Cartagena, Lorca y otras poblaciones de tierra de Murcia ya estaban sometidas entonces a los reyes de Castilla.[10]

When they were assembled, they marched north. Hearing of their approach, FG called on his men to meet him in Muñó and, when they had gathered, asked them for their opinion as to whether they should fight:

> Fablo con sus vassallos en que se acordarian,
> queria oir a todos que consejol' darian,

                    sy querian yr a ellos o les atenderian,
                    qual seria la cosa que por mejor ternian. (200)
Gonzalo Diaz answers for the count's "varones." It is his opinion that it is
not the right time for fighting the Moors, they should avoid combat if
possible, by truce or tribute, which is better than paying with one's life,
for they are far fewer in number than the enemy. FG, though angered,
responds in controlled fashion. Man can not avoid death and should make
sure that he dies honorably, a truce will make them a vassal people. Then
comes a stanza which seems apropos of nothing at the moment, but is put
in by the poet because of what he is planning for later on in his work.
                    Por enganno ganar non ha cosa peor,
                    quien cayere en este fecho cadra en grrand error,
                    por defender engannno murio el Salvador,
                    mas val ser engannado que non engannador. (211)
"enganno" four times in one stanza to let the reader know that it is, or
will, be a key word, that it will be important. FG continues: It would be
deceitful to accept a truce since Christ died to end deceit, their ancestors
'guardaron lealtad," were always honest in their dealings, avoided doing
evil, strove to protect the lords in spite of injustices that might be done
to them. Cornered in a small area, their forebears fought, suffered, died,
and eventually won, leaving their example and their land. Castilians must
now fight and be like them, instead of relinquishing what their ancestors
left them through fear of death.   Though far fewer in numbers they will
beat Almanzor, and they, his Castilians, will make him, FG, better than
others in Spain, to his great and their even greater honor. With this he
moved with his troops from Muñó to Lara and waited for the enemy to
arrive. (l99-224).
        The next example of this asking for advice occurs before the battle
of the Era Degollada against King Sancho Garcés which follows
immediately after that of Lara. The Navarrese king had unprovokedly and
treacherously invaded and ravaged Castilian territory while FG and his
men were away fighting the Moslems at Lara. FG tells his men that
although Navarre is far stronger, the Castilians have only to show they
aren't afraid and the enemy will leave the field. He himself will die or
see how well his men help him, and he won't mind dying if only Sancho
dies too. (297-307)
        This battle has a second part in which the "conde de Pyteos e conde
de Tolosa" leads the action against the Castilians who have not had time
to recover from the wounds suffered at the Era Degollada. But:
                    "el conde don Fernando, maguer muy mal ferido," (332c)
wanted to resume the fight immediately.   His men, needing to rest and
recuperate spoke bitterly to him: they had always to go about armed, their
life seemed like that of devils, he seemed like Satan to them and they like

his "criados," they were like Satan's host that never tired of taking lives. He was sorely wounded and needed rest and if he died, Castile was lost. Then Nunno Layno spoke for the others, asking for a delay until FG had recovered. He then accused the hero of "codiçia" (339c), (covetousness, one of the seven deadly sins), whereas they, his men, had "mesura," that Castilian virtue. (It has been noted that this charge of "codiçia" is unjustly made here, because FG was not fighting for his own advantage, but rather for the advancement of Castile. It is the same charge that was made against Alexander in the *Alexandre* as a reproach that was deserved for he went on and on to satisfy only his own insatiable ambition and desire for conquest.)

    Non rrecuden las cosas todas a vn lugar,
    deve aver el omne grrand seso en lidiar,
    sy non, podrra ayna muy grrand yerro tomar,
    podrrya tod el grrand prez por y lo astragar. (340)

This failure to use his "gran seso" is the great sin of Roland in the *Chanson de Roland,* in which pride clouds the good judgement of the French leader and is responsible for the defeat at Roncevalles. When Oliver wants him to call for help, because the enemy are so numerous that they cover "li val e les montaignes," the valleys and hills, Roland is too afraid of being thought a coward to blow his horn to recall Charlemagne for help. The poet at this point comments:

"Rodlanz est proz ed Oliviers est sages." (l093).

Roland is brave, overweeningly brave to the point of folly, confident to excess of his own power and ability, guilty of *hubris*. Oliver is "sages" which here corresponds to the "mesura" and the "grrand seso" the poet has just mentioned (339d). Since our poet is on the point of naming Charlemagne and his twelve peers, it is clear that here too his thinking is shaped by the French poem. Nunno Laynez continues to no avail, for his count:

    avya grrand conplimiento del sen de Salamon,
    nunca fue Alexandrre mas grrand de coraçon" (345cd).

FG agrees with don Nunno, but continues, countering everything that has been said: Man must not put off what can be done now lest he leave nothing to show for having lived on earth. Since good deeds are all man can leave at his death, he must put off the desires of the flesh. The poet now cites Alexander, David, Judas Maccabeus, Charlemagne and each of his twelve peers by name, men who are remembered today for their good deeds.[11] None of FG's Castilians, "caveros o peones," could answer his arguments and they went on into battle (332-3540).

  There is no discussion as to whether to fight before the battle of Hacinas because our hero absents himself, goes back to see his friend Pelayo in the hermitage and then merely reports to his men what he had learned there. (441-444). Later, however, during the three day battle, while they are resting at night after a day of combat, FG harangues them in a passage (estimated by Marden at five stanzas (519-523) which is missing from the manuscript but preserved in the *PCG*). He tells them to exert themselves the next day, not to be dismayed by how much they have suffered, in the morning help will come, they will win, and the enemy will be forced to leave the field, will flee, the Castilians will pursue and avenge themselves.

Once more near the close of the poem, in a passage preserved only in the *PCG* , FG assembles his men and speaks to them at length, protesting that he is innocent of Sancho I's charge that he had tried to seize ("alçarse con") Leonese land against his king. He says that he would never do such a thing, that he will go to Leon to prove the injustice of the accusation and that he expects to run into great trouble and danger, but that as an honorable man he has no other recourse. This final speech, put into his mouth by the poet, again shows him as he has been portrayed since the beginning of the poem. He is always fearless, honorable, the servant of God and Castile. There can be none better.

One has only to make a count of the stanzas in these speeches to realize how much importance the poet gave to them. In all, he has devoted fifty-one out of the total of seven hundred fifty-two in the whole poem to them, and while his leaders have a good bit to say, the majority of the speaking is done by FG. Most of what he says is clear, graphic, solid. He plays on the emotions of his men and appeals to their manly virtues, extols the value of bravery as against cowardice, points to the need to fight to keep their children from slavery, exhorts them to honor and duty, and to make the most of their opportunities.

It is interesting to note what Correa Calderón says about coincidences and parallels between the two works:[12] intervention of the marvellous, participation of the gods and saints in the struggles of men, scenes of the dreams of Agamemnon and FG, enumeration of the combatants and their enemies, realistic notes which refer to the daily life of the heroes, similarity of the harangues, concept of death as an irremediable fact, feeling of honor and future glory, horror of slavery, deciding of a battle by a single combat between two leaders, realism of the battle scenes, and the simile of the warriors as "leones bravos, hambrientos." For him, as stated, these are only similarities, not direct influence, because of the dates he accepted for the two works.

Miracles

One of the best known threesomes in the poem is the "miracles" which are found in connection only with the battles against the Moors. There are none for those against Navarre. Just before the battle of Lara there occurs the "fuerte sygno" predicted by the hermit Pelayo: a chasm opens up and a horse and rider fall in and are lost as it closes over them.[13] The Castilians are terrified and want to leave because they believe they have been abandoned by God:

"mejor seso fizieramos si fueramos tornados.
Bien vemos que Dios quiere a moros ayudar. (255d-256a)

(These two verses, reconstructed by Marden from the corresponding prose of the *PCG,* are part of four stanzas supplying a lacuna in the manuscript.) FG tells them that they should not show cowardice, that it is all because not even the earth can withstand the pounding of their horses' feet, that he wants nothing more than to face Almanzor. Reassured, they enter the fight and win.

The second miracle is that of the flaming serpent, the "sierpe en llamas" that preceeded the battle of Hacinas, almost certainly based on the heavenly portent of the eclipse before that battle under Ramiro II, It was recorded first in the *Sampiro,* then in numerous Latin chronicles, in the *Toledano* and the *Tudense,* and even in the records of the monastery of St. Gall in Switzerland.[14] The *PCG* (Chap 693) says: Et en aquel dia, assi como cuenta la estoria, escurecio el sol et duro quanto podrie ser una hora." Some of the other chronicles say that a flame issued from the sea and passed over the land eastward setting fire to cities, killing people and animals. Berceo combined several of these in his *VSM,* rejecting the part that spoke of the destruction of the cities, "lo al apos esto todo es juglaria," to warn the public that it wasn't all necessarily true. In our poem the eclipse became a flaming serpent that roared across the sky, terrifying the Christians who were already apprehensive over the coming battle. One could well expect this to have been based on a comet, meteor, or meteorite, but listings of these in books of astronomical records show none of these for 939, the year of Simancas. In folklore, comets had long been considered fearful apparitions, harbingers of disaster, and our poet used the "sierpe en llamas" to demoralize FG's men.

Vieron aquella noche vna muy fyera cosa,
venie por el ayre vna sierpe rrabiosa,
dando muy fuertes gruytos la fantasma astrosa,
toda venie sangrienta, bermeja commo rrosa.

Fazie ella semblante que feryda venia,
semejava en los gruytos que el çielo partya,
alunbrava las vestes el fuego que vertya,
todos ovyeron miedo que quemar los venia. (465-466)

By the time the terrified men woke FG from his sleep, the "sierpe" had disappeared, and when he understood their frantic statement as to what had happened, he too thought it had come to help the Moors, but was able to calm his men. His explanation reveals much of the poet's ideas, superstitions, beliefs, or myths (one can choose one's own term according to one's understanding of these matters today concerning unexplained natural phenomena). These all too often cause damage or destruction and are feared for that reason. Speaking of stars our hero tells his men:

"Los moros, byen sabedes, se guian por ellas,
non se guian por Dios que se guian por ellas,
otrro Cryador nuevo han fecho ellos dellas,
diz que por ellas veen muchas de maravillas."

Here he ridicules the enemy who are foolish enough to imagine a new "Cryador," and are so ignorant they let themselves be guided by stars, which is the not true of the Castilians.

"A y otrros que saben muchos encantamientos,
fazen muy muchos malos gestos por sus esperamentos,
de rrevolver las nuves e rrevolver los vientos,
muestra les el diablo estos entendymientos."

It is the devil that empowers them to do these things.

"Ayuntan los diablos con sus conjuramentos,
aliegan se con ellos e fazen sus conventos,
dizen de los passados todos sus fallimientos,
todos fazen conçejo, los falsos carbonientos."

Only by allying themselves with the devils can they do all this.

"Algun moro astroso que sabe encantar,
fyzo aquel diablo en sierpe fygurar,
por amor que podiesse a vos mal espantar,
con este tal enganno cuidando nos toruar." (473-476)

Then FG says that they know that Christ has taken away the Devil's power and they have nothing to fear. All power is in His hands, He can give and He can take away, and He is the "Sennor" to be feared (478). FG calls on his men to reject the Devil and to go to bed and sleep. Which they do. The poet shows his feeling of superiority over the Moors, who are wandering in error because of their beliefs, while he and Christians are possessors of the truth and know how wrong their enemies are.   He has again demonstrated that the hero is a true Christian, holding the true beliefs. The faith of Castilians is restored, their fears removed. God is on their side and has promised to help them.

With both the rider and chasm and the fiery serpent, FG proves his fitness and ability to serve as leader and passes another of the tests which, according to Lord Raglan, all heroes must face in their rise to the top.[15] Milá y Fontanals delicately questions whether the second and third miracles really happened:

"Consideramos ...de dudoso origen varias circunstancias
de la batalla de Hacinas, entre ellas la asistencia de
Santiago, y acaso de invención del autor del poema la
aparición de la serpiente." [16]

We are more than inclined to agree. Where then did the poet get the ideas he set down in his verses here?

Beverly West discusses the folkloric origin and meaning of the flaming serpent, showing that it goes far back into the past. Comets were considered to be harbingers of disaster, and were variously explained by soothsayers according to the needs of those for whom they were interpreting the omen.[17] One might add that there is Biblical precedent for this miracle taken from the the story of the battle of Jericho in which the sun stopped moving for three hours in its course across the sky to allow the children of Israel time enough to finally tumble the walls of the city. (*Joshua* Chap 6). In the *Alexandre,* Darius tells his leaders of a dream he had (951). When battle lines were set :

"desçendíen unos fuegos, e unas iradas flammas,
quemauan'le las tiendas e todas las posadas." (905cd).

And immediately after that:

"Departíen se las flamas cuemo rayos agudos,
quemauan les lanças que tenien en los punnos" (906ab).

So, our poet may have used here some bit of folklore with which he was familiar,an idea from the story of Jericho in the *Bible,* the Latin *Crónica de Sampiro*, or the *Alexandre,* but most probably he used Berceo's *VSM* because he had been borrowing from it so often, and because the stars moving around and the flaming star that set fire to towns are closer to "lo al apos esto todo es juglaría." If it was the last named work from which he drew his idea, it is gratifying to see how much he cleaned away the extraneous material, which cluttered up Berceo's account.

The third miracle, the appearance of Santiago and his heavenly host on the third day of the battle of Hacinas when the Castilians are on the point of defeat, is the high point of the battle. As shown in the previous chapter, our poet destroyed the connection of San Millán de la Cogolla with the count, and reestablished that of San Pedro de Arlanza. Of equal or greater importance is that he again showed Christ as the guiding and sustaining power in FG's life. Such Divine intervention and help in mankind's affairs is accorded only to those whom He chooses to favor. There can be no more convincing sign than the appearance of Santiago that the count and all Castile are God's chosen instrument to carry out His plans for Spain.

Prayers

One other matter that needs comment before starting to discuss the military events themselves is the prayers. It should be no surprise that our poet-monk puts prayers five times into the mouth of his hero. The first comes while he is still in the mountains and has just learned of how the Moslems were over-running Castile. Rather surprisingly for an uneducated Christian lad reared apart from the learned world by a charcoal burner, he addresses Christ saying that the latter can turn the wheel (of fortune), a Greek conceit which is found two other times in the poem. Castilians have gone through enough affliction, it is time for him to leave his mountains for he was not born to live like a wild animal, and he must learn of things out in the world (l78c-l8l). The second prayer comes when he is recognized and accepted as lord by the Castilians. Here he shows a real humility as he faces his responsibility in the task of liberating his Castile from the "premia" it is in, so that what had been lost may be regained, so that vengeance may be taken, and so that the "Cryador, Sennor, Rrey de los Rreyes" may consider Himself well served by FG. Too long have Castilians suffered as captives of the "gente descreyda." Young and old alike do not know which way to turn. He starts by asking for help for he is a sinner:

"Dame, Sennor, esfuerço, seso, e buen sentydo," (l85a)

(which will allow him to perform his task without falling into Roland's fatal mistake of *hubris*). The prayer ends with:

Sennor, esta merçed te querria pedir,
seyendo tu vasallo, no me quieras fallir;
Sennor, contigo cuedo atanto conquerir,
por que aya Castiella de premia salir. (l89)

Humble before his Lord, determined to do His will, he is ready for the great task of serving his Creator. Here we see the bargain with the Lord: If You do Your part, I'll do mine.

The third prayer comes in the cave when he realizes he has almost profaned holy ground, and asks the Lord and the Virgin for forgiveness. Again he requests help for Castile and against the "gent pagana," (231) and after their victory at the battle of Lara, FG and his Castilians offer thanks to God and Saint Mary. A new note comes into his fourth prayer, again in the cave, in which he rails against the Christians who have joined the "descreyentes" in fighting him and Castile. He alone stood up against the Moslems and with the Lord's help he resisted and conquered. As God promised though the prophet Isaiah, He will not fail His vassals, and His aid is needed now:

"Sennor, da me esfuerço e seso e poder" (401c).

This differs from the previous "esfuerço, e seso, e buen sentydo" (l85a), possibly because there are so many more of the enemy now that Almanzor has assembled troops from all Africa to add to those he had in Spain. FG has done his part and the Lord has no reason to fail him at this point. He concludes with the wish that he :

"pueda a Almozor o matar o vencer" (40ld).

It would be interesting to know why the poet did not have FG offer prayers before the battles against Navarre. It may well be because the hero was warring for his own purposes, to avenge wrongs done to him and his Castilians, and not as as crusader in the battles against the Moors, fighting for his Maker, whose faithful vassal he always was, doing his Lord's will. In the poem as a whole there are parts or all of thirty two stanzas in FG's prayers to his God or to Christ, asking for help against the Moors. And here again we have the idea of the bargain: our hero will be faithful to his God who surely will not fail him.

El Sitio de Carazo

The first military action of FG, the siege of Carazo, is really an introduction to the battle of Lara. It is a relatively minor engagement in which the young leader tests his ability to fight, and to organize and direct his men. It serves also as an introduction or build-up for the battle of Lara and the poet devotes only two stanzas to the fighting here, showing how little significance he attached to it. The attitude of the Christians is shown by the verse:

"fazian a Dios serviçio de puros corazones." (192d).

Since the fortress had been retaken earlier by Christians, probably by FG's father, the poet did not see fit to dwell on it, but the people certainly had no objections to hearing the victory ascribed to their hero. The episode serves as psychological motivation to rouse Almanzor to anger, making him vow vengeance against the young Castilian upstart for the affront to his honor and reputation that lay in an unknown's daring to attack a castle in his, Almanzor's, domain. The Moor reacts predictably and sends out his summons:

que veniessen ayna peones e caveros",
sus rreyes que veniessen de todos delanteros" (l95cd).

They come "de toda el Almería" and Almanzor, "sannudo e yrado," moves them against Castile. When FG hears of their approach, he summons his

Castilians and tells them of the threat they face. After the discussion as to whether to fight, as stated above, he leaves them to go hunting, meets Pelayo, and returns to his men. The next day the battle takes place.

Battle of Lara

When the fighting starts there are are a thousand Moors to one Christian. As in the *Chanson de Roland* (l084-5), the enemy covers "oteros e llanos" (251c), advancing with trumpeting and shouting so that the noise stirrs the hills and plains, and the Devil must have thought the "cruzados" would be filled with fear. Then occurs the portent or miracle: the ground opens up and a horse and rider are engulfed as it closes over them. FG allays the terror of his men by telling them that even the earth can not resist the Christians who make it sink. In the battle the Castilians are careful to surround and protect their leader and when he calls out "Castyella" they redouble their efforts, advancing towards Almanzor's tent. Hearing the bad news about how many of his men have been killed and wounded, how many of his kings lost, the Moorish leader is roused to arm himself. He mounts his horse, but then seeing how badly things are going for his side, he flees, denouncing Mohammed:
 "¡Ay, Mafomat, en mal ora en ty fyo!
 non vale tres arvejas todo tu poderio-" (268bc).
After a half-day's pursuit the Christians turn back, give thanks to God and Saint Mary for the wonder that had been done for them and begin collecting battle-field booty:
 "copas e vasos que eran de fino oro, e rricas maletas e muchos
 de çurrones... llenos de oro e plata, pepiones, tyendas,
 tendejones, espadas, lorigas, guarniciones, arquetas de marfil"
 (273b-275a)
so much that they had to leave "dos partes" behind.[18] They went to the monastery of San Pedro de Arlanza where they gave thanks for their victory, and offered to San Pedro the "joyas" they had won, while FG gave his "quinto" in fulfilment of his promise. Menéndez Pidal has discussed the "quinta/o" in his Vocabulario to the *CMC*, saying that it came from an Arabic custom which accorded to the king one fifth of all that was taken as a the result of battle. Other leaders were granted lesser amounts. However, its codification into law forbidding others to have one fifth, proved that the basic rule was being broken. Our poet either reflected here the practice of granting the royal portion to leaders below the rank of king, or intentionally conferred that right upon FG in order to elevate

his Castilian hero, if not to the status of king, at any rate to an equality of worth which deserved that amount.

Luciano Serrano mistakenly called this the battle for Carazo and said that the account here was taken from that of the battle of Osma, a conclusion he reached based on the *Sampiro*.[19] The engagement, as the poet tells it, conforms, however, to no early Latin or Spanish source and, as given, is known only through our poem. It must be considered either as our poet's rendering, his "refundición de un cantar" that was current in his day or, less likely, an episode completely original with him.

In this account of battle of Lara the poet gives only seven stanzas to the military action. He does not tell of a blow struck, a rider unhorsed. He merely says the men fought hard and protected their count; enemy troops were killed and wounded; at the shout of "Castyella" the Moors turned and fled, and it was a wonder that three hundred horsemen could beat so many. The poet is saving his real story for the second battle against the Moors, which will be the show-piece of the poem.

While the battle of Lara was still raging, while the booty was still being collected and taken to San Pedro de Arlanza, while the Castilians were still suffering from their wounds, Sancho, king of Navarre, took advantage of their absence fighting for the Lord and struck behind their back into FG's territory. The poet thus intentionally kept the pressure on the Castilians allowing no respite to his hero and the men who loyally follow him. In just reprisal for the wrongs done Castile, FG pushed a day's march into Navarre with his men and reached the Era Degollada. In a battle whose action was vividly described, as compared with with that of Lara, Sancho was killed by FG who himself was wounded, but there was still no rest for the Castilians, because an ally, the French count of Poitou and of Toulouse arrived belatedly to aid his relative, King Sancho. Our hero pushed his men into battle again over their protests, deaf to their entreaties for time to heal, saying that new wounds would make them forget the old ones. Only when the defeated French had left with the body of their fallen leader, whom FG had killed, did the Castilians have time to recuperate. The first battle against Navarre will be discussed in the next chapter, but the above has been given, following Carazo and Lara, to show how the poet continued the pressure on the hero, and to enhance his early military accomplishments: three victories over the Moors, one over Sancho, and then over the French count in a continuing crescendo of action. Sancho was the first of the kings that the hermit Pelayo had prophesied FG would slay. Two more will be disposed of in the battle of Hacinas, filling out another of the threesomes so dear to the poet. Skipping the first battle against Navarre, we go on instead to the battle of Hacinas, the high point of FG's military career. The account of this engagement is a real achievement by the poet who composed it as a series of scenes in praise of God and FG.

The Battle of Hacinas

Just as the siege of Carazo is an introduction to the battle of Lara, giving its circumstances and the psychological motivation of Almanzor, who must have vengeance against FG, so also does the battle of Lara serve the same purposes for that of Hacinas. It starts immediately after the French disappear down the road, a stanza that locates the episode in time:

> Dexemos tolosanos trystes e deserrados,
> ya eran en Tolosa con su sennor llegados;
> tornemos en el conde de los fechos grranados
> commo avia oydos otrros malos mandados:
> Que venia Almozor con muy fuertes fonsados,
> que traya treynta mil vassallos lorigados'
> non seyan los peones por ninguna guisa contados,
> estavan çerca Lara en Munno ayuntados. (380-1)

The second scene is a vivid picture of all the troops that Almanzor assembled, which tells us of the enormous importance that he gave to this campaign which was supposed to crush forever the man whom he had considered as only an upstart. The poet says that when Almanzor was defeated at Lara, he went back to Morrocco and summoned his troops from "toda Afrryca," calling them as to a religious war:

> "e fue commo a perdon tod el pueblo movydo" (382d).

Then follows a listing of "turcos, alarabes" with all their various weapons, "almohades, and benimerines (aves marinos) with their camels loaded for a long campaign, all covering the roads. They crossed the sea to Gibraltar where they were joined by Moors from Cordoba, Jaen, and all Andalucía, from Lorca, Cartagena, and all Almería, from west to east, a vast horde which did not pause until it reached Muñó.

The third scene is a visit to the hermitage where FG had met Pelayo and where his future successes and troubles had been predicted. When he is told that his friend had died a week earlier, he prays telling his "Sennor" that when he realized that kings of Spain out of fear had made themselves vassals of Almanzor, he turned from them even though he had to stand alone. With the finality of desperation he prays:

> "Sennor, da me esfuerço e poder,
> que pueda a Almoçor o matar o vencer." (401cd)

Falling asleep he dreams that his friend Pelayo comes to him as told in the last chapter, promising victory. Asleep again, San Millán appears to him in a second dream, tells him how to arrange his forces, and promises to appear with Santiago and help win the battle. With confidence restored he returns to his men.

The fourth scene concerns what FG tells them when he finds that they are furious at his absence. He calms them saying that help from above was assured to him by a voice from Heaven:
> "Conde Fernan Gonzalez, lieva dende, ve tu via,
> tod el poder de Afryca e de Andaluzia,
> vencer lo has en canpo deste tercer dia" (427bcd).

And FG continues with an explanation of what Pelayo and San Millán had said to him as told above in the section on the discussions with the men. Then he sets up his troops with their leaders and their places in the battle lines, just as is done in the Greek epic also, as demonstrated by Correa Calderón. He arms twenty men as knights and they all retire for the night.

The final scene of the introduction is that of the "flaming serpent." The way FG calms his men lets us see again how he understands the human heart and his knowledge of what moves men to act for good or ill, qualities that every leader must have in order to be successful, another of Lord Raglan's tests for kingship. Then all retire a second time and sleep until cock-crow, when:
> "començaron las alas los gallos a feryr" (481 b).

They arise, hear mass, confess, repent of their sins, and arm themselves. Thus prepared, the Castilians take their places on the battle field.

It must be remembered that the account of Hacinas gives the poet an opportunity to indulge in several threesomes: the army is divided into three parts, the battle lasts three days, pursuit ends on the third day, and the second and third of three kings are killed by FG. The action, the most spirited of the poem, is graphic and sustained, with much detail and color, giving a feeling of reality to the account.

The battle starts with praise for the hero: "leal cabdiello, fermoso castyello", his shield bristling with the enemy's "cuadryellos" showing that he was in the thick of the battle. Then the count opens a hole in the lines of the Moors, blows resound afar, the field is bloody, many die on both sides. A gigantic king from Africa faces FG. (One thinks of David and Goliath, although in that battle the single combat between those two men decided the whole fight for the two armies that watched their two heroes.) They lower their lances, and strike blows hard enough to split a tower, stunning both men, but our hero recovers in time to bring his opponent to the ground. The Moors surround the Castilian whose men rally round and save him. The count's horse is wounded with its entrails dragging on the ground and dies, the count on foot is hard pressed, but his men again succor him and bring him another horse, all of which draws a prayer of thanks from him for his deliverance. Like a wolf among sheep

FG goes on, and the poet leaves him in full action to tell of Gustyos Gonzalez, his right hand man who is the leader of the first division, "haz" of the army. Where he goes, blood flows:
"yvan grrandes arroyos commo fuent que manava" (499c).
Foot soldiers were falling on both sides, and the hills rang with the sound of the blows. Diego Laynez leads the other "haz:"
fazia grrand mortandad" en los pueblos paganos (501c).
The poet brings the action of the first day to a close with the Christians considering that they had probably done better than the enemy. They drive Moors out of their "posadas," and retire, fully armed, for the night.

The next morning the Moors again start their noise to strike fear into the Castilians. The Christians again hear mass and are ready, drawn up in battle order at the "primer campana," shouting their battle cry of "Santiago", and needing all their skills. Again the poet gives a series of epithets applied to his hero: "corazon syn flaqueza, sennor d'ensennamiento, çimiento de nobleza, mas bravo que serpiente" who struck and killed those of the "mala semiente" (513-514a). The poet wisely shortens this day's action and avoids boring his public. After eating, the two armies retire for the night, still wearing their armor.

The count calls his leaders together later that night and they come with all their wounds and suffering. In a passage which is missing from the poem, but supplied by the *PCG*, (Chap. 700) we read the harangue to his men, which was summarized above, in which he promises them victory the next day after the "hora de nona" (3p.m.) because help will come to them from above. When day dawns, both sides arise and arm themselves and go forth to the field. The Christians cross themselves and pray "de todos sus coraçones." On this third day of fighting the action is fiercer than before, no one dares oppose the count, the noise of the blows can be heard afar (*PCG* Chap 700). Gustyo Gonzalez is killed by a king from Africa. At the report that many of his best men have died, FG urges his army to fight harder and they respond with renewed effort. Then he meets the king who had killed Gustyo Gonzalez, splits his shield, pierces his armor with sharp steel, strikes him dead from his horse. Many horses with empty saddles can be found. FG is sure that the Castilians are on the point of defeat so he prays to his "Cryador" saying that Castile will lose its leader, will fall into the power of the Moor Almanzor, and it will be better not to outlive the day. Then he asks why God is angry with him, why He is destroying Spain for its sins, why He has not kept his promise to help, and then:
"yo no te falesçiendo ¿por que me falesçiste? (545)
This is almost like the cry of Christ on the cross, "My God. my God, why hast Thou forsaken me."(Mark l5:34) And there is the overtone of a reproach: he had kept his part of the agreement, but God had failed to keep His word. Then he turns his burden of saving Castile over to the Lord:

"resçibe Tu, Sennor, en guarda est condado," (546c)
This is very like the last words of Christ on the cross: "Father, into Thy hands I commend my spirit." (*Luke* 23, v.46), and coming immediately after verse 545d is probably another intentional parallel. Then he says that if he can get to Almanzor he will not leave him alive and will thus avenge all the Christians who have died in battle.

While he is expressing his displeasure with God, FG hears a voice from heaven :
"Ferrando de Castyella, oy te crez muy grrand bando."
(550d)
He raises his eyes and sees the holy apostol with a great band of "caveros, todos armas cruzadas" who attack the Moors who are terror-struck at the unexpected sight:
Dixo Rey Almanzor: "Est non puede ser.
¿Dond recreço al conde atan fuerte poder? (554ab).
The Moors turn and flee, and the Christians pursue for three days. Returning to the battle field, they search for their dead and accept FG's suggestion that they take the bodies to a holy place, San Pedro de Arlanza, where he himself is to be buried. They do so and then make their ways home. This whole episode from the visit to the hermitage, and the promise of victory made by Pelayo on authorization from Christ, to the fiery serpent that lets FG prove the power of faith in God rather than in the Devil, to the victory brought about by the appearance of Santiago and his heavenly host, all is planned, directed, and carried out by the "Sennor" on behalf of His chosen people.

The question can be asked as to what the historical facts were, as far as can be ascertained, what the poet had to work with. We start with the assumption that our poet based his work on a juglaresque account of Simancas. The *Crónica Silense* record of that battle, based on that of Sampiro, ca 1010, and then expanded and made more vivid by Pelayo, bishop of Oviedo a few years later, says that Abderrahman came north from Cordoba to Simancas. Ramiro II made ready with a large army, and God gave a great victory to the Catholic king two days before the feast "sanctorum Justi et Pastoris." 80,000 Moors were killed, King Aboiahia was captured and taken to Leon, and jailed there. The rest of the enemy fled and were pursued to Alhandega where most of them were killed. Abderrahman himself barely escaped alive, "semiuiuus euasit." Much booty of gold, silver, and precious clothing was taken. The *Silense* says that God gave a great victory, and Aboiahia was captured by the "recto juicio Dey." The *Crónica de Pelayo* adds the eclipse to the *Silense* account: "reuersus est sol in tenebras universo mundo per unam horam."[20] No date is given for this battle, which we know occurred in 939.

The *PCG*, (Chap 693) however, as another in a long series of erroneous dates, says that Simancas was in 907. Its account, expanded to include the fictional elements of the *PFG* , is much the same as that of Sampiro. One addition is that Ramiro, wanting blood more than booty, pursued the fleeing enemy, and surrounded them in the castle of Alhandiga. The Christians returned to Leon with their prisoner Abenahia, after collecting great booty of gold, silver, precious stones and many other things, and with many captives. In his account of the battle in the *VSM* (366-459). Berceo names "Remiro" and Abderrahman, and says that San Millan appeared with Santiago, mentions no pursuit, and says that the battle occurred in the "campo de Toro," that the sixty "duennas" were to be given to the Moors, and arrows reversed their flight. All these are changes in Berceo"s retelling. The *PFG'* s version is far more dramatic. The participation of the hermit Pelayo and San Millán in the dreams, and of Santiago in the battle make it vastly more important than that of the *VSM*. Kings Ramiro and Abderrahman of historical fact in Berceo's work are replaced in the *PFG* by FG and Almanzor. Our poem's version is organized according to a well thought-out plan, developed step by step in a sequence that provides suspense, as vividly described battle actions go well or ill for the hero who fights better than any one else, who kills two enemy kings, and who repeatedly rallies his men. The poet makes his greatest contribution in the portion in the hermitage, which is possibly modeled on part of the *Troyana.*, in the dreams which bring in both the all powerful hand of God which will save FG, and in the the failure of San Millán to appear, effectively destroying any connection between that saint and the count of Castile. This total episode is clearly the high point both of the military career of the hero and of the poem.

---

[1] One translator give the meaning: a Summer military expedition.

[2] Pérez de Urbel, *Historia*, I, p. 419.

[3] Georges Cirot, "La chronique léonaise," *Bulletin hispanique*, XIII, No. 4. (1911) p. 413.

[4] M. Menéndez y Pelayo echoes the Tudense's sentiments in *Antología de poetas líricos castellanos*, V, p. 11. Speaking of FG he sayshe was: "más afortunado y sagaz que heróico, más hábil para aprovecharse de las discordias de León y de Navarra que para ampliar su territorio a costa de los moros."

[5] Much of the above is based on Pérez de Urbel's *Historia*, I, Chapter 14, on Manuel Marquez-Sterling's *Fernán González, First Count of Castile: The Man and the Legend*, Univ. Mississippi: Romance Monographs, 1980, which draws heavily on Pérez de Urbel, but gives a different interpretation to parts of Pérez's work, and adds from other sources, on "Orígenes de León y Castilla," by Cristina Grande Gallego,

Margarita Cantero Montenegro, and Jesús Cantero Montenegro, in *Historia de Castilla y León,* coord. Enrique López Castellón. Vol. II, (Reno: 1983), and on Justiniano Rodríguez, *Ramiro II, Rey de León,* (Madrid, CSIC, 1972).

6 E. Correa Calderón, "Reminiscencias homéricas en el 'Poema de Fernán González,'" *Estudios dedicados a Menéndez Pidal,* (Madrid: CSIC, 1953) pp. 359-89. (Hereafter *Reminiscencias)*

7 R. Menéndez Pidal, "Historia troyana en verso y prosa," *RFE,* , Anejo 18, (1934).

8 For a delightful parody on this type of listings see Stephen Leacock's "On the Classical Antiquities."

9 Juan Manuel was so impressed by the speeches of FG that he modeled two of his stories in *El conde Lucanor* on our count's exhortations to his men. See *El conde Lucanor. Ejemplos 16, 37.* Written 1328-1335, it was first printed in 1575.

10 Serrano, *PFG,* p. 21.

11 Marden and others since him have attributed this listing of the twelve peers to the *Turpin.* This has recently been questioned.

12 E. Correa Calderón, *Reminiscencias,* p. 387.

13 In Marden's note to (254) he says that he omitted the second verse because it was not prosified in the *PCG.* Amador de los Ríos, *Historia crítica,* III, p. 342, had pointed out how much the *PCG* text resembled this stanza. Menéndez Pidal said that in Pedro de Medina's *Libro de grandezas y cosas memorables de España,* Sevilla, 1549, the knight who was swallowed up was called Pero Gonçalez *(Romancero de FG),* pp. 484-5. The *C1344* says this Pero Gonçalez was from Puente de Fitero. Gonzalo de Arredondo calls him Pero Gonzalez. The story of course is taken from Roman folklore, the account of the self-immolation of Curcius who rode into the chasm that had opened up, in order to save the city, after a prediction had said that Rome could be saved only by the sacrifice of its greatest treasure, which Curcius said was its brave men.

14 Henrique Flórez, *España sagrada,* 23. (Madrid: 1767). Flórez gives parallel entries for the *Annales compostelani, Cronicón burgense* (sic), *Cronicón complutense,* and *Cronicón de Cardeña.,* all of which record flames that destroyed various towns along a path from west to east.

15 Lord Raglan, *The Hero, a Study in Tradition, Myth, and Drama.* (London: Methner & Co. Ltd., 1936). pp. 190-1.

16 Milá y Fontanals, op. cit. p. 292.

17 West, op. cit. pp. 61-3.

18 This "dos partes" means "two thirds." See Chapter Nine, citation from the *Fuero Juzgo.*

19 Serrano, *PFG*, p. 20. Of the battle he said "El poeta la consideró digna de una hazaña de FG localizando en ella una batalla perfectamente histórica que dió el Conde al reconquistar, hacia 934, la ciudad de Osma y derrotar en ella por completo al ejército árabe. La semejanza de Carazo y Osma es notable: los cristianos invocan en Osma el nombre de Dios, ordenan las haces o cuerpos del ejército; preparan los caballeros de toda la comarca para tomar parte en esta campaña; matan los cristianos a muchos miles de moros, cautivan otros tantos y regresan a tierra de Burgos cargados de botín." He seems to have made a momentary lapse here because his description corresponds in most details to Simancas, which was probably the model of our poet for the battle of Hacinas.

20 Cirot, *La chronique léonaise, Bulletin Hispanique,* XIII, No. 4, (1911). pp. 413-4.

Chapter Seven

The First Battle against Navarre

"feziste te amigo de los pueblos paganos" (288b)

The introduction to the first battle against Navarre is twenty-eight stanzas in length, as against only nineteen for the battle action itself, showing how important the poet considered this preparatory material. In the wars against Islam, FG is the champion of God, doing His holy work, and the hand of the Lord is ever with him ready to help. In the case of Navarre the situation is entirely different, because Christian should support Christian against their common enemy, the Infidel, but Sancho Garcés of Navarre had cravenly and treacherously overrun Castilian land while FG was away, "estava a Dyos faziendo plazer" (281a), fighting the Moors. Treachery of any type involves deceit, which takes us back to the word "enganno" (used four times in stanza 211) which FG said Christ had come to the world to remove from us.
"Por enganno ganar, non ha cosa peor," (2lla)
is exactly what King Sancho did, overrunning Castile when the man he should have supported as another Christian had his back turned.

Because FG is not fighting Islam this time, there is no need for the poet to have his hero saved by God's help. Instead he makes this battle a test between the two leaders in which vengeance, justice, and right, not Navarrese power, prevail and where "enganno" is punished. There has been treachery and the poet speaks of the "tuertos" of Sancho against Castile which FG and his Castilians as the aggrieved parties must set aright.

Following the battle of Lara, after the Castilians gave their gifts to San Pedro de Arlanza and returned to Burgos, they got word that Sancho Garcés and his Navarrese had overrun Castile. Their reaction understandably was:
"de todos los del mundo somos desafyados" (282d).
because now they had been attacked by Moors and Christians alike. FG, roaring like a "leon bravo," prayed for the Lord's help in putting an end to such "soberbia," such arrogant pride. He sent a man to King Sancho who respectfully delivered the count's message: FG had a complaint, a real grievance, for Sancho had been pushing him

around for some time, had overrun his lands twice in a year, had allied himself with pagans against Castilians in war against Christians just because the latter didn't want to put themselves into Sancho's hands (288d). Now either make amends or accept FG's challenge. The answer was disdainful: FG must be lacking in good judgement and must have received bad advice. Sancho is surprised that after one victory in pitched battle against the Moors FG should defy him and he, the king of Navarre, will seek out the Castilian who won't be able to hide in towers or behind walls or escape by sea.

When the messenger reported to FG, the latter summoned all his men: "varones, rricos omnes, infançones, escuderos, peones," but without giving them a chance to speak, reminded them of Sancho's wrongs, told them that they should fight because such arrogance was not to be tolerated, and closed by saying :

"que nos venguemos dellos e todos y muramos" (300b).[1]

(The MS, the PCG, Marden, and Geary all read "o" in this verse rather than the "e" which Janer, Serrano, Menéndez Pidal, Zamora Vicente, and Victorio Martínez all give. This seems strange because it would be better to avenge wrongs and live rather than to avenge them and die. The word should be "o.") The poet ends this by saying that cowardice would be a great villany on their part and that the Navarrese will withdraw if they see that the Castilians are not afraid. He, FG, won't mind dying if he can kill Sancho. With this he leads his men into Navarrese territory to the Era Degollada.[2]

From the Catholic point of view, King Sancho had been guilty of committing four of the seven deadly sins. He had shown pride in his arrogant disdain for the Castilians, he had been guilty of covetousness, seizing their land and possessions, through lust he had been led to steal, and he had answered with anger the request that he make amends for his wrong-doing. In view of this it is easy to see why FG and his men should have the moral support of their poet and the public in whatever they do to secure justice for themselves.

Sancho met them at the Era Degollada and seeing FG's anger did not delay; lances were lowered and battle was joined, with the two leaders seeking each other and meeting between the two massed armies. They wounded each other so severely that Sancho knew he was going to die:

"man a mano del cuerpo el alma fue salida" (316d).

FG was also badly hurt and his men thought that it was due to their sins; they hurried to rescue him, drove the Navarrese away, feared he was dead, raised him up, cleaned his face, remounted him, and the battle continued until the Navarrese fled. Sancho's body was sent back in honor to Najera. (The MS says "a Navarra" but as they were a day's march into Navarrese territory, it is clear that Menéndez Pidal's correction to "Nájera" is right.)

In the account of the action the poet uses numerous phrases of the type that Correa Calderón cited in his article: "abaxaron las lanzas, fueron a feryr, oye el omne a lexos las ferydas sonar, astas quebrar, espadas retennnir, yelmos cortar, fyerros de las lanças al otra parte salieron, como sy fuesse muerto grrand duelo fizieron." In comparison with Carazo and Lara, the description of this battle is vivid, graphic, and filled with action in which the two angry men, driven by real emotions, pit themselves against each other in a struggle to the death of one and the severe wounding of the other. Both are worthy opponents, deserving of respect for their courage and determination. As was to be hoped and expected, the victory fell to the right man and to the right cause. Justice prevailed in FG's triumph.

Sequel

"El conde de Pyteos e conde de Tolosa" (328a)

In a sequel to the battle in which the Navarrese king dies, the count of Poitou and Toulouse in France comes belatedly and ill-advisedly to help his relative, Sancho. The battle is rejoined with Navarrese and French fighting together against the Castilians, and again the hero and his men are the victors.

> El conde de Pyteos e conde de Tolosa
> -pariente era del rrey, esto es çierta cosa-
> tomo de sus condados conpanna muy fermosa,
> movyo pora Castiella en ora muy astrrosa.   (328)

He did not hurry, and when he arrived at the mountain pass of Getarea the Navarrese reached him with the news of their defeat, of the many dead, saying that they had waited for him for two days before starting the battle. They advanced to the same place where the first fighting had occurred, determined to avenge Sancho's death. FG paid no attention to his wounds and went to meet the enemy against the wishes of his men who wanted time to recuperate. Saying that new wounds would make them forget the old ones he pushed them into battle, citing examples of brave men whose fame came from what they did, not from taking their ease; time lost can never be regained; they will be remembered only for what they do. The Castilians advanced to the Ebro River where the "tolosanos" unsuccessfully tried to keep them from crossing. The poet several times calls them "pytavinos" and once even names "gascones," (because the French troops were made up of these three groups), but strangely does not mention the Navarrese who were also in this fight. As the tide of battle went against the French, the poet, in one of his few humorous sallies, says:

"no's pueden tolosanos fallar byen dest mercado" (364d).

Setting a fierce example, FG ranged the battle field as men fell around him. Finally he cried out for the "buen conde" to meet him, and most Toulousans fled, leaving their leader almost unprotected. Then our hero, who usually showed no cruelty, forgot "bondad e mesura" and struck the Toulousan a mortal blow that dropped him dead from his horse. FG then acted nobly:

"oyredes lo que fyzo al conde tolosano" (373b),

He stripped the body of his slain enemy, washed and dressed it in expensive raiment, and laid it on an "escanno" he had taken from Almanzor (one thinks of the Cid's "escanno" taken from King Búcar), with a thousand candles to light it suitably. He had it placed in a magnificent coffin, covered with vermillion cloth, studded with gilded nails, and loaded on a sumpter mule. He ordered the three hundred captured Toulousans freed from the prison where they had been put, and sent them back home as an honor escort for their fallen leader, and with money for their journey. [3]

Dating the Poem

Marden based his dating of the poem on the identification of the French count and on the capture of Acre and Damiata in the Crusades. Recent discoveries make it necessary to re-examine the matter. For this it is best to go back to the first stanza of the episode of the count. The MS reads:

El conde Pyteos & el conde de tolosa
paryentes eran del rrey don sancho esto es cosa çierta
tomaron de sus con(xxx)dados conpan(xx) muy fermosa
movyeron para castylla en ora muy astrrosa. (328)

The part in the first parenthesis is crossed out in the MS showing that the copyist started to write "conpannas" and corrected his mistake to read "condados" as best he could. The corresponding part of the *PCG* (Chap. 696) reads:

llego el conde de Tolosa e de Piteos,

which shows that the writer knew that he was dealing with one man, but not so the copyist in the fifteenth century. Marden concluded that the latter had made two men out of one, destroying meter and rhyme with his changes, and edited the verses to read:

El conde [de] Pyteos e (el) conde de Tolosa

>   -paryente(s) era(n) del rrey, (don Sancho) esto es çierta cosa-,
>   tomo de sus condados conpanna muy fermosa,
>   movyo pora Castyella en ora muy astrrosa.

Later in verse 640d, the poet mentions Acre and Damiata. Marden says that both were taken by Christians in 1249 in the Sixth Crusade, victories which were widely celebrated in Christian Europe. He found that two men had been both "comte de Poitou" and "comte de Toulouse."[4] The first was Guillaume IX, duc d'Aquitaine who was also Guillaume VII, count of Poitou. He won Toulouse from Beltrán/Bernard, and held the county for only two years, 1098-1100. The second was Alphonse Jourdain (1250-1271), brother of Louis VIII of France, who married Jeanne, daughter of Count Raymond of Toulouse, in 1249 and was recognized by her people in 1250. At his death in 1271 Poitou reverted to the crown and the title disappeared. This Alphonse played a "papel prominente" in the Sixth Crusade. (The truth is that he was best known for being held hostage after Saint Louis had left for Acre, and was held until a large ransom was paid.) The naming of Acre (a strongly fortified, all-weather sea-port about seventy miles south of modern Beirut) and Damiata (on the Nile delta) in 640cd led Marden to say: "...la mención de Damiata puede ser eco de la conquista de esa ciudad por San Luis en 1249, año en que quedó también Acre en posesión de los cristianos. Este último punto y lo del doble título nos dan derecho á creer que el Poema se escribiera en el año 1250 ó muy poco después," a date that has been accepted by scholars ever since. (His use of the Subjunctive "escribiera" avoids the certainty that the Indicative would imply.) Juan Victorio Martínez recently said that the poem was most likely written within the years 1250-52.[5] Information that has recently come to light makes it necessary to re-examine the date.

Marden was mistaken in stating "1249, año en que quedó también Acre en posesión de los cristianos," because that city was taken by them in 1191 and remained in their hands until 1291 when the Crusaders withdrew from the Holy Land. Its capture after a siege of two years was the cause for great rejoicing in Europe, but was a bitter-sweet victory because it cost over 100,000 Christian lives.[6]

Marden was correct when he said that Damiata was captured in 1249. It too was a victory that brought great jubilation in Europe, but unfortunately the triumph was short-lived because the city was surrendered to the Sultan in 1250, after costing the lives of tens of thousands of Crusaders (most of them to sickness), forcing Saint Louis to give up his Egyptian campaign, withdraw to Acre, and pay an enormous ransom for hostages. In both of these seeming successes so many died that they were Pyrrhic victories that Europe could ill afford.

For Marden to be right the poet would have had to incorporate mention of Damiata into his poem before the celebration over the capture of the city had turned to dejection and before a full understanding of the total cost in lives of men had been reached This would have had to be before the news of the fall of Damiata in May of l250 had reached Europe.

An examination of the passage in which the two cities are named shows that it is another instance of ironic contrast or reversal, that favorite stylistic ploy of the poet. It occurs in the portion about the "mal arçipreste" (See Chapter Eight) whose hunting dogs discover FG who has escaped from jail through the help of Sancha, daughter of King García Sánchez of Navarre. Hiding by day in the woods and brush, our hero and his liberator are scented and discovered:

> Fueron luego los canes do yazien en la mata,
> el conde e la duenna fueron en grran rrebata,
> el arçipreste malo quando vio la barata,
> plogol' mas que sy ganase a Acre e Damiata. (640)

The "arçipreste," overjoyed at the happy prospect, threatens to deliver them back into the king's hands if the "duenna" does not allow him to enjoy her favors. She pretends to accept, then grapples with him, and while he is tightly held, FG still in shackles creeps over and kills the priest with the latter's own knife. This ironic reversal of a happy prospect could not have failed to please the public for whom the *juglares* had composed the episode. (Milá y Fontanals and Menéndez y Pelayo listed this episode as one of the early juglaresque portions of the poem.)[7] The poet used the ironic reversal inherent in the initial joy over the capture of Acre, which was offset by the terrible loss in lives, and in the taking of Damiata, with the dismay and dejection over its loss the next year as a parallel to the initial joy of the "arçipreste" and the ultimately overwhelming cost of his death. Marden may not have known that the city was in Christian hands less than twelve months and he clearly did not realize that the poet had referred to Acre and Damiata not as a matter of topical interest, but rather in a consciously thought out stylistic device to heighten the contrast of the ironic reversal of the errant priest's fate.

El conde de Pyteos e el conde de Tolosa

It would appear, therefore, that Marden did not understand the poet's mention of Acre and Damiata and there is evidence that the identity of the French count must also be questioned. Let us now look again at the "conde de Pyteos e conde de Tolosa" who served as the other criterion for the dating of the poem.

In 1958 there was in the library of the Real Academia de la Lengua a volume that listed the dates given by Marden in his study for the two men who held the double title. In 1971, unfortunately, they could not find the same book which may have been the one Marden used. Different information is given by Alphonse Brémond in his *Nobiliaire toulousain,* 1903.[8] He lists three men who were "comtes de Toulouse" near the end of the eleventh century and on into the next.

Toulouse (Raymond comte de) quatrième du nom,
    dit de Saint Gilles 1093-1105
Toulouse (Bertrand comte de) fils naturel
    du précédent lui succéda de 1105-1112
Toulouse (Alphonse Jourdain comte de)
    fils légitime de Raymond de Saint Gilles
    et d'Elvire de Castille, succéda á
    Bertrand de 1112-1148.

There is here no mention of Guillaume VII of Poitou, who we know from another source really was also count of Toulouse, and not only once but twice. Brémond apparently followed an ancient local tradition that never recognized the claim of Guillaume VII of Poitou as legitimate because medieval Salic Law denied succession to any female, and Guillaume VII was enforcing his wife's claim to the county. Might prevailed, however, and the Poitevin took over control of the county of Toulouse. He was the *de facto* count on two occasions, even though some refused to recognize him.

Confirmation of Marden's discovery of the double title held by Guillaume VII is given by Alfred Richard in his *Histoire des comtes de Poitou,* 1903,[9] published too late for Marden to use in his 1904 edition of the poem. What Richard tells is important to our poem as well as interesting in itself for the glimpse it gives of the mind-set and of some practices of a portion of Europe during the three centuries while the *PFG* was evolving. He says that Sancho Ramírez, king of Aragon, in 1086 married Philippie, daughter of Guillaume IV, comte de Toulouse After his death she married Guillaume VII, comte de Poitou. Her father turned the county over to his brother, Raymond de Saint Gilles who assumed the title in 1088. When this Raymond set out for the Holy Land in 1098, to head the Third Crusade at the

Pope's request, he left the county in the care of his illegitimate son Bernard, but Guillaume VII invaded to enforce his wife's claim to the county as legitimate daughter of Guillaume IV of Toulouse. Two years later our count of Poitou also left for the Holy Land, leaving Philippie in charge in Poitou, whereupon Bertrand reassumed control of Toulouse. By now Raymond had established himself as Governor of Tripoli and was prosperous, but our Count Guillaume VII suffered a tremendous defeat in which thousands of his Crusaders were killed, and he was back in Poitou by October 1102. In 1109, Bertrand set out for the Holy Land leaving his legitimate half-brother Alphonse Jourdain, aged two, (who had been born in the Holy Land and baptized in the Jordan River) nominally in charge. In 1113, our count of Poitou gathered support and retook control of Toulouse. In 1118 a crusade was preached for an expedition to fight the Moslems in Spain, but he declined to go. Later he changed his mind at the request of Alfonso el Batallador of Aragon, collected a force of six hundred horsemen, and crossed the Pyrenees to help Alfonso in the battle of Cutanda, near Zaragoza in 1120. Richard writes:

> Il se croisa donc, et à la fin de l'année il s'en fut à la tête de 600 chevaliers se mettre à la disposition d'Alphonse le Batailleur, roi d'Aragon; au printemps de 1120 l'armé de confédérés continua ses précédents succès qui furent couronnés le 18 mai par la victoire de Cutanda, dans laquelle les Musulmans firent une perte énorme.

Zurita confirms this in his *Anales de la corona de Aragon*, 1562-9.[10]

> Esta batalla según parece por las historias antiguas, se dio junto a Cutanda cerca de Daroca; y fue muy nombrada porque se hizo en ella gran matanza en los moros. El de Puitiers se halla con el rey. Toma el rey a Zaragoza y su reino...El conde vino a servir al emperador con seiscientos de caballo...Los moros entregaron la ciudad (Cutanda) al emperador a diez y ocho del mes de diciembre del mismo año en la cuarta feria en la era de 1156 (año 1118).

Further and equally convincing evidence comes from the *Annales compostelani* ca 1248,[11] in which we read that in 1118 Zaragoza was besieged for seven months, that seven battles were fought, and the city, castles, and villas were taken. Then (Alfonso) encircled Calatayud and besieged it.

> Deinde Calatayud firma obsidione vallavit, et acceptis obsidibus cum Guilemo Pictatavensis (sic) Comite, qui in auxilium eius venerat, ad Castrum Cotanda, contra

Sarracenos pugnaturus, iter direxit: ibique Sarracenis
expugnatis, Castrum Moabitarum dirupuit, & ipsum Castrum
Cotandam cepit.
Then he strongly besieged Calatayud, and when this was done,
with William count of Poitou who had come to aid him,
he went to Cutanda to fight the Sarracens and there, when the
Sarracens had been beaten he destroyed the (fortified) camp
of the Moabites and took the camp of Cutanda itself.

This entry in these annals had to be based on a tradition, either oral or written, of the presence and participation of the count of Poitou and Toulouse in the fighting at Cutanda, transmitted from 1118 to 1248. That it crossed the whole breadth of the peninsula to the far northwest corner is proof that the role of Guillaume VII was important enough for the chronicle in northwest Spain to record the activities of this foreign nobleman in Aragon.

If all the above were not enough, there is one final piece of evidence to authenticate Guillaume VII's activities in Spain. In the *Crónicon Sancti Maxentia* [12] of the home church of Guillaume VII in Poitou we find:

XV kalendas juli, comes Willelmus dux Aquitanorum
et rex Aragundiae pugnaverunt cum Abraham et aliis
quatuor regibus Hispaniarum, in campo Costanciae (sic);
et divicerunt et occiderunt quindecim millia Moabitarum
  et innumerabiles captiverunt. Duo milia camelorum
ceperunt et aliis bestiis sine numero et plurima
alia subjugaverunt castella.
15th kalends of July, count William, duke of Aquitaine
and the king of Aragon fought with Abraham and four
other kings of the Spaniards (Moors) on the (battle) field
of Costancia (Cutanda); and they defeated and killed
fifteen thousand Moabites and captured innumerable
others. They took 2000 camels and other beasts without
number and subdued many other castles.

Yes, there was a count of Poitou and Toulouse who fought in Spain but not at the Era Degollada against FG as the poem tells us. The Arlantine was not aware of the kernel of the historical truth that lay at the heart of the juglaresque material he used so fancifully in creating his work. His poem was not intended to be a historical document. It was and is a work of fiction with the special purpose of presenting its hero as the embodiment of the hopes, ambitions, and Christian zeal of those who peopled, built, and struggled for the Castile of the early years. Judging from Zurita's account, which he took from an earlier source in Latin, from the

Crónica de San Juan de la Peña, 1248, or possibly from a *cantar* still available in his day, it is clear that Guillaume VII, comte de Poitou et de Toulouse, made his presence sufficiently felt in Spain, 1118/1120, to have been incorporated into the historical records of the Spain of his day and possibly even into a *cantar* in the first half of the twelfth century. Marden correctly identified the double title held by the two men but lacked the evidence that would have allowed him to interpret it correctly.

An interesting addition to the story is the role played by Guy Geoffrey Guillaume (GGG), VIe comte de Poitou and VIIIe duc d'Aquitaine, at a time when Aquitaine comprised an enormous part of what is now France. Father of our "conde de Pyteos," he was asked by Raymond Béranger, count of Barcelona, to help in the continuing wars against the Moors. On his way to Spain he traversed the duchy of Gascogne. When its ruler quite understandably didn't want to allow an intruder with an army to cross his lands, GGG fought and defeated him, and added the title of "duc de Gascogne" to those he already had. Then in Spain he helped take the rich city of Barbastro and the surrounding countryside from the Moors. Both were ravaged by the victors and many Moors, both men and women, were taken as slaves. French histories give the date as 1063, while Spanish records show 1065. Months after the victory of the Christians, with nothing significant happening in military action, GGG became disgusted with the idleness and returned to Poitou.[13] The French *épopée Le siège de Barbastre* shows the kind of idleness that made GGG feel disgusted. It deals among other matters with the purported events before and after the defeat of the Moors, and tells of the Christian knights who preferred dalliance with high born Moorish maidens to military action.

Acre and Damiata have been shown to be invalid as a criterion for the dating of the poem. The role of Alphonse, count of Poitou and Toulouse, 1250-71, ransomed by Saint Louis, was less important for what he did in the Holy Land than that of Guillaume VII who was count of Poitou and Toulouse not only once but twice, 1098-1100 and 1113-24, known in Spain possibly for his fiasco in the Holy Land, but far better for his outstanding part in the conquest of Cutanda. With Marden's second criterion weakened if not invalidated, what more likely date can be suggested for the composition of the poem?

To answer the question we go back to the episode of the battle of Hacinas to the point where Almanzor summons his troops from "toda Afrryca."

[Los] turcos [e] alarabes, essas gentes ligeras

> que son pora en batallas vnas gentes çerteras,
> trraen arcos de nervyos e ballestas çerberas,
> destos venien llenos senderos e carreras.
> Venien los [almohades] e los auen marinos,
> trrayen en sus camellos sus fornos e molinos,
> venien los moros todos de oriente vezinos,
> de todos estos eran cobiertos los caminos. (383-4)

In this listing of the different "gentes" and their weapons, our poet was following the Homeric pattern as Correa Calderón pointed out.

It is verse 384a that gives us a clue as to a more probable date. The MS clearly reads: "los aues marinos" which makes no sense in a listing of "gentes" and their supplies and equipment for a long campaign. Zamora Vicente and other recent editors of the poem follow Menéndez Pidal's suggestion (*Reseña*) and give "auen marinos" which rhymes correctly in the stanza. It is agreed that this should be "aben merines/benimerines." The Benimerines were a tribe that did not come over to Spain from North Africa until 1275, so the poem could not have been written before that time.[14] The fact that they did not enter Spain until then has been disregarded by all in view of Marden's seemingly solid evidence and the reasoning for his "1250 ó muy poco después." Since these two criteria can no longer be held to be valid and since the completed poem was prosified in the *PCG*, 1289, the proposal is now made that 1280-85 is a more likely date for the composition of the *PFG*.

"Pariente del rrey era"

We now come to the second verse of the stanza as given in the MS in an attempt to determine what historical basis it may have:

> parientes eran del rey don sancho esto es cosa çierta,
> (328b)

The necessary correction back to the singular form of the verb is obvious once the two men have been recognized as only one, and the last two words must be inverted to restore the rhyme. The inclusion of "don sancho" must have been an internal gloss, destroying the meter, inserted by the copyist to inform the reader that it was Sancho to whom the count was related and it too had to be dropped. The King Sancho of Navarre of FG's time had died in 926 and never fought the Castilian, so Marden dropped the "don sancho." There is nevertheless a grain of truth in the legend because there was a count of Toulouse who died at Carazo and whose name found its way into the records. The *Códice de Meyá/Roda* and the *Crónica najerense* [15] both contain the following in their genealogies. (Abbreviations extended).

> Comitu[m] tolosan[orum] genealogia
> Pontius accepit uxorem filiam garcie sancionis & gen[uit] regemundu[m]. Rex mun[di] gen[uit] regemundum quem occiderunt in carazo.
> Pontius (count of Toulouse) married the daughter of García Sánchez and begat Raymond. Raymond begat Raymond whom they killed in Carazo.

The second "King of the World" was therefore the great grandson of García Sánchez, FG's contemporary and brother-in-law. He was not, however, the count of Poitou. His death occurred almost a century after Carazo was captured at the start of FG's career. He did not die in the siege which our poem says was the hero's first victory. But popular tradition retained the fact that a count of Toulouse had been killed in a battle at Carazo and that fact entered legend and appeared in the *PFG*.

Counts of Poitou who were "parientes del rrey" abound. One is found in Richard's *Histoire* which tells us that in 1069 Alfonso VI asked for the hand of Agnès (Inés), daughter of GGG, who was father of Guillaume VII. She joined Alfonso in 1074 but was repudiated five years later and replaced by Constance de Bourgogne. Zurita tells of another royal *parentesco* of this same Inés[16].

> "Nótese lo que aquí se advierte. En la historia de San Juan de la Peña (1248) se escribe que doña Inés que casó con el rey don Ramiro (el monje), fue hija del conde de Poitiers...escribe aquel autor que muerto el rey Alfonso el Batallador, sacaron a su hermano de la monjía y le dieron por mujer la nieta del conde de Puitiers. Pero lo que se ha de tener por cierto y constante conforme a la razón de los tiempos a mi juicio es que fuese hermana del postrer Guilllelmo."

The "a mi juicio" shows the record had become so confused by Zurita's day that he rejected the statement as he found it. Ramiro "el monje" did succeed his father to the throne, which made still another "conde de Pyteos e Tolosa" the relative of another king.

Since this Inés had first been married to Alfonso VI of Spain, her father, either Guillelmus VI, "conde de Pyteos" or his son Guillelmus VII, the "conde de Pyteos e conde de Tolosa" of our poem, was doubly "pariente del rrey." No wonder that the tradition came down through the years insisting that the French count was related to royalty. Interestingly enough, the last man to hold both titles of count of Poitou and Toulouse was the younger brother of Louis VIII, King of France. And finally, Eleanor of Aquitaine, grand-daughter of our Guillaume VII, "comte de Poitou et de Toulouse" married Henry II of England. He came down to southern France to try to enforce his wife's claim to Toulouse, and the now well mixed-up tradition of "paryente del rrey" had another chance to go around again beguiling enthralled listeners.

The *PCG* (Chap. 696) says: "Llego el conde de Tolosa e conde de Piteos" which shows that the writer of that MS knew that he was dealing with one man. Five times he writes only "Conde de Tolosa", omitting any mention of Poitou. Three times he refers to the soldiers as "los de Tolosa," and twice he writes of "tolosanos e gascones" (the latter had a part in the fighting due to GGG's conquest of that region), but not once does he mention the "petavinos" who also are named in the poem. It is in the *Crónica de 1344*,[17] however, that we see how far the confusion had spread during the half-century between the *PCG* of 1289 and the *C1344*. In its first mention of our count it states: "el conde de Piteos e el conde de Tolosa non llegaron. " A few lines later we find: "el conde Petavinos de Tolosa..." The confusion which had already begun in the MS of our poem where the initial reference to the man is: "el conde Pyteos e conde de Tolosa," with Pyteos as a first name, now becomes worse with the *C1344'* s final reference to him: "El conde Pretavinos de Tolosa..." None of these errors is due to the poet, and it is hard to understand how any copyist(s) could have strayed so far from the original and entangled further an already mixed-up name in so short a passage.

Yes, there was a "conde de Pyteos e conde de Tolosa" who was indeed "paryente del rrey" who did in fact take part in the battle of Cutanda in Aragon, though not in that of the Era Degollada. as stated in the poem. We can be sure that the poet invented only part of the sequel. And since much of the materials must have come to him orally in the *cantares juglarescos*, we would do well to amend the line from Berceo's cautionary admonition "al non escribimos si non lo que leemos" by adding the phrase "o lo que oímos," in recognition of the probable oral source of the episode.

The above proves that the poem's account of the participation of Guillaume VII, count of Poitou and Toulouse, was based on fact. What of the historicity of the first half of the battle? Pérez de Urbel stated that there were numerous clashes between Castile and Navarre as the leaders of both areas tried to expand their territory. He dates with assurance only the one in 960, when Sancho I of Leon, García Sánchez of Navarre, and Abderrahman of Cordoba united to remove FG's puppet, Ordoño IV, from the Leonese throne and restore Sancho who had been thrown out by FG. Pérez de Urbel believed that the Sancho who was killed in this battle was the son instead of the father of García Sánchez, because the father had died in 926, and because documents show that the son had been in Leon supporting his cousin Sancho I in 957 when troubles with Ordonno IV were starting. His statement that Prince Sancho faced the Castilian alone while Sancho I and the king of Navarre were still in Cordoba is hard to accept because this would require the relatively inexperienced young man to attack his battle-hardened, successful uncle at a time when Sancho I and García Sánchez together were so inadequate that they had gone to Cordoba to seek help. Further, this would change a prince to the poem's king, and disregard the death of the Sancho of the poem's battle, since Prince Sancho lived to inherit the throne of Navarre, and it would also destroy a set of three kings killed by FG.

The accusations made by FG against King Sancho were true for the period of the battle of the Era Degollada:
>traxyste a Castyella grrand tiempo a la pella
>dos veces en el anno veniste a corrella. (287cd)

And it was also true that:
>"Por fer mal a Castyella e destruyr castellanos,
>feziste te amigo de los pueblos paganos,
>feziste guerra mala a los pueblos cristianos," (288abc)

for it was only when Sancho I and García Sánchez, two "pueblos cristianos," had allied with Abderrahman to secure for themselves a preponderant strength that they invaded Castile, determined to rid themselves of their troublesome relative. There is, therefore, historical support for Pérez de Urbel's conclusion that the battle of the Era Degollada was based on the events of 960.[18]

One further comment must be made now to show what the poet does repeatedly. We go back to the beginning of the Era Degollada episode which immediately follows the battle of Lara:
>Mientrra que el conde estava a Dios haciendo plazer,
>lidiando con los moros con todo su poder,
>el rrey de los navarros ovo se a mover,
>cuydo toda Castyella de rrobar e correr. (281)

Throughout the poem the Arlantine makes one episode grow out of another with little or no time interval between. After the Christian victory at Carazo the reader is told that as soon as news of the Christian victory reached Almanzor he sent word for his followers to assemble and that on their arrival they started north and met FG at Lara. Before that episode is finished, Sancho of Navarre, as shown above, has invaded Castile, is defeated and killed by the

count. Before FG's wounds have healed, he refuses his men's request for a ten-day delay, and leads them against "Pyteos e Tolosa" who dies and is escorted back home in honor. The next battle is the most important military engagement of the poem, and we know that only a short time has passed since the Era Degollada because the funeral party is scarcely allowed to arrive at Toulouse:
"ya eran en Tolosa con su sennor llegados" (380b),
before Almanzor has sent word "por toda Afrryca" for his armies to assemble, and when they are ready, they move north to Muñó against FG. Not until the end of the battle of Hacinas, with the burial of the Christians at Arlanza, which closes the second main section of the poem, does the poet give any suggestion of a pause. At this point one may infer a time lapse before the start of the next episode of the "Cortes en Leon," with the ensuing capture and jailing of the count. The latter is freed by the Navarrese princess (Sancha, acording to the poem), and they go back to Burgos, where they are immediately married. The celebration of the "bodas," heightened by the jubilation of the Castilians who had gone to free him and had accompanied him back to Burgos, is interrupted by the news that Sancha's brother García Sánchez, king of Navarre, has already invaded Castilian territory to punish the count and to take back his sister. Menéndez Pidal says at this point: "Antes de esta copla (686) falta una que dijese cómo el conde enuió sus cartas por toda Castilla que fuessen luego con ell caualleros e peones."[19] He did the same for stanza 282 where he followed the *PCG*' 's account which, like the poem, tells of Sancho Garcés' invasion while FG is away again fighting the Moors. In neither case, however, does the poet think it necessary to have the count take time to send out a call for his men to assemble. He has structured his work so that in the earlier case above, FG's army is still with him after the battle of Lara just prior to the battle of the Era Degollada. In the second case, his Castilians met him on the way back from prison in Castroviejo and accompanied him to Burgos where they remained fully occupied in celebrating both his return to them after a year in prison and also his marriage to Sancha who had freed him. The poet has knowingly and intentionally omitted any time-lapse in these several portions giving the effect of continuous pressure on the count. In the poem he seven times uses the word "premia" to express FG's feeling of the unremitting, enormous pressure of his task of doing God's will and work in defeating all of Castile's enemies.

The main episodes of the poem were put into verse by *juglares* at an early period, some undoubtedly in the lifetime of the hero, as shown by the retention of proper names of the leaders of FG's army, and the poet adapted them to his needs. As such, they are not original with him. His contribution here, other than obvious surface decorations, lies in the far more important task of selecting, ordering, and retelling existing materials in such a way as to best embellish his story.

We are now in a position to change Marden's: "Es fábula todo el cuento tocante al Conde francés y el auxilio que prestara al rey de Navarra" to read," "Es fábula una parte del cuento..." because there was a historical basis for the presence of the French count fighting at Cutanda as ally of the king of Aragon, though not for the king of Navarre. We also change Zamora Vicente's "El episodio del conde es puro lugar poético." to "El episodio del conde es en parte lugar poético."[20] Our poet used existing materials to create his own version of the legends about FG and he treated them with poetic license as was his right.

---

[1] Study of the Escorial MS, my photocopy, and John Geary's facsimile edition of the poem all show that the word given as "e" in 300b looks like an "o" which is different from the "e" of 299d." The *PCG*, Marden and Geary all read "o." Janer, Serrano, Menéndez Pidal, Zamora Vicente and Victorio Martínez all read "e."

[2] Zamora Vicente has a long footnote here on the site of the battle. The Era Degollada lies in the Valpirri/ Valpiedra/ Valpierre/ Vall Pirri between the River Najerilla and another that is roughly parallel to it. Both flow towards the northeast into the Ebro. In stanza 356 in the sequel to the battle, the Castilians go on to the Ebro and fight their way across, driving the Toulousans from the far bank. (359b). Menéndez Pidal (*Reseña*) says: "Valpirre es la llanura que hoy se llama Valpierre. entre Briones y Nájera...Es un llano muy pedregoso...[compárese Berceo *San Millán*, 14, "Por medio de Valpirri, un sequero logar"] : el padre Anguiano, *Compendio hist. de la Rioja*, lib.3, cap. 19, dice que en Valpiedra o Valpierre "hay una piedra que hasta hoy llaman del conde." Stanza 746, in the third battle against Navarra, says it was a "fuerte vallejo" good for hunting, producing "grrana con que tiñen vermejo," and "al pye le passa Ebro much yrado sobejo"/ Valpyrrel' dizen todos, e assi le llamaron/do el rrey (García Sánchez) e el conde anbos se ayuntaron. (747).

[3] In his *Historia general de España*, (Madrid:, 1608,) I, p. 524-5, Juan de Mariana tells of a battle in 1157 which is strangely parallel to the Era Degollada and its sequel: two battles in the same place, twice in the same year, help from the French belatedly comes after the Navarrese have lost the first battle and again the Navarrese and their allies lose, the prisoners are treated honorably. It is possible but highly improbable that our poet knew of this battle of 1157 and adapted some of its details to his purposes.
Essentially the same account is found under the entry "Valpierre" in the: *Diccionario geográfico-histórico de España* of the Real Academia de Historia, Sección II, (Madrid: 1846) and Pascual Madoz's *Diccionario geográfico-*

estadístico- histórico de España, 16 vols. ((Madrid: 1845-50), under the entry "Bañares."

4 C. Carroll Marden, "An Episode in the *"PFG," Revue Hispanique,* VII, (1900), pp. 22-7. and also the introduction to his edition of the *PFG,* pp. xxix-xxxi.

5 Juan Victorio ed., *PFG,* (Madrid: Cátedra, 1981). He says that the poet was probably trying to flatter King Fernando III , by comparing him with our Count Fernando, into contributing to the monastery of San Pedro de Arlanza. He concludes that since this King Fernando died in 1252, the poem must have been composed 1250-52. pp. 27-9.

6 Stephen Runciman, *A History of the Crusades,* 3 vols., (Cambridge: III, 1955.) pp. 261-71. See also Zoé Oldenbourg, *The Crusades,* trans. from the French by Anne Carter, (New York: Pantheon, 1965), pp. 449-457. Another cause for shock and depression over the Christian capture of Acre was the news that Richard the Lion-hearted, in charge of the city for a time, had in cold blood ordered the execution of three thousand of its Moslem defenders against the terms of the surrender treaty.

7 Manuel Milá y Fontanals, *De la poesía heróico-popular castellana,* ed. Riquer y Molas, (Barcelona: 1959), p. 259.
    Menéndez y Pelayo, *Obras de Lope de Vega,* VII, (Madrid: 1897), p. cxciii.

8 Alphonse Brémond, *Nobilaire toulousain,* (Toulouse: 1863), p. 464.

9 Alfred Richard, *Histoire des comtes de Poitou,* I, (775-1126), (Paris: Picard & fils, 1903). Chapter on "Guillaume le jeune." Quotation p. 482.

10 Jerónimo Zurita, *Anales de la corona de Aragón,* ed. Angel Canellas López, (Zaragoza: 1957), p. 141.

11 Henrique Flórez, "Annales compostelani," *España sagrada,* XXIII , p. 320.

12 Paul Marchegay and Emile Mabille, *Chroniques des églises d'Anjou,* recueillies et publiées pour la Société de l'Histoire de France. (Paris: 1969), From the "Cronicon Sancti Maxentii Pictavensis," pp. 351-433.

13 Richard, op. cit. pp. 289-93, 308, 351.

14 Rachel Arié, *L'Espagne musulmane au temps des Nasrides (1232-1492).* (Paris: Brocard, 1973.) pp.69-70.
    Histoire des Benou l'Ahmar, rois de Grenade, extraits du Kitab al 'Ihbar (Livre des examples) trad. fran. par M. Gaudefroy Demombynes, dans *Journal Asiatique,* neuvième série, t. XII, Paris: 1898 p.22.
    M. Ben Cheneb, ed. *Al Dahira,* (anonyme) (Alger: 1920.) "L'armée marinide puis le sultan ses familiers, son escorte et ses viziers debarquèrent aux environs de Tarifa le 21 safar 674/ 18 juillet 1275."

15 Georges Cirot, La chronique léonaise," *Bulletin hispanique,* XIII (1911), p. 438.

16 Zurita, op. cit. pp. 1135-6. Menéndez Pidal says that Guillaume VI had two daughters of whom the first married Alfonso VI. The second married Pedro I of Aragon, son of Sancho Ramírez. A daughter of Guillaume VII married Ramiro el monje. *Poesía árabe y poesía europea*, (Madrid: Espasa Calpe, 1955) 4th ed. p. 37.

17 Menéndez Pidal, *Reliquias* , p. 159.

18 Pérez de Urbel, *Historia*, II, pp. 553-6. and *Glosas,* pp. 239-43.

19 Menéndez Pidal, *Reseña*.

20 Marden, *PFG,* p. xxix.
Zamora Vicente, *PFG,* p. 98, footnote to 328a.

Chapter Eight

Cortes in Leon and Aftermath

"Enbio Sancho Ordonnez al buen conde mandado" (564a)

The third main section of the poem is just as carefully sequenced as the previous two. The introductions to the battles have been shown to be as important as or more so than the portion devoted to the fighting. In this last fourth of the work too, several episodes themselves become the introduction for the one that follows. A glance at the outline of Section III given in the chapter on structure, in slightly expanded form here so as to show causal relationships, will make clear their integrated connection.

III   Liberation of Castile from Leon
     A Cortes in Leon; leading to capture and imprisonment of FG in Navarrese jail; release by and marriage to Sancha which causes
     B Second battle against Navarre with capture of García Sánchez and his release through intervention of Sancha; third battle against Moors; third battle against Navarre.
     C Cortes in Leon; quarrel over debt, imprisonment, release by Sancha; negotiations over debt leading to liberation of Castile

Section III starts with "cortes" in Leon and the sale of a horse and hawk by FG to Sancho, turns to the capture and jailing of FG by the Navarrese, changes to the intervention of a Lombardian, inserts a troubadoresque interlude with an escape from jail and encounter with an "arcipreste malo," and adds the meeting with the Castilians on their way to free FG, followed by a wedding and celebration. Then come an invasion and battle with capture and jailing of García Sánchez, release after a third intervention by Sancha, the third battle against the Moors and the third against Navarre. Finally the poet settles down and finishes the story of Sancho and FG, which has been made dramatic and vivid by the third jailing and the third release on intervention by Sancha before the eventual independence of Castile is reached. The successful interweaving of all these threads shows that the poet prepared and followed his plan with great care. He had to put together all the above disparate elements in such a way that he glorified his hero and the Castilians.

It will be remembered that the siege of Carazo, the first military action of the poem, was motivated by the young FG's determination to free his Castile from oppression, from its age-old "premia." The first battle against Navarre was caused by his determination to avenge injustice and remove the "premia" that would result if he accepted King Sancho's treacherous raiding of Castilian territory. The second battle against the Moors was due to Almanzor's desire for revenge against the upstart who had defeated him, and to FG"s fight against the "premia" of the Moorish Conquest. Motivating forces are much more varied in the last section of the work. The final battle of the poem was apparently imposed on the poet solely by the tripartite structure he had chosen as the main framework for his poem. We now consider the several episodes in detail.

Cortes

The first main section of the poem traced the history of Gothic Spain. The second established the military supremacy and personal prowess of the hero over Moors and Navarrese. As the third main section opens, Sancho Ordonnez, king of Leon, appears for the first time. The main purpose of III, A is the freeing of Castile from subservience to Leon. Sancho summons FG to "cortes," saying that all the other nobles are there and they are waiting only for the Castilian to appear. That the king should send a special message to the count after the others had assembled and that they should all wait for him to arrive shows the status and importance of the man. His reaction to the message shows why he had delayed in obeying the summons.

> Ovo ir a las cortes pero con grrand pesar,
> era muy fiera cosa la mano le besar;
> "Sennor Dios de los çielos, quieras me ayudar,
> que yo pueda a Castyella desta premia sacar." (565)

Here we have in one stanza the situation, the psychologically motivating factors, and the stated purpose of the last main section of the poem. The keynotes: "la mano le besar" and "desta premia sacar" must be remembered for they will appear again in the closing. This stanza is a restatement of the driving purpose of the count and his Castilians which the poet told in an early stanza at the start of FG's career.

> Varones castellanos, este fue su cuydado:
> de llegar su sennor al mas alto estado,
> D'un alcaldia pobre fizieron la condado,
> tornaron la despues cabeza de rreygnado. (l72)

For this they have followed FG through suffering and victory at Carazo, Lara, Hacinas, the Era Degollada, and in Valpirri. They have triumphed repeatedly over the Moors doing God's will, and they have proved their superiority over their Christian neighbor, Navarre. In all this there has been no mention of duty to their king. Now when a major portion of their common, continuing task has been accomplished in the battles won, their liege lord summons their count who obeys, albeit late and reluctantly. The *Fuero Juzgo* (ed. cit.) states:

> Libro V Titol IV Ley antigua. Todo omne que no quiere venir por mandado del rey, ó que diz por enganno que non le oyó, é que non vió su mandado, pues que fuere provado este enganno; si es omne de mayor guisa, peche tres libras doro al rey. E si non oviere onde pague, reciba C azotes, e non pierda su ondra.

There was, of course, no, chance that this law might be enforced. But for the count to acknowledge subservience publicly by answering the summons to "cortes" and then kissing his sovereign's hand before the assembled nobles was a humiliation that FG would not willingly accept, and was the reason for his almost anguished prayer for help in taking Castile out from under this "premia," this crushing burden. His appearance at "cortes" was a matter of great joy for the Leonese nobles, as a refusal to attend might have led to great unpleasantness, even to open fighting. All were glad to see him, except for the queen who had "muy grrand enemistad" with the count. This unexplained enigmatic statement leaves a feeling of uncertainty that will remain until later because the poet now changes the thread of his story again.

Taking his rightful place in the assembly, FG quickly disposes of the business at hand, and then gives personal counsel to those who request it. He had come on a superb steed which he had taken from Almanzor. (One remembers the Cid's horse Babieca taken from the king of Seville.) Sancho sees the horse and hawk and decides that he must have them. FG offers them as a gift, but the king insists on paying. The price is set at one thousand marks of silver, to be paid on a stipulated date, and a penalty is imposed: the price is to be doubled for each day repayment falls into arrears, and the

contract is signed in "cartas por ABC." (This type of contract didn't come into usage until long after the time of FG. It provided that the terms of the agreement be written twice with a line , often of ABCABC etc., between. The parchment or paper was cut through the ABC's in a wavy line so that only when the two parts were brought together and found to fit perfectly was it clear that no substitution had been made in the wording.) The doubling of the amount to be paid is "al gallarín." This is the adaptation of the oriental tale of the man who obligated himself to pay with one grain of wheat on the first square of a chess-board, two grains on the second, four on the third, etc. He soon saw that he would never be able to fill the thirty-second square. (It is interesting to note that the MS says "cada dia cada dia," not "al gallarín," a change adopted only by modern editors of the text.) Sancho clearly did not know the tale and was as lacking in cash as he was in knowledge of mathematics and fell into a trap without knowing that he had done so, for the poet says of him:
  Assaz avia el Rrey buen cavallo comprado,
 mas saliol' a tres annos muy caro el mercado,
 con el aver de Francia nunca seria pagado,
 por y perdio el Rey Castiella su condado. (574)
Here the poet uses the last verse of the stanza to foretell the eventual ending of the story of Sancho and FG.

  The matter of the horse and hawk as sale price for the whole county of Castile has called forth numerous explanations and much discussion. One of the earliest attempts was made by William Entwistle in 1924 who suggested what he admitted involved a tenuous connection. Quoting from Jordanes' sixth century history of the Goths, he showed that at one point Jordanes rejected a portion whose doubtful authenticity is expressed in the words "it is said." It told of the Hunuguri who "it is said" redeemed their people from servitude, "for "the price of a horse."[1] Then the idea was picked up by Menéndez Pidal who accepted the statement totally because it strengthened his theory of the Germanic origin of the epic.[2] He overlooked the fact that the story concerned the Hunuguri, not the Germans or Goths. In 1976, L.P. Harvey alone, and then in 1982, in collaboration with David Hook, discussed the whole matter as given in Arab histories.[3] They said that there are several which deal with the treachery of Count Julian and his betrayal of Gothic Spain to the Moors in 711. Four of these accounts involved the purchase of a horse or horse and hawk. The last of the four was written only a few years after the death of FG in 970 and therefore well in time for it to have entered the growing legends about the Conquest and eventually about the count of Castile. In the most romanticized of these, Julian promised to go back to Africa and, when he returned, to bring with him hawks such as king Rodrigo had never seen. He of course meant that he would return with the Moorish invaders, but Rodrigo had no way of knowing. Harvey and Hook say that similar accounts are found in other European cultures as well as in the Orient. In the *Cavallero Zifar*, written some fifty years after the composition of the *PFG*, there is the loss of a kingdom for the price of a dog, a horse, and a hawk. Harvey and Hook say that in our poem there seems to be no moralizing in the loss of Castile: no Sexual Lust, no Inordinate Desire, no Immoderate Request unpunished, no Test of Kingship, as in some variants of the horse and hawk theme. To these must be added the fifth failing: the Deceptive Bargain, by which Sancho lost what was to become the most important part of Christian Spain, because as the poem says:

por y perdio el Rey Castyella su condado   (574d)

Pérez de Urbel and Menéndez Pidal discuss the "roboratio" or corroboration of a sale, exchange, or major gift in which the person who receives may give a jewel, cloak, or other token payment, even a horse or hawk, in return. The latter quotes Fray Benito de Montejo who says:" A la segunda época reducen lo que varias de nuestras historias refieren de la entrega de un azor y un caballo por nuestro conde al rey de León, pero los más, como una especie de cuento, novela, indigna de crédito. Mas yo no veo que den razón alguna para esta calificación. Antes bien, hallándose un gran número de escrituras de aquellos tiempos, que se solemnizan y corroboran con la entrega por la parte agraciada de algún caballo rojo, bayo, morcillo o otro color apreciable que se suele expresar, me parece igualmente haber mediado tal entrega en el pacto..." He continues with an example of the value of the "azor" and other birds of prey.[4] The whole story which the poet is telling is aimed at showing how FG secured the liberation of Castile by legitimate peaceful means. This makes Castile the long delayed "roboratio," given as token in exchange for the horse and hawk, which are the the "merchandise" of the sale. Such an inversion is an ironic reversal exaggerated to absurdity. It is likely that the "juglares" had worked out the sale in this way to heap scorn on Sancho and to further glorify their hero as the canny leader who bested the king by his greater shrewdness.

Pérez de Urbel says that such a gift to the king was often the mark of respect shown to the monarch by his vassal and it may be that FG did give the two animals to his liege lord.[5] In any case, the *juglares* changed the story so that it disparaged the king and showed our count as a cunning and shrewd man who outsmarted his ruler. And the poet tells the episode in such a way as to use his favorite device of ironic reversal to heighten the contrast between the beginning and the end of this extremely Deceptive Bargain.

The next portion concerns what happens in Leon after the close of the "cortes. Before leaving for home, FG is approached by Queen Teresa who proposes to him a marriage to the daughter of the king of Navarre. She then writes to her "nephew" and urges upon him a stratagem by which he can capture the Castilian. FG and his men, unaware of her duplicity, see this as a way to peace and stability. Arrangements are made for a meeting with King García Sánchez to settle marriage terms, but when FG goes, he is treacherously captured at Ciruenna and jailed in Castroviejo in Navarrese territory not far from the border with Moorish territory. A count of Lombardy on his way to Compostela appears and is allowed to visit the prisoner. He then goes to see the princess who served as bait for the trap and urges her to free the Castilian. She goes to see FG and releases him on his promise to marry her, carrying him on her back because he is still shackled. Traveling by night to avoid detection they are hiding by day in the undergrowth when the hunting dogs of an "arcipreste" scent them. The priest sees this as an opportunity to have his pleasure at the expense of the woman by threatening, if she refuses, to turn them over to the king. The princess pretends to agree but when the disrobed priest approaches, she grapples with him and FG crawls over and kills him with a knife presumably taken from the prelate's discarded clothing. Riding the mule of the dead man they go on their way and meet meet the count's men who have made a statue of him, sworn fealty to it, kissed its hand, and with it in their front rank have gone to free their leader, swearing not to return without him. After a joyful reunion, the whole company goes on to Burgos where the marriage takes place and the festivities begin, celebrating both the wedding and the return of the count after his year's incarceration. Let us now look at this section in detail.

The count and his men had been received with joy at "cortes" by the king and his court of nobles. All were highly pleased, except for the Queen who had "muy grrand enemistad" with the count. This unexplained statement introduces a feeling of foreboding. As he had done in earlier parts of his work the poet has planted here the first of numerous seeds in the story he is telling.

Teresa

"que avya con el conde muy grrand enemistad. (4567d)

The poem left Teresa after the cryptic announcement that the presence of FG in the court was a burden to her:
> a la Rreyna sola pesaua por verdad,
> que avya con el conde muy grrand enemistad. (567cd)

Who was she and why the enmity? In the poem, which calls her Teresa, she writes to García Sánchez:
> "Oras tu tynes tyenpo de vengar mi hermano," (580a)

which makes her the sister of Sancho Garcés, whom FG had killed in battle, and aunt of King García Sánchez. In the *PCG* (Chap 709) she writes:
> "perdiemos al rey don Sancho nuestro padre,"

which makes her the sister of García Sánchez, whereas in the poem she writes:
> "perdi al Rey tu padre que yo grrand bien queria," (579c),

which makes her the aunt of the king. So, she is variously the sister or daughter of King Sancho Garcés, and the aunt or sister of King García Sánchez. Zamora Vicente writes:

> "La reina era Teresa, hermana de Sancho Abarca, aquel gran rey de Navarra que murió en combate singular con el conde Fernán González (copla 316) en la batalla de la Era Degollada. De ahí su enemiga por el castellano." [6]

In this he follows the poem and the ballads which followed the poem, continuing the confusion. Who was she in fact? In Flórez's *Reynas católicas* we find the following in a document of Santius rex (Sancho Ordonnez of the poem):

> die kalendis aprilis
> era DCCCCXCVII
> (March 29, 959)
> Signatures: Santius rex hoc vere conf[irmat]
> Veremundus rex conf.
> Tarasia regina conf.[7]

This Teresa was the wife of King Sancho I of Leon. The footnote identifies her as the daughter of Assur Fernández, count of Monzón. When FG became too active in the area west of Castile, King Ramiro II of Leon appointed Assur Fernández, of a family that had long been one of the foremost of his realm, as count over the area in question thus effectively blocking the Castilian from further expanding his county in that direction. This was important, for Monzón lay to the west of Castile and south of Saldaña, held by Diego Muñoz to whose son FG had married one of his two daughters. FG had expected this political alliance would put one relatively enormous stretch of land under his control. But he was blocked by Ramiro. The two "consuegros" kept on in their joint efforts until Ramiro stripped them of their properties and jailed them. There they remained until it was expedient for the king to release them and restore them to their former holdings, probably because he needed FG's military strength against the Moors. While they were in prison he sent Assur Fernández to Burgos to keep matters stable in Castile, and then his younger son Prince Sancho went there to represent the royal person . The count of Monzón and the prince remained in Burgos only until shortly after FG was free again, as shown by the fact that their signatures figure in documents for a time and then disappear not long after our count returns, when his signature reappears in documents.[8]

It matters little that the real identity of Teresa and her relationship to the other principals in the poem were lost in the evolving legends about the count of Castile. What is important is that she lived in the songs of the *juglares* in the growing, evolving *cantares* about FG and therefore in the memories of the people. After her real identity was lost, the legends retained the enmity, but then it was necessary to invent a reason for it under the new identity. They did so by making her the sister of Sancho Garcés whom FG killed in battle, providing the correct psychological motivation for the enmity but garbling the story of why she hated the Castilian. Why did she feel this way?

It is probable that the real Teresa accompanied her father when he went to administer Castile while FG was in jail. Daughter of a powerful family, she had spent her youth with the rivalry and ill-will between the two families as an ever present fact of her life. Her position rose along with that of her father when he took Castile under his governance in 943/4. She must have felt a great pleasure as she contemplated her father's taking over control of the county of the man who was "enemistado" with her family, and undoubtedly enjoyed her enhanced role in the scene. It is probable that at this time she met Prince Sancho of Leon when he came to represent his father in Burgos. Then FG returned and she had to leave along with her father, going back to Monzón with diminished prestige, and certainly holding an increased and now personal resentment against the Castilian. Later the acquaintance with the prince became important and they were married.[9] When her husband came to the throne as Sancho I at the death of Ordoño III, she found she was Teresa, Queen of Leon, enjoying all the perquisites of her new position. Suddenly her family's old nemesis, that count of Castile whose return once had removed her father and her from the highest position in Burgos, was in her husband's royal court and her anger flared up. She had been forced out of her high position because of this man who had for years been an enemy of her family. She had long harbored her anger and a wish to avenge the wrongs done to her and her family. This is her personal "vieja saña retenida," and she bided her time, "aguanto y aprovecho," for revenge. When she saw an opportunity she quickly planned a strategem to even scores with the Castilian.

What of the historical facts of the jailing of FG? Dozy cites Ibn Hayân saying that the "roi des Basques" (sic, i.e. the Navarrese) captured FG in a battle.[10] This of course was unacceptable to the *juglares* who were intent only on extolling the count and had to remove that disgrace to their hero. It happened that FG's first wife Sancha, the Navarrese princess he had married about 931, had died at the end of 959. This left Castile's flank exposed on the northeast and no one was more aware of the fact than the count. He had put his puppet Ordoño IV on the throne of Leon in 958, forcing Sancho I to flee.[11] In 960, however, when the latter obtained the firm support of his uncle, the king of Navarre, and of King Abderrahman of Cordoba, the puppet was driven out, Sancho returned to the throne and Teresa was married to him to seal an alliance between him and the Ansúrez family. At some point, probably in 960, FG was captured, imprisoned by García Sánchez and held in jail for about a year, while the Moorish king kept on insisting that FG be turned over to him.[12] Queen Mother Toda, the old conniver, was still at work and she undoubtedly had her hand in arranging the second marriage of FG, this time to her grand-daughter the Navarrese princess Urraca, daughter of García Sánchez. Pérez de Urbel shows that after Sancha's death, Urraca's signature, which had appeared in Navarrese documents up to this time, now disappeared, and an Urraca signed as FG's wife, only to reappear in Navarrese documents after the Castilian died in 970. He concludes that our count did marry Urraca and that evolving tradition lost sight of the second wife or intentionally combined the two Navarrese princesses, called both of them Sancha, and used her first to get him into and then twice to get him out of prison.[13]

It must be recalled at this point that the battle of the Era Degollada was caused by an invasion of Castilian territory by Sancho Garcés while FG was away fighting the Moors on behalf of his God. This blow in the back by one who should have been his ally, was treachery, "enganno," and the *juglares* did not let the public forget it. To keep FG's reputation unsullied by any suspicion of his being less able in combat than his opponents, they again had recourse to treachery, this time on the part of Teresa and García Sánchez, which would keep a defeat on the battle field from dishonoring the count.

Since it could be imputed to the same Navarrese royal family, they strengthened the case against Navarre by thrusting the opprobrium of this second "enganno" upon García Sánchez. And they started it off with Teresa's stirring up the nobles in the Leonese court at the end of the "cortes" where FG had just been well received by his king and by those same nobles whom she now turned against him. She wrote to her "nephew" García Sánchez, laying a cleverly devised trap. The poet omitted the details of the message, but the public, knowing the story, was drawn in to participation by having to supply the content of the letter from Teresa. The poet merely sketched the framework of the incident:

> Antes que el partyesse, vna duenna loçana
> Reyna de Leon, de don Sancho hermana
> prometiol' al buen conde e fizol' fiuza vana,
> cuntiol' com al carnero que fue buscar la lana. (576)

Here we have the announcement of an approaching ironic reversal:

> Demostro le el diablo el enganno ayna:
> cometyol casamiento al conde la Reyna:
> por que finas la guerra le daria su sobrina.
> Seria el danno grrand syn esta melecina. (577)

The message to her "nephew" told him to call FG to a meeting to discuss marriage to his sister (really his daughter), which would re-establish the political alliance that had ended with the death of Sancha, his first wife. It is easy to understand how much the combining of the two women into one Sancha simplified and strengthened the juglaresque story. Teresa's desire for revenge is clear in:

> si yo fuese Rey com tu ya vengadol' auria,
> Oras tu tyenes tyempo de vengar mi hermano,
> por este tal enganno coger lo as en mano,
> tomaras buen derecho d'aquel conde loçano,
> a vida non le dexes aquel fuert castellano. (579d-580)

To arouse García Sánchez himself to act, she finished by kindling his sense of filial duty, and roused his pride by saying that had she (a woman) been king she would have already avenged her brother's death. The *PCG* followed the poem here, but the *Cl344* had Teresa add that she and her nephew could share the guilt for the "omecillo," the homicide.

Both the count and his men approved of the proposal for the new alliance with Navarre:

> Quando oyeron las gentes d'aqueste casamiento,
> todos tenian que era muy buen ayuntamiento,
> que seria de la paz carrera e çimiento, (581abc)

And they were right, for marriage to a Navarrese princess would remove the dangers that threatened Castile from the northeast, and would thereby keep Sancho I quiescent in the west. That left only the Moors whom they had repeatedly shown they could handle. Then the poet clearly foretells the disaster to come:
>   mas ordio otras redes el diablo pezineto.   (581d)

Vistas en Ciruenna-Traición del rey navarro

With the place and time for the meeting set in Ciruenna to the satisfaction of both men, FG appeared with an escort of five/six men as agreed, but when he saw García Sánchez had come with thirty, he realized he had been betrayed and exclaimed:
> "Santa María, val, ca yo so confondido,
> creyndo me por palabra yo mismo so vendido."   (585cd)
>   ...
> Con este mal enganno que el rrey a cometido,
> lo que me dixo el monje, en ello so caydo.   (586cd)

He fled with his escort to a hermitage/church where he took shelter. His "escudero" threw their swords in through a window, and then left with the other "escuderos" to take the news back home. The Navarrese could not get to the hard pressed Castilians, but at the end of the day FG surrendered on condition that their lives be spared. At this moment, God showed his anger as the altar was split from top to bottom and the church building along with it. (The poet says that as verification of this, the public can still see the damage for themselves.) (592-3) This is closely parallel to the veil of the temple being rent from top to bottom at the moment Christ expired on the cross. FG was put into irons and taken to prison in Castroviejo, but he secured the release of his escort who he said were innocent parties in the capture. They too went back to Castile with the latest news, and there was a great mourning for their imprisoned lord. In the jail, meanwhile, FG was closely guarded and treated badly:
> ...teniendol' fuerte sanna mala presion le dieron
> commo omnes syn mesura, mesura non le fizieron.   (597bc)
>   ...
> nunca fue omne nado en prysion mas coytado.   (605d)

This harsh treatment will be avenged later in the poem.

Then Sancha frees the prisoner. The satisfaction of a Castilian public must have been immense on hearing of how their hero escaped from prison. That one woman countered the treachery of another who had long been known as an enemy of the count, and at the same time let him win a bride was a matter for great satisfaction. The account of how she aided and abetted the man she then married must have delighted all Castilians. That Urraca did this without her father's knowledge made a fool of him, which was what he deserved for his part in the treachery of Teresa's nefarious plot. An offer of marriage was real and may in fact have been used to bait a trap in which FG could be taken. It may even have been an offer made by García Sánchez voluntarily to strengthen his position against the Moors. Toda, the shrewd conniver, may have originated the idea. In any case, the imprisonment did occur, and the wedding really did take place not long after the Castilian was freed. One can easily understand that, betrayed and imprisoned by the man who had until a few months before had been his brother-in-law, FG should have been seething with anger, and that he would have promised anything to get out of jail, even to marrying. The juglares knew this and made it a motivating factor in their version. The fact that the "donzella" was the daughter of the man who had jailed FG and that she acted in secret made the count's revenge all the sweeter.

El conde lombardo

The following episode introduces a visitor whose role is to serve as a link between FG and the Navarrese princess Urraca. We do not know why the poet used a count from Lombardy here. Serrano says that it may be due to a bishop in the XIII century who was of a prominent Lombardian family that had settled in Burgos.[14] As stated before, Milá y Fontanals and Marcelino Menéndez y Pelayo concluded that the episode was one of the early portions of the poem. Georges Cirot likened it to vaguely similar stories in other literatures, but missed the main thrust of the telling.[15] No one saw that it is a complicated account, with portions coming from the most unexpected sources. At first reading it is merely the poet-monk's moral tale of the misadventure of a churchman, an "arcipreste" whose erring conduct reaped its just reward. As was his custom, our poet began with an introduction that was at least as important as the main story. A count from Lombardy on his pilgrimage to Santiago de Compostela asked about the country through which he was passing and was told of the treacherous capture and jailing of its count. He was allowed to visit FG in the prison and the two men were greatly impressed with each other. Leaving the jail he went to see the "donzella" who had served as bait for the trap in which the Castilian was caught, and told her that she was doing a great disservice to Christendom, that she should do anything she could to secure the prisoner's release, and that Castile would be lost if she didn't. He said she would be blamed for the disaster, adding that if she could marry the prisoner, she would be considered lucky by "las duennas" and would be honored by all "los d'Espanna," and that she could not marry any better "enperador o cavallero."

La donzella enamorada

After he left, the "donzella," who in all probability was the princess Urraca, sent her serving lady to the jail to see whether the Lombardian had been exaggerating. The "duenna" reports favorably for FG.

> "Rruego vos lo, sennora, por la fe que devedes,
> que vayades al conde e vos lo conortedes,
> tal conde com aqueste non lo desamparedes,
> sy muere de tal guisa grrand pecado faredes." (625)

We know from the *Siete infantes de Lara* what such comfort to the prisoner might entail.

The princess is immediately smitten without having seen FG and her response is clear and strong:

> "Quiero contrra el conde vna cosa fazer,
> al su fuerte amor dexar me vencer,
> quierom' aventurar e yr me lo a ver,
> todo mi corazon fazer le he a entender. (627)

She goes to the prison to FG:

> -"Buen conde, dixo ella, esto faz buen amor,
> que tuelle a las duennas verguença e pavor,
> olvidan los paryentes por el entendedor,
> ca de lo que el se paga tyenen lo por mejor." (629)

She continues, saying that if he will promise to marry her, she will release him from jail; if he refuses, he will die in prison. He of course accepts, promising on his part that he will never take any other wife. She then takes him out of the prison quietly so the king won't be alerted and thwart them. They flee, with the "donzella" carrying the count on her back because he is still shackled and can not walk. They keep going until the approaching dawn makes it dangerous for them to continue and they stop in "vn monte espeso" to await the night.

El arcipreste malo

Their escape is momentarily halted by an "arcipreste" riding on a mule, who is out hunting with his dogs and hawk. When the hounds discover the couple in hiding, the priest is overjoyed, more than if he had won Acre and Damiata, and threatens to turn them over to the king unless, as he says, the lady allows him to "cunplir mi voluntad" with her. FG refuses, but she pretends to accede to the demand, and when the disrobed priest is unable to help himself, she grapples with him, the shackled count crawls to them and kills the "arcipreste malo" with a knife that he presumably has taken from the priest's discarded clothes.

In 1973, Fernando de Toro-Garland's article "El arcipreste, protagonista literario del medievo español" threw virtually the first real light on this episode. He connects it with the Arcipreste de Hita. Quoting Milá y Fontanals and Menéndez y Pelayo, he connects the "arcipreste" with the "primitivo y más antiguo cantar juglaresco" as shown in the *Rodrigo o Crónica rimada.*. That "tema" served the poet of Arlanza for whom the priest is "entre ingenuo y crédulo," and whom he ridicules with a mixture of "broma y sátira." Quoting the *Leyes de partida*, Toro-Garland tells of the various grades and duties of "arciprestes." It was forbidden to them to hunt with dogs and hawks, though they were allowed to fish and hunt with nets and snares. So when our poet says to his public:

"d'un Arcipreste malo que yva a cazar,
oyeron los podencos en el rrastro entrar. (639cd)

they know that they are dealing with a law breaker who will deserve what he gets. In the end he is despoiled of his dogs, his mule, his clothes, his "mudado açor," and his very life (651c). Here indeed is an intentional ironic reversal as the poet shows by naming Acre and Damiata.

Toro-Garland says that the great weakness of the priest here is his sexual obsession:

dexa me con la duenna conplir mi voluntad. (634d)

which leads directly to Juan Ruiz. Any princess who could carry a man on her back can serve as prototype to the unforgetable "serranilla" of the *Libro de buen amor,* who carries the near-perishing Juan Ruiz through the snow and ice to her cabin and there has her will of him. The princess of our poem too is a "duenna esforçada" (649d). This episode is completely self-contained, with no loose ends or connections and as such could have been omitted without affecting the rest of the poem. (We add that it is a tongue-in-cheek moral tale like so many of those which Juan Ruiz tells.) Toro-Garland agrees with Milá y Fontanals and Menéndez y Pelayo that this episode of the "arcipreste" must have been one of the early portions of the stories in the traditional materials about the count. This is as far as Toro Garland goes.[16]

It is time, now that Juan Ruiz has been introduced, to see what is involved in the whole episode of the jailing and escape. It will be immediately recognized that this is part of the Provençal tradition of the troubadors. Arab influence also is not to be doubted as can be seen in *The Ring and the Dove* which was known in Spain well before the composition of our poem. From it can be taken the themes of the lady who falls in love from merely hearing about the man, and of the go-between who tells the lady of the virtues of the man. Both of these are in this episode of our poem with the count of Lombardy and the "duenna." There is also the convention that arose which made it a Christian duty for the lady to rescue the lover from the suffering which his love imposed on him by giving herself to him. This is Christianized into a promise of marriage in our poem. Other troubadoresque conventions can be found: the princess speaks of "buen amor" (629a) and the "entendedor" (629C) which Zamora Vicente gives as meaning "amante" in the footnote to this verse. One of the conceits used in Troubador poetry is that of the man freeing the lady from high up in a tower where she is prisoner. Our poem reverses this and has the woman free the man. To make the reversal stronger, one might wish that our poet had said that his hero was kept deep in a dungeon instead of merely in prison. [17]

To go further and connect the Provençal tradition with Spanish poetry, we refer to Joseph Anglade's *Littérature méridionale au moyen âge,* 1921. He tells of numerous types of songs of which the "sirventès" is often used for mockery. This is allied in mood to the Spanish "escarnio" that was popular with the people for so long. Speaking of the "pastourelle" which is the prototype of Juan Ruiz"s "serranillas," Anglade says that in the northern French poems, the shepherdess succombs to the blandishments of the man, whereas it is different in the southern type in which she rejects him.[18] One can cite "La vaquera de la Finojosa" by the Marqués de Santillana for an example of this latter type of ending. The completely burlesque parody and heavy irony of Juan Ruiz's portrayal of the mountain maiden who slings the exhausted priest on her back to carry him off to her lair, where he can but submit to her amorous advances, is but a reworking, some sixty years later, of the Navarrese princess who carries the shackled FG on her back to safety.

La imagen de piedra y bodas

The poet now leaves his story of FG and the princess painfully making their way towards Castile and takes up that of the "duelo por Castyella" over the count's capture. The count's leaders assembled and discussed what to do. Once before the Navarrese had treacherously attacked while the count and his men were away fighting the Moors, and their reaction then was:

de todos los d'Espanna somos desafyados   (282d),

because they were assailed by Moors and Christians. Again Navarre has struck treacherously and has captured their count. Their reaction is now expressed in equivalent wording:

caymos en la yra de todos los d"Espanna (602c).

Leaderless, they assemble and, in Castilian fashion, discuss what to do. Nunno Laynez, the one who remonstrated with FG before the battle with the count of Poitou and Toulouse urging ten days' rest, now with a reversal in attitude, says that the count's worth is increasing while theirs is becoming less because they are doing nothing. He recommends that they make a statue of their count, that they kiss its hand and swear fealty to it as if it were their count present in the flesh. They follow his proposal and set out with the statue in front of their ranks, promising to bring back their leader or never to return themselves.

The poet now switches back to FG and the princess who, seeing the dust raised by the approaching armed force, are filled with fear that it is either the Moors or the Navarrese. Then FG recognizes the Castilian banner and allays her terror. The rejoicing is great as they meet and the count tells them that the lady is their new "sennora." Retracing their route, they reach Byl Forado (modern Belorado) where a blacksmith strikes off the shackles from FG and they go on to Burgos. There the marriage "a bendiciones," like that of the daughters of the Cid, takes place and is followed by a long celebration in which festivities of all kinds entertained the people. These end abruptly when the news comes, in less than a week, that García Sánchez has invaded Castile. A father could do no less to vindicate his honor and to teach his erring daughter a much needed lesson.

A final word here is fitting to show a further connection of our poem to the Provençal troubador tradition. A previous chapter introduced Guillaume VII, count of Poitou and then also of Toulouse, who came down into Spain as a crusader in the battle for Cutanda and won such renown for his part in the fighting that the news spread to the far northwest corner of the peninsula. Only once in the material above was his first and most important title given: Guillaume IX, duc d'Aquitaine, who just happened to be the earliest troubadour whose name is known. During his presence on Spanish soil in 1118 or 1120, he must have picked up the seeds of Arab poetry so fundamental in Troubador poetry. We know that it took root and flourished in the fertile soil of the courts of kings and high nobles from the duke's day through to the reign of Alfonso X, contemporary of our poet. The king's sponsorship of and help to the poets of the Troubador school of poetry was shown by Menéndez Pidal in his *Poesía árabe y poesía europea*.[19]

---

[1] William J. Entwistle, "The Liberation of Castile," *Modern Language Review*. XIX, (1924), pp. 471-2.

[2] R. Menéndez Pidal, *Los godos y la epopeya española*, 2nd. ed. (Madrid, Espasa Calpe, 1969), pp. 48-51.

[3] L.P.Harvey, "Fernán González's Horse," *Medieval Spanish Studies presented to Rita Hamilton*, ed. A.D.Deyermond, (London: Tamesis, 1976). pp. 78-86.
L.P. Harvey and David Hook, "The Affair of the Horse and Hawk in the *PFG*" *Modern Language Quarterly*, LXXVII, (1982) pp. 840-7.

[4] Fray Benito de Montejo, *Memorias de la Real Academia de la Historia*, t. III, pp. 296-7. See also endnote 24 of Chapter Three.

[5] Pérez de Urbel, *Glosas*, p. 258.

[6] Zamora Vicente, *PFG*, footnote to 567c.

[7] Henrique Flórez, *Memorias de las Reinas católicas de España*, cited by Barrau Dihigo in "Notes et documents sur l'histoire du Royaume de León", *Revue Hispanique*, IX (1903), pp. 349-454.

[8] For a detailed discussion of the Ansúrez family, see Menéndez Pidal's entry for *Carrión* in his Vocabulario to the *CMC*.

[9] Pérez de Urbel, *Historia*, II, p. 564: "La reina Teresa Ansúrez aparece ya al lado de Sancho el Craso en cartas del comienzo de 960" when he made a donation to Celanova and Teresa signed with him.

10   Reinhart Dozy, *Recherches sur l'histoire et la littérature de l'Espagne pendant le moyen âge*, I, (Amsterdam: Oriental Press, 1965), p.98, cites Ibn Hayân who says that FG was taken prisoner in a battle and jailed by the king of the Basques (García Sánchez).

11   Reinhart Dozy, *Histoire des Musulmanes de l'Espagne (710-1110)*, Nouvelle édition par Lévy-Provençal, Leyde: 1932. V. II. p. 98. Dozy cites Ibn Haldûn.

12   Reinhart Dozy, *Recherches sur l'histoire et la littérature de l'Espagne pendant le moyen âge*, I, (Amsterdam: Oriental Press, 1965), p. 98.

13   Pérez de Urbel, *Historia*, II, pp. 579-85.

14   Serrano, *PFG* p. 25.

15   Georges Cirot, "Sur le 'Fernán González'," *Bulletin hispanique*, XXIII, 1921, pp.1-14, states that the *Rodrigo* says that FG was taken at vistas at Bañares by Sancho Ordonnez de Navarra, jailed at Tudela, and freed by Constança, sister of the king. Cirot suggests that : "Peutêtre l'auteur du *Rodrigo* ou celui dont il s'inspire, avait-il une malice contre un archiprêtre ou en général contre le clergé de cette ville (Tudela)!"

16   Ferdinand Toro-Garland, "El arcipreste, protagonista literario del medievo español," *El arcipreste de Hita: el libro, el autor, la tierra, la época*, Actas del 1er Congreso Internacional sobre el Arcipreste de Hita, (Barcelona: SERESA, 1973), pp. 327-325.

17   John Lihani, "Notas sobre la epopeya y la relación entre el *PFG* y el *Libro de buen amor*," *Homenaje a Fernando Antonio Martínez*, (Bogotá: 1979), pp. 474-85.   Lihani says:" En cuanto a la estructura de las serranillas, ésta parece derivarse de varias fuentes incluyendo fuentes gallegas y francesas, pero las ideas temáticas, en una forma invertida, son resultado de un intento, por Juan Ruiz, de parodiar directa o indirectamente el episodio del *PFG.*"

18   Joseph Anglade, *Littérature méridionale au moyen âge*, (Paris, E. DeBaccard, 1921). Sirventès, pp. 40-1. Pastourelle, pp. 44-5. On p. 26 he says he doubts that there was influence from Arabs through Spain, that it was "autochtone." Menéndez Pidal , on the other hand, has since then shown how strong the Arab influence was. See next note.

19   R. Menéndez Pidal, *Poesía árabe y poesía europea*, (Madrid: Espasa Calpe, 1955), 4th ed. pp. 13-78.   RMP traces the "zéjel" with its "estribillo" from the blind Muccádam, ca 900, through the muwaxxaha to Aben Guzman who died about 1080. He outlines its spread into Europe by way of Andalusia. "He llegado a la convicción de que el zéjel se propagó también por Europa, y que el primer caso de imitación que podemos señalar es precisamente en las obras del primer poeta lírico que conocemos: Guillermo IX, duque de Aquitania, en una lengua neolatina. La canción árabe apadrina así el nacimiento de la poesía lírica de las naciones modernas de Europa." p. 28. He tells of Guillaume IX's role in poetry development, saying that he couldn't have been the first to

write poetry showing the influence of "poesía árabe." He also tells of GGG's outstanding role at Barbastro.

Chapter Nine

The Last Three Battles

En antes que ovyessen las bodas acabadas, (685a)

The first three battles may well have been based originally on real occurrences. The last three, however, are totally ficticious in the form in which we have them in the poem, although other conflicts must have taken place between Castile and Navarre that could have given rise to *cantares* not reflected in the *PFG*. Just as the poet gave careful introductions to the battles discussed up to this point, so does he give one for the next. The siege of Carazo was the introduction to the battle of Lara, which gave rise to that of Hacinas. Similarly the next combat comes from what has immediately preceeded. In the poem the sister of the king of Navarre had gone without his knowledge to see the prisoner, had released him, and then, to make matters worse, had fled with him to Burgos. It was to be expected that the king should set out to avenge the betrayal and double insult. Again there is no lapse in time. In fact there is an overlapping of events for the king invades while the wedding celebrations are still in progress. This reaction of an irate head of the family who intended to bring back not only his sister who had eloped, but also a recaptured prisoner, and so be doubly avenged, was strong psychological motivation for the episode. FG again had to rouse his men to action, virtually calling them traitors if they did not fight.

The ensuing battle of Valpirre in which the Era Degollada is located, near the Ebro River, was fierce, with many men dying on both sides, the Castilians suffering the worst of the losses. Finally the two leaders met face to face:

"Partase el canpo por nos amos, hermano" (694d)

and, inevitably, FG won running his foe through with his lance:

metyol' toda la lança por medyo la tetyella,
que fuera la espalda paresçio la cochyella (696cd).

(These same details, "partir el canpo" and "por medyo la tetyella," were both pointed out by Correa Calderon in his article "Reminiscencias homéricas.") The king was taken prisoner and jailed in Burgos.

This capture and jailing of the king of Navarre are totally ficticious, nowhere recorded in chronicles known today, although the poet says here:

Segund nos lo leemos, e diz lo la lienda, (688a)

The episode was needed by the *juglares* to balance and offset the historically true imprisonment of FG, and also by the poet who included it in the story of the count to be part of another threesome. It had to do so in such a way as to remove the disgrace of FG's capture and jailing. How better could it have been done than by having the hero overcome, capture, and jail the man who had been able to seize and imprison him solely through treachery? Of course the count did so in an honorable manner, through his good right arm and his thrusting lance which transfixed the valiant king of Navarre. The latter remained in jail for twelve months (thirteen according to the *PCG* (Chap 713) Of the incarceration suffered by the king the poem says:

> la presyon fue tan mala que peor non podieron,
> por ningunas rrehenes nunca dar le quisieron,
> non era maravyella que negrua la fyzieron. (699bcd),

This was only to be expected because FG had been more than harshly treated in his imprisonment in Castroviejo. As García Sánchez meted out, so also was it measured unto him when it was his turn to suffer imprisonment. Navarrese treachery by both Sancho Garcés and García Sánchez had to be punished. It was secured by having the first killed and the second seized and jailed.

After García Sánchez had suffered for a year, the new countess went to her husband's men, his trusted and faithful supporters, and asked them to intervene on her behalf. It was not right, she said, since she was wife of the count, for him to keep her brother in jail, "cavtyvo y lazrado"

> "Yo saque de presyon al conde don Fernando
> ¿por que es el agora contrra mi tan vyllano? (701ab)

Pérez de Urbel objected to the statement in the article on the structure of the poem that the imprisonment of García Sánchez was invented by the Arlantine. He thought that instead of having García Sánchez jailed in the third imprisonment, it would have been much fitter for FG to have been incarcerated three times.[1] Not so, for the story as given is more effective for a Castilian public. The treachery of the Navarrese king had to be punished and his jailing entered legend as the proper and fitting vengeance that FG was determined to exact, and also supplied a third incarceration for the poet's structure. The battle of the Era Degollada was fought to obtain revenge for an "enganno" of Sancho Garcés against Castile. The second battle turns into vengeance for the "enganno," of Teresa and of García Sánchez that caused FG's capture. The poet pointed out, as quoted above, that the count was badly mistreated while he was in jail (597bc). Now the count exacts his full measure of revenge by making the imprisonment of García Sánchez as harsh as possible. It is no wonder that FG's wife, though loyal to him, should have been sorry for her brother and asked the count's men to to help secure his release. She is not only a "duenna esforçada" who frees FG and carries him on her back to safety, but also a sister who, although belatedly, feels a proper fondness for her brother.

At this point there is a break in the MS of the poem. For the material that has been lost it is necessary to turn to the *PCG* (Chap 714). The first thing to notice is that FG's wife is now correctly the daughter of the Navarrese king, which shows that this portion entered legend before the two women were combined into one. The young countess, also called Sancha, asks the count's men to help her secure the release of her father and says : "Et este es el primero ruego que uos yo rogue." This is additional proof that the original of this episode which the poet was following was composed at a time when the *juglares* knew that the count had been married twice and that it was his young second wife, daughter of the Navarrese king, who was speaking here not long after her marriage. As will be seen in the next chapter, they knew that the jailing in Leon was the first. At that time Sancha had called her husband's men together and asked their help, had gone to Leon with them and then had herself secured FG's escape But now we have the first request of the second wife. The men intercede and the count agrees to do as they ask. FG has his brother-in-law/father-in-law set free and unshackled, and then does him great honor. The king is clothed, fed, and treated as befits royalty, and then FG provides him with all he needs for the journey back to Estella in Navarre.

It was in the first main section of the poem that the poet referred to his sources, "ditado, lienda, escrito, escrytura." Since then he has not referred to them. But now, as stated above, he writes:
Segund nos lo leemos, e diz lo la lienda (688a)
The *PCG* prosifying the poem says: "...lo que agora dira aqui la estoria." Speculation as to whether the poet was using a prose text or was following a "cantar" has been only that -speculation. There could have been a verse source for the beginning of the episode, and then a prose "estoria" for the portion which the *PCG.* followed or vice versa. One suggestion is that of Luciano Serrano who thinks that this battle may have been adapted from the accounts of that of Atapuerca. There are good reasons for his suggestion. He posits his proposal on a duplication of names as follows.

The *PCG* has said that there was a Count Fernando of Castile who was married to a Sancha at the time of a King García Sánchez of Navarre. Later (Chap 804), there was a King Fernando of Castile who was married to a Sancha at the time of a different King García of Navarre. In l054, the second King García, brother of the King Fernando of Castile, invaded Castilian territory, would not withdraw, in spite of the latter's pleas, forced his brother to fight and was killed. The duplication of names and another invasion by the Navarrese, Serrano believes, were the cause of a confusion that led easily to the ascribing of the occurrence to Count Fernando in place of King Fernando.[2] It was clear that the juglaresque tradition recognized a need for a counterweight to balance the historic capture and jailing of FG by the Navarrese king so as to prevent any diminishing of the worth of the hero. Therefore the trapping of the Castilian was made the result of treachery, which then was offset by FG's honorable capture and jailing of García Sánchez, proving he was the better warrior, in retaliation for the capture and jailing of FG by his brother-in-law. Such a transfer from one Fernando to another would not have been hard for the *juglares* to make. Serrano may well be correct.

Repeated victories over the Moors and over Sancho Garcés have already established FG's military prowess. Included in these are his killing of three kings. The poet seems to think, therefore, that now he has no need to dwell on the course of the action in this second battle against Navarre which serves principally to allow the capture of García Sánchez. In his account of the action the poet puts in only a few of the warfare wordings of the previous combats. No poet can exhibit a continually changing vocabulary for the same type of occurrences. As Correa Calderón pointed out in his *Reminiscencias hómericas,* warfare had not changed from the time of the Greeks and we add that the terminology could not have appreciably changed either.

The poet now inserts three short episodes before he tells of the third battle against Navarre. Although it takes the events out of sequence it will be best to discuss the last battle at this point. The psychological motivation for this last combat is the burning desire of García Sánchez to avenge the dishonor he suffered in his capture at Valpirre and the subsequent jailing in Burgos. As might by now be expected the situational motivation once more is the absence of FG and his men who are for a last time away in Leon fighting the Moors at the request of their king. Although the poet refers to an as yet unidentified source: "assi commo leemos," there is no known historical clash commemorated in the poem's third meeting of Castile and Navarre. There is no reason or need for this last battle. The poet was merely filling out his planned threesome of battles between the two neighbors, and was not averse to reworking some of the materials he had previously used as may be concluded from the fact that there is a striking replication of ideas. In fact the third occurs in the same Valpirre where the two other battles against Navarre had taken place. Before the first fight, Sancho Garcés insulted FG by saying that the latter must have had bad advice, and must be "loco e de seso menguado"

(292c, 293a) to defy Navarre after his single victory over the Moors in "batalla campal." This same Navarrese disdain and pride is repeated before the third encounter. García Sánchez has just returned to his home after being released from a year's jailing in Castile and, enraged, tells his men why they must now fight Castile.

> Dixo les que tal cosa non queria endurar,
> d'un condeziello malo tantos dannos tomar,
> que con el non queria otra mient pleytear,
> mas que queria morir o se queria vengar. (737)

The father's attitude towards FG was the cause of his downfall. It is also that of the son whose disdain is clear in the "condeziello," the petty upstart count, who has wounded his pride to the point where he must have vengeance. Disregarding FG's three victories over the Moors and the two over his father and himself, he attacks again with foolhardy abandon, proving that it is he who has neither "mesura" nor "grrand seso en lidiar" ((340b), and he does indeed his "prez por y lo astragar." (340d). Leaving Estella, García Sánchez invades and overruns Castile at a moment when the Castilians, as by now can be expected, are away doing their king's bidding in answer to his call to fight the Moors. The Navarrese are able to reach the gates of Burgos where the king hopes to seize his sister/daughter and take her home with him, thus further dishonoring the count, but she is able to foil his efforts, "sopos byen guardar" (740bc). When FG returns and finds the depredations of the Navarrese, he sends word to his enemy to return what has been stolen or be ready to fight. Earlier under the same circumstances Sancho Garcés had told the messenger that:

> "Non le mejorare valia de vna meaja." (291d)

The son replies to FG's messenger in almost the same words:

> "dixo que nol' daria valia d'un dinero," (744c)

Without delay the two armies meet and the two leaders seek each other out. In the fertile Valpirre, with the angry Ebro flowing by, almost reflecting the mood of the combatants, the foes meet in a "lid campal," a term that reflects the poet's intention to characterize this as a major engagement. The fighting could not have been fiercer, all did their utmost, there was great noise, action, clash of weapons, blood in streams, but the utmost efforts of the Navarrese could not match those of the Castilian:

> mas eran con el conde todos desventurados.(75ld)

At this point we have the final two lines of the incomplete MS.

> Quiso Dios al buen conde esta gracia fazer,
> que moros nin cristianos non le podian vençer (752ab)

The *PCG* (Chap 7l6) says: "Et fue alli el rey don García vençudo con todo su poder", to which the *Cl344* adds: "e el conde don Fernan Gonçalez le dio una ferida de que morio despues...," a detail that either was omitted from the retelling by our poet in order to avoid the killing of a fourth king, or was added only later by the compilers of the chronicle.

Two of the three battles against Navarre, as will be remembered, were caused by treacherous invasions of Castilian territory while FG was away with his men fighting on behalf of their king. Not for nothing did the poet use the word "enganno" four times in one stanza (211). Revenge was needed for the "tuertos" and it was gained by the Castilians through their bravery, determination, and fighting. There is no intervention from above, no hand of their "Cryador" helping them as there was at Hacinas against the Moors, no Santiago and his heavenly host. They rely only on themselves. And the final two verses are the clear indication by the poet as to the inevitable triumph of Castile, the inheritor of the Gothic leadership, which will bring it to primacy and supremacy in all Spain. The last two battles against Navarre are closely linked in theme and were discussed together even though they are separated in the poem by the third one against the Moors which will now be dealt with.

Third Battle against the Moors

dexien "¡Fernan Gonçalez, dexe te Dios rreygnar!" (723d)

One of the artistic achievements of the *Poema/Cantar de Mio Cid* is the portrayal of the Cid, Ruy Diaz de Bivar. Starting as an exiled freebooter forced to fight, he becomes a mercenary for a Moorish ruler, captures and rules the city of Valencia as a *de facto* king by right of conquest, and finally, restored to Alfonso's favor, he watches as his liege lord presides over the judicial trial that accords him justice for the affronts to his honor done him by his sons-in-law. Here at the end of the poem the Cid is an almost hieratic figure, towering over those present in his honor, dignity, prestige, and all-encompassing influence. During this time his allegiance to his king has never wavered, and he has shown repeatedly by word and deed that his fealty is sincere. Alfonso finally feels a measure of shame at the injustice of the treatment he has wrongly forced upon his loyalest subject. The triumph of the Cid in the trial restores his honor and brings the poem to a most fitting close.

The poet-monk of Arlanza, who knew the legends of the Cid and probably had read a version much like the one we have today, has not been able to match the portrayal of that hero. Yet in his own way he did what he could with the materials he had to work with, and it is clear that he was aware of the necessity to show his hero as more than a mere military man. From the count's first appearance the Arlantine has given us an FG who is obsessed with the fight against the the enemies of the true Faith, and who is the servant of his "Cryador," always doing His will. Against the Navarrese and their French allies, with no help from his Maker, he fights to avenge the wrongs done treacherously to him. From facing the overwhelming numbers of Moors, he turns to meet fellow Christians who should have been his allies, and depends solely on his own bravery and skills and on his ever loyal Castilians. He is always conscious of the need to consult with his men, to secure their advice, or to let them know why it is necessary to go again into battle. When in our poem he is first summoned to "cortes" he is already recognized and accepted as the foremost of the subjects of the king whose obedient vassal he is and will continue to be, almost to the end of the poem. To the two dimensions of fighter and servant of God we have already seen are now added the third and fourth of faithful vassal and sage counsellor of all those who seek help with their problems. In the following episode we will see another facet or stage in the portrayal of the hero. The beginning of the next portion is missing from the poem and has to be taken from the *PCG* (Chap 715).

The scene opens with Sancho I sending word to FG that Abderrahman has again invaded Leonese territory and "quel rogaua mucho quel fuesse ayudar." The loyal subject immediately sets out with the men who happen to be with him at the time and sends word to all the others "que se fuessen empos ell," to meet him in Leon within the week. As stated above, it is significant to note that the king "rogaua" the count to come with help, whereas the latter told his men to come. When the Castilians arrive, Sancho is very happy and receives him well, judging that FG has come in good time. After the arrival of the whole contingent they decide to go out to fight the Moors rather than to stay in the besieged city.

The poem now resumes its account. The Moors hearing of the arrival of the Castilians, raise the siege and move to Safagun (Sahagún), which they besiege, and then ravage the nearby area of Tierra de Campos. When the relieving forces under FG start out to meet the enemy, the Leonese nobles and their men expect to go with the Castilians, and are infuriated when FG forbids them to accompany the expedition. At Safagun they force the Moors to raise the siege of the city, pursue and meet them in a "lid campal," a term which show that the poet intends this too as a major battle. Now comes the beginning of the important part of the episode.

>Avyan a toda Canpos corrydo e rrobado,
>llevauan de cristianos grrand pueblo cabtyvado,
>de vacas e de yeguas e de otrro ganado,
>tanto lleuavan dello que non serya contado.

The poet tells of the Christians who had been captured by the Moors:

>Grrandes eran los llantos, grrandes eran los duelos,
>yvan los padres presos, los fyjos e abuelos,
>matavan a las madres los fyjos en braçuelos,

> e davan a los padres con los sus fyjuelos. (717-718)

The satisfaction of the Moors with their booty is shown by:

> Yvan con muy grrand rrobo alegrues e pagados, (7l9a)

The poet gives only three stanzas to the military action of this battle, for his main interest lies in another matter. He tells of the devastating effect of FG's fierceness against the enemy, and of the king of Cordoba who:

> "bendezie a Mafomad quando dend fue escapado." (721d)

Then comes the reason for the episode. FG forbids his men to keep any of the booty:

> non dexo de la prea nulla cosa llevar,
> mando yr a los catyvos todos a su logar,
> dezien: "!Fernan Gonzalez, dexe te Dios rreygnar!" (723bcd)

There had long been laws governing the disposition of the spoils of battle. The following will serve as an example of their most common provisions. It is taken from the *Fuero Juzgo:*

> Libro IX Titol II Ley 7 Ley antigua
> Qual galardón deve aver el que recobra siervo ajeno ó otras cosas los enemigos.
> Todo omne que desespera su vida, é se mete entre sus enemigos é recobra dellos algun siervo ó algun aver, si después viniere el segnor del aver ó del siervo, e lo conociere, el que lo torna deve dar al sennor las dos partes por merced y él deve aver la tercia parte por su trabajo. E otrosí decimos si algun omne conseiar ó mostrar alguna cosa á siervo, por que fuya de los enemigos, é se tornare pora su sennor á aquel que lo ficiere aya la decima parte del siervo por su trabajo.[3]

It is easy to understand that most attacks had been and continued to be judged desperate. A further provision was that if any captives or booty were not released until the day after they had been taken or later, all the captives and all the booty retaken from the enemy were to be the property of the person or persons who recovered them.

It will be remembered that García Sánchez took Castilians captive and led them off to Navarre, for they were considered to be spoils of war (742c). The Moors here have just taken great numbers of men, women, young, old, grandparents, and babes-in-arms. The cows, mares and other live stock they carry off are of the highest value and concern to the common people for they are the breeding stock from which will come the future living and wealth of the "pueblo." Without these animals they would change from being independent freemen to serfs and spend the rest of their lives at the orders and will of those for whom they are forced to work. As captives they would be led back to Cordoba or elsewhere as slaves, the men to spend the rest of their lives at the harshest of physical labor until death released them, the women to toil as slaves, and/or to be taken into the beds of their captors, a "lucky" few possibly spared to be married to Moorish men. The aged and the babes would in great likelihood be killed with little consideration, for the verse says here that fathers were beaten with the bodies of the little children (718cd). This is clearly modeled on stanzas 91-95 which tell of like horrors suffered at the hands of the Moors in the Conquest.

The people whom FG ordered released recognized his generosity and fairness towards them, for the liberators were entitled to keep all the booty which had been in the hands of the enemy overnight. The *PCG* says here that FG told them "que fuessen todos libres e quitos" (Chap 715), which means that they were again free men and were exempt from paying even the one-third that they might have been held for, at the very least. The episode ends with the Castilians returning to Leon.

> El conde don Fernando con toda su mesnada,
> quando ovo el rrobo a sus casas tornada,
> por verdat avya fecha muy buena cabalgada,
> a Leon el buen conde luego fyzo tornada. (724)

There were also provisions against intentionally delaying the retaking of Christians and their property in order to profit from the "next day or later" clause, showing that such was a fairly common practise.[4] It is clear now why the Leonese nobles were so incensed: "ovyeron leoneses desto fuerte pesar." (715d), when FG adamantly kept them from accompanying the Castilians on the expedition into the Tierra de Campos, which clearly would last several days. He had made it impossible for them to take advantage of the expected victory coming from the valor and fighting ability of the Castilians which would give them a part in what they expected would be a profitable victory for the Christians. They not only missed out on the booty from the personal property the Moors had brought with them but also from what was originally property of the Christians, released or retaken from the enemy. The overriding matter here is that FG did not even keep the one third which was his legal portion for booty returned the same day of the battle, much less the whole of what was not recovered until the next day or later, as had to be true for the great bulk of what was taken during this campaign. No wonder the freed captives cried out, "Dexe te Dios rreygnar."

FG of course was thoroughly familiar with the laws concerning booty and knew what he was doing to the Leonese nobles in depriving them of any share in it. Besides, he was repaying them for their hostility towards him in Leon. Even more important was that he was determined to keep them out of this area for it was one which he had long coveted. It lay between the Pisuerga and the Cea Rivers where he had at various times tried to increase his influence. It was an area that he may have been trying to expand into when King Ramiro II had him thrown into jail. Pérez de Urbel has shown documents in which FG made gifts to the monastery of Sant Facund (Sahagún), which made its monks look favorably on the Castilian.[5] Any presence of the Leonese in the area would diminish his chances of consolidating power there, so he did his best to keep them out. At the same time, the fact that he returned freedom and property to the Christians he had rescued from their Moorish captors boded well for his influence among the people in the Tierra de Campos were he ever to make an overt, determined move to take over the land between the Pisuerga and the Cea. Of course they cried out: "Dexe te Dyos rregnar."

---

[1] Pérez de Urbel, *Glosas*, p. 237.

[2] Serrano, *PFG*, p. 23. Serrano says "En un poeta del siglo XIII no parece extraña la confusión de reyes, cronología, y datos geográficos, dada la igualdad de nombres de los protagonistas, el motivo de la agresión y el recuerdo popular de haber muerto un rey navarro en tierra castellana a manos de su soberano, llamado Fernando."

[3] *Fuero Juzgo*, ed. cit. p. 159.

[4] The custom of taking prisoners as slaves continued for centuries. In the *Siete partidas*, Partida II, Título XXVI, Ley 7 forbade letting the enemy take property (and prisoners) so that it could be repossessed. It specifically states : "a menos que se hiciera con engaño el dejarselo en poder por aquella noche," to prevent the "liberators" from profiting from the "overnight" provision.

[5] Sahagún lies on the Cea River. The Tierra de Campos lay between the Pisuerga and the Cea Rivers It was this area that FG coveted and considered rightly his, and into which he tried to expand. When Ramiro made Assur Fernández count of Monzón, this was part of the territory that was involved. By gifts to the monastery of San Facundo, FG tried to gain the favor of the Church in that area.

Chapter Ten

Inversion of the Prison Episodes[1]

"faredes contra mi como buen sennor e buen rey" (*PCG Chap 719*)

In the poem the jailing of FG by his brother-in-law, King García Sánchez of Navarre has been shown to be a highly fanciful account designed to explain away the historical capture and jailing of the count in such a way as to leave the count's honor and prestige unblemished. The *PCG* tells of three incarcerations by Ramiro II, García Sánchez, and Sancho I. The prophecy by Pelayo foretells only two, and the poem gives only two: the first at the hands of the king of Navarre, and the other at the hands of Sancho I of Leon. The *Crónica de Sampiro* , ca 1000, records that King Ramiro II jailed FG. What can we believe? It will be best to look at the accounts of the imprisonments as given by the several Latin chronicles.

Pérez de Urbel says that the first record of this occurrence, in the *Annales compostellani,* was written down about forty years after the event, "son de aquel mismo siglo." They record, laconicly that:

> fuit captus comes Ferdinandus Gonsalvi et filii eius in Aconia (sic) a rege Garcia et transmisit illos in Pampilonia.[2]
> Count FG was seized with his sons at Aconia (sic) by King García who transferred them to Pamplona.

This has already become garbled, a mere forty years after the event, both as to where it occurred, and as to the place of the jailing, which later vary still more according to local tradition.

The next record, in the *Sampiro*, is of a different incarceration. It tells us that:

> Fernandus Gundisalvi, & Didacus Munionis contra Regem Dominum Ramirum tyrannidem gesserunt, necnon & bellum paraverunt. Ille vero Rex, ut erat prudens & fortis, comprehendit eos, & unum in Legione, alterum Gordone, ferro vinctos, carcere trusit. Multo quidem tempore transacto, juramento Regi dato exierunt de ergastulo. [3]

FG and Diego Muñoz exercised tyranny (illegal assumption of power) against King Ramiro and prepared for war. As that king was prudent and strong, he seized them and put one in jail in Leon, the other in Gordon, shackled, in irons. Much time having passed, having sworn an oath (of fealty), they left jail.
The *Najerense* differs only in adding that both men were stripped of their posessions. There is no mention of a jailing under Sancho I. The facts given above are those followed by later records also.

The next account of a jailing is by far the most important for it shows that legends had been growing for which there is no preserved text. It might be termed the fossil remains, all we have today of a previously existing entity. It also shows a considerable advance in the development of the legend about the hero's incarceration in Navarre. The *Najerense, ca II60,* over a century befoe our poem, says (abbreviations extended):
    Predictus comes .f. gonzalvet fuit captus et filii eius in Cironia. in ecclesia sancti andree apostoli a predicto rege pampiloniae. G. sanctii. & transmissus pampilonia inde clavillum inde tubiam. Vnde cum sanctia eiusdem regis .G. sorore qui prius ordonii regis legionensis postea comitis albari harrameliz de alava extiterat uxor. habiens nesciente fratre colloquium liberatus est dato prius eidem sacramento .quod si eum inde educeret: eam duceret in uxorem. Quod et fecit.[4]
The aforesaid count Fernán González was seized and his sons in Cirueña in the church of Saint Andrew the Apostle by the aforesaid king of Pamplona. G. Sánchez. who transferred [him] from Pamplona to Clavijo, thence to Tobía. From there [after] speaking with Sancha sister of King García who previously had been wife of King Ordoño (II), afterwards of count Alvaro Harrameliz of Alava, her brother not knowing, he (FG) is liberated, having promised her first that if she freed him, he would marry her. Which was done.
As can be seen, this is essentially the story we have in the poem, and shows how far the legend had advanced in the century and a half since the *Sampiro* was written. To the simple account in the *Anales compostelanos* of the seizure and jailing it has added the "enganno" of the king's sister against her brother. It gives the information that Sancha had previously been married twice before wedding FG, but there is no indication that the *juglares* knew that he was

married twice nor that it was FG's first wife to whom Ordoño II and Alvaro had been married. The count's two wives have been fused together into one named Sancha. The fact that FG married the woman who freed him is in the story. The church where the capture took place is named. (In the area of the capture there still can be seen the ruins of a small church or chapel of San Andrés.) The place of the jailing is uncertain. Teresa has not yet entered the legend. There is no suggestion of an inversion.

According to the *PFG*, as already discussed, the first imprisonment occurred when the count was tricked into a meeting with García Sánchez to settle on terms for the marriage of FG to Sancha, sister of that Navarrese king. The latter came with over thirty men instead of the agreed-on five/six and the Castilian was seized and jailed at Castroviejo. Later a count of Lombardy visited the prisoner, and told the princess that she would be doing Christendom a great disservice if she left FG in jail. She went to see him and released him on his promise to marry her.

Georges Cirot studied the several accounts in detail. He found from documents that named the Navarrese princess as *Sanctia Sanctionis*, that she was indeed the sister of García Sánchez and that she really had been the wife of King Ordono II and of Alvaro Harrameliz, count of Alava and Lantarón, before marrying FG. From a document of 94I in which four sons and a daughter of the count and Sancha are named, Cirot concluded that in 960 when the Navarrese jailing took place, the sons could have accompanied their father to the meeting, as stated in the *Najerense*. Since Castroviejo, Tobía, and Clavijo are only a few miles apart, there must have grown up varying local traditions of the event with the exact location of the prison depending on who told of the occurrence. Since the count was separated from his men/sons, all three sites may have been involved. Cirot raises two objections. He says that the account of the *Najerense* cannot be accepted unlesss the jailing be advanced twenty-five years (because there is documentary evidence that FG and Sancha were married ca 931), and the sons must then be dropped. He adds, "C'est beaucoup demander." Later in the article he notes that FG's first wife, Sanctia Sanctionis, died near the end of 959 and that he then married an Urraca, daughter of García Sánchez, but he failed to see the relationship of the two marriages and the poem. He was so close to the solution to the problem! We shall return to Cirot's objections later.[5] At any rate, chronicle and poem agree in broad outline and in numerous details as to the Navarrese jailing which is recorded even in a Moorish history.[6]

It is otherwise, however, with the Leonese imprisonment, which is missing from the ending of the poem. The *PCG* (Chaps. 717-9) gives what is generally accepted as the last few episodes of the original versification. In it we read that Sancho I summoned FG to "cortes" under penalty of forfeiting his county, and there accused him of trying to take lands away from the crown and of being in revolt. The count heatedly protested his innocence and the justice of his conduct, whereupon the king, enraged, had him thrown into jail. Sancha, now the wife of FG, heard of her husband's plight, went to Leon dressed as a pilgrim on her way to Santiago de Compostela and secured permission from Sancho I to visit her husband in his cell. There she exchanged clothes with him and he left the jail in her place. Apprised of the situation, Sancho angrily summoned Sancha but eventually forgave her.

The testimony of Sampiro has been questioned by some scholars who have preferred to accept the Leonese imprisonment as occurring under Sancho rather than under his father. Fray Justo Pérez de Urbel brought together a great deal of hitherto unknown documentary biographical material concerning the count. An example of the customary formula for closing a document in territory lying under the control of FG ran much as follows: "Ramiro ruling in Leon and Fernán González count in Castile." On several occasions from 935 on, all mention of the king is dropped and the formula even becomes: "Fernán González, count by the grace of God" or "by the will of God," showing that the unruly brother-in-law of the king was trying to shake off the feudal yoke that held him subject to Leon. For a short while in 941 we find: "Ramiro in Leon and under his rule Fernán González count in Castile." This submission did not last overly long for in 943 the count tried to expand westward into the territory lying between Leon and Castile. He was summarily checked by Ramiro who appointed Assur Fernández, of a prominent family that had long been opposed to our Castilian, to be count of Monzón, the region in question. FG thus was effectively shut off from occupying this area which he had been coveting. Ramiro II then sent Assur Fernández to Burgos and in November 943 he was signing as count of Castile. By May of 944 the region was sufficiently stabilized and under his control for young Prince Sancho to come to Burgos to represent in person the authority of Ramiro II. At this time, the signature of FG, which had previously stood at the head of the witnesses to official documents disappears, and only later, in 945, reappears, but now below that of Sancho and Assur Fernández, attesting to the fall of the man. Still later it again stands at the head of the list and the names of Sancho and Assur disappear. It must have been about that time that Ramiro and the count dropped their hostilities and cemented their good will with the marriage of Prince Ordoño to Urraca, daughter of FG and Sancha.

Pérez de Urbel concludes that the Sampiro account shows that FG really was jailed by Ramiro II. This means that in point of historical fact the Leonese jailing occurred before the one in Navarre, and the juglaresque legends of the count and then the poem transferred it to a period twenty years and three kings later. He explains the transfer as follows. Early *juglares* knew that FG had a wife named Sancha, that he married a woman who freed him from jail in Castroviejo, and a woman already his wife helped him escape from jail in Leon. In the course of succeeding generations, they lost sight of the fact that he had remarried after the death of *Sanctia Sanctionis*. Therefore, in the poem, the Navarrese jailing had to preceed that in Leon.[7]

Two possible explanations have been advanced for the historical jailing of FG and Diego Muñoz by Ramiro II. One is found in a history in Arabic that says they failed to come with troops to help their king when he was again beset by the Moors, a breach of the obligations of the two vassal counts. The other is that Ramiro II saw the danger in allowing the ambitious Castilian to continue unchecked in his efforts to expand into the area west and south of Castile. This would have given FG most or all of Monzón, and as FG had already struck south of the Duero River and had retaken Sepulveda, he would then have controlled an enormously expanded Castile. This new area added to the county of Saldaña held by his *consuegro*, Diego Muñoz, and his own Castile which was now made up of seven small counties united into one, would have represented an accumulation of territory and power that Ramiro II could not tolerate in the hands of an ambitious man. He therefore jailed both counts.

Pérez's theory of inversion satisfactorily disposes of Cirot's two objections: that the *Najerense* account cannot be accepted unless the Navarrese imprisonment be advanced twenty-five years and the sons then be dropped. It is the Leonese jailing that must be advanced twenty years from 965 to 944 or 945, and the sons may well have been with their father when he was captured. By the time the *Najerense* was finished, the two women had been combined into one Sancha, and the two episodes were partially fused. Inversion of the jailings had not yet taken place, for the *Najerense* still gives the Leonese incarceration as under Ramiro II, but does not mention one under Sancho I. By a century later when our poem was composed, inversion had entered the tradition and the Leonese episode had been shifted from Ramiro II to his son Sancho I. This is as far as Pérez goes.

Pérez's theory carries the weight of considerable documentary evidence to support a carefully reasoned argument and explains motives for the two jailings as well as their evolution away from historical fact. It would have to remain theory, however, if there were no other source of proof for it. There is such proof in the poem itself and in the *PCG*, carried over from earlier stages of the legends about the count. It has often been noted that the *cuaderna vía* in which the work is composed cannot hide the vigor and spirit of the earlier juglaresque poems. We find many of the epithets so popular with former singers of epic exploits. The audience is addressed directly and called on to listen to some exciting bit. Some writers, believe that they have found remainders of assonance in the prosification of the poem. Further analysis uncovers portions that were carried over from previous tradition without an understanding of how they fit into the account and what they really mean. Some verses and even whole stanzas don't ring true, or seem out of place in the thirteenth century retelling. When read with the idea that inversion has taken place, these verses take on a meaning and naturalness that confirm the belief that they too were originally based on fact and were at a relatively early period incorporated into the legends and thus preserved. We shall now consider these passages.

In the poem itself the first matter to consider is the prediction of the hermit Pelayo at the beginning of the career of FG that he would be jailed twice. Early *juglares* knew that the Castilian had indeed been imprisoned on two occasions and they composed their verses accordingly. At some point in the evolution of the legendary materials, these incarcerations were enhanced by the inclusion of the hermit's prophecy, (almost certainly an addition of our Arlantine. See Chap. V above.) We read that FG came to the meeting with García Sánchez accompanied by the stipulated five/six men. García treacherously appeared with over thirty attendants and the count knew that he had been tricked. There flashed through his mind the scene in the hermitage with Pelayo. He could again hear the words of his new found friend:

"Dos veçes seras preso crey me synes dudança" (238d).

Once before he had been imprisoned by Ramiro II, but in the fifteen years since then he, FG, had made and unmade kings, had set aside

his ruler's treaty with the Moors, and had dealt with them on his own terms.[8] Long since he had discounted the possibility of a second capture, but now it was coming true, and he cried out in bitterness:
"lo que me dixo el monje, en ello so caydo." (586d)
This verse is correctly placed in the Navarrese episode but it does not ring true. When would a prophecy of two jailings be seen as fulfilled? Only on the occasion of the second. And so it was in the earlier versions of the legends. If the verse is to assume its proper meaning and take on its original naturalness it must be restored to its correct place in the second jailing of the count. Early *juglares* knew that the capture at Cirueña was not the first, but our poet of the thirteenth century no longer knew it. The anachronisms of this reference to the hermit's prophecy of "dos veces seras preso", which was added by our poet in his "anointing" of FG at the hermitage, almost escapes detection. It is significant and corroborative that the *PCG* in its prosification of the lost ending merely records that FG was cast into jail, with no mention of the prediction of the hermit. That is, of course, because the early versions of the Leonese imprisonment made it the first incarceration and the "dos veces seras preso" was in no way a part of that incident.

The next matter to consider is the identity of the Navarrese princess who served as bait for the trap in which the count was caught and who freed him from Castroviejo. After talking with the prisoner, the count of Lombardy:

    demando la donzella por qui fuera cuntido,
    commo el conde ouiera a ser della marydo.
    Mostraron gela luego la fermosa donzella   (614cd, 615a)

It is clear from these verses that the tradition which the poet was following held the princess to be a maiden, "donzella," that she had not been previously married. Therefore she was not the woman who, according to the *Najerense*, had married Ordoño II and Alvaro Harrameliz before wedding FG. And it was known also to previous *juglares* whose tradition our poet was following that Sancha, the count's wife, was the widow of an emperor and a nobleman, for in the poem the Lombardian says to the "donzella:"

    "Sy tu eres de sentydo esto es lo mejor
    sy tu nunca ovyste de caballero amor,
    mas deves amar este que non enperador,
    non ha omne en el mundo de sus armas mejor." (621)

Note well the "enperador" and the "cavallero" which apply properly to the first two husbands. The *PCG*, (Chap 710) prosifying these verses, says:
> "Et si tu as en ti seso o ameste a algun cavallero en alguna sazon, mucho mas deves amar a este ca non a emperador nin cavallero en tod el mundo tan bueno como este."

These words are not pure chance. Where then did they come from? The answer is that they are from a previous telling of the legends in which the poem's first marriage of Sancha is recounted. They are entirely appropriate to an argument in 931 when Queen Toda had to convince her daughter that she had nothing to lose by marrying FG, a promising young man. It was true that she had been married to an emperor, Ordoño II, and to Alvaro Harrameliz, count of Alava and Lantarón, enjoying the exciting life first of a royal court and then that of a highly placed count. Now she could choose either to enter a convent and spend the rest of her life shut off from the kind of world she had been reared in, or she could marry FG. (Years later FG accepted marriage as the best way to get out of jail, an irony the *juglares* never thought of.) Appropriate to an incident of 931, the emperor and knight are out of place in an account dealing with 960, for Sancha had disappeared after signing a document of Sept. 4, 959, and must be presumed dead in 960.[9] Finally, the proposal of marriage to a Navarrese princess who is a "donzella" has nothing to do with the woman who had been twice married. It is clear that at some point in the evolution of the legends the two women were fused into one, as is common in folkloric materials for the purpose of simplification. Both women were called Sancha and then references to both were erroneously combined. When the name Sancha was given to the heroine of the Castroviejo escape it was necessary that the Navarrese imprisonment be made the first because FG married the woman who freed him from that jail and was later released from a Leonese jail by a woman who was already his wife. With the fusion of the two women into one, inversion was inevitable.

  The arguments advanced so far have been made to prove that the first imprisonment of the poem was originally the second. It remains to show that the poem's second jailing was the first in earlier versions. We are forced to turn to the *PCG* (Chap 719), which preserves the lost ending of the poem where we find what has become the traditional account. After helping FG escape from the jail in which he had been cast by Sancho I in Leon, Sancha is summoned before her irate nephew, the king. She says to him, choosing her arguments cannily, that she had counted on his "mesura," his restraint or self-control, that preeminent Spanish virtue, that she as daughter of a king and the wife of a great man will be treated as befits a lady of her rank. Then she adds, most curiously, "et vos non querades fazer contra mi cosa desguisada, ca gran debdo e con vuestros hijos, et en mi deshondra gran parte auredes vos." What did she mean? The answer centers around the word "debdo-deudo." The meaning which applies here is that of *parentesco*, relationship.

If we follow the tradition of the poem, reflected in the *PCG*, she was aunt of Sancho through her sister, Queen Urraca of Leon. Sancho's children then would be her great-nephews and nieces, certainly not a "gran parentesco." Punishment would, it is true, reflect on him to a certain extent. But, unfortunately for this relationship, Sancha died at the end of 959, and this scene is of 965. If we keep Sancho I as king and change the wife to the Navarrese Urraca as proposed by Pérez de Urbel, we are faced with an equally tenuous relationship. In this case, Sancho is cousin of Urraca who is then second-cousin of his children, certainly no closer a tie than in the preceeding case. Punishment of Urraca will reflect on him in much the same degree as in the above relationship. But, and this is not conclusive, histories and chronicles record only one child for Sancho I and the statement refers to "hijos" in the plural.

If however we follow the order of events as given in the Latin chronicles and place the Leonese imprisonment under Ramiro II, the woman in question as wife of FG in 944 or 945, is Sancha, daughter of the late King Sancho Garcés of Navarre, and sister of the reigning monarch García Sánchez. She is sister-in-law of King Ramiro II of Leon, aunt of Prince Sancho and of Princess Elvira, as close a relationship as is possible outside of the royal family itself. It is likely that Queen Urraca of Leon had stood as godmother, *padrina*, at the baptism of her niece and namesake Urraca, daughter of FG and Sancha. And it is equally probable that Sancha was god-mother of her *tocayo* Prince Sancho and of his royal sister Elvira. This latter relationship would suggest for "debdo" another meaning, that of duty or obligation arising from the promises made by god-parents at the baptism, as defined by Menéndez Pidal in his vocabulary to the *Cid*. Punishment by the king against his sister-in-law, aunt and probably god-mother of his children, "hijos," historically true in the plural, would reflect strongly on him, making him share in the dishonor to her. The real meaning of that statement by Sancha becomes clear and takes on its intended significance only when the Leonese episode is placed under Ramiro II where it belongs. It is obvious that when the two wives were combined into one the two prison accounts had to be and were inverted, a change that occurred before our poet took up his work.

Beverly West points out that FG goes through several of the stages of the Raglan Initiation/Leadership criteria. One of these is marriage to a queen, which in our poem becomes marriage to the princess Sancha/Urraca. She also notes that Sancha too passes through some Initiation Tests, and cites her strength, courage, fidelity, and wit.[10] What is probably one of our poet's contribution to the character portrayal in the legends about the count is shown in his freeing of the Christian captives he rescued from the Moors in Tierra de Campos, and in his restoring to them the livestock on which their future welfare depended. Here he shows himself to be a leader who understood the life, needs, and problems of the common man. The Arlantine makes very clear FG's concern for them as human beings, in sharp contrast to the Leonese nobles who wanted to profit from the disaster they had suffered. The count's generosity as leader is intended to benefit the people. It is doubtless true that part of his purpose was political, to induce the people of the Tierra de Campos area to support his cause if the need were to arise, but the poet makes no mention of this, leaving solely the impression of his great-heartedness.

The interesting aspect of Sancha's actions is that they show she has much the same qualities as FG. In all his combats he is the "esforçado" leader, just as she is the "duenna esforçada" who carries her man to safety on her back. Then she helps him to escape the "arcipreste" through her ingenuity and wit in fooling her would-be attacker. FG had proved himself to be an "esforcado" leader in military matters, and at the end of the work outdoes Sancho in ingenuity and wit. Sancha gives her own display of ingenuity and wit in helping her husband escape from his prison in her clothes. Finally she completely outshines her nephew, the inept Sancho, as will be shown in the next chapter, as she justifies her help to FG and wins both the king's permission to leave and an escort to take her to the man who had until that morning been her nephew's prisoner. She shows herself to be a worthy equal to the count who owes his freedom, his welfare, and probably his life to her. The final qualities shown by Sancha are those of filial piety, and a generosity which matches that of her husband. The parallel between FG and Sancha is striking.

The poet used a common and effective device known to and much practised by churchmen, that of contrast. Through it he strengthens and ennobles his portrayal of a Sancha who stands out against a Teresa, embittered, unforgiving, intent only on her self-seeking vengeance. This is the very antithesis of the strong, outgoing, self-sacrificing-if-necessary wife of the hero. The contrast of the forces of good and evil continues, without being designated as such, the struggle of "Dios y el Pecado "that filled the first main section on Gothic Spain. Our poet-monk again lets his training and knowledge as a churchman show through the verses here. Teresa had long been part of the legends, but the high degree of unremitting vindictiveness she shows in our poem, in all probability, due to our poet's priestly thought processes, is made to contrast with and thus enhance the portrayal of Sancha whose good qualities match those her husband.

---

1   The major portion of this chapter appeared in 1954.See:J.P.Keller,"Inversion of the Prison Episodes in the *Poema de Fernán González,"*   *Hispanic Review,* XXII, (1954), pp. 253-63.

2   Henrique Flórez, *España sagrada,* XXIII, p. 32. Flórez gives the title *Annales compostellani*   while Pérez de Urbel uses the more common   *Anales compostelanos.*
Pérez de Pérez de Urbel, *Glosas* p. 250.

3   *Silense,*   ed. cit., pp. 328-9.   Pérez de Urbel says that the notice was in the *Sampiro*   first, ca 1000.   "Glosas," p. 251.

4   Georges Cirot, "La chronique léonaise,"   *Bulletin hispanique,*   XIII, (1911), p. 416.

5   ----------, "La chronique léonaise,"   *Bulletin Hispanique,*   XXIII, (1921), p. 283.

6   Dozy, *Recherches,* ed. cit. p.98.

7   Pérez de Urbel, *Historia,* I, pp. 581-3.

8   Reinhart Dozy, *Histoire, II,*   ed. cit. p. 164.   Dozy cites Ibn Haldûn who says that Abderrahman concluded a separate peace with FG.

9   Pérez de Urbel, *Historia,* I , footnote, p. 583.

10   Beverly West, op. cit. pp. 45-7.

Chapter Eleven

Liberation

"ferdinandum gundisalbiz qui castellanos de subiugo
legionensis dominationis dicitur extrasisse"
(*Crónica najerense*)

The Latin quotation above, from the *Crónica najerense*, ca 1160, says: "Fernán González who is said to have taken the Castilians out from under the yoke of Leonese domination." The "dicitur," "it is said," shows that the chronicler recognized that the assertion was not necessarily true. When the count died in 970, Castile was still a vassal state subservient to Leon. Not until 1033, when Fernando I, who was known as "el Magno" became king, did Castile achieve full status as an independent monarchy. In the mind of the people, however, it had been free for decades, no longer under the yoke of Leon. What hidden truth was preserved in the words of the chronicle that led to the popular tradition that Castile was and had been free and separate from Leon?

Normally, under the feudal system, a nobleman swore fealty to his liege lord, accepted his orders, and appeared in person when summoned to the royal court. Normally, a count was appointed by the king to control an area that was his only at the pleasure of the crown, and could be removed at the royal whim. We know from the *Sampiro* that Ramiro II had named FG to be count of Castile, that later he removed and jailed him, and then restored him to his former position and power. We know that the alliance of FG, García Sánchez, and Sancho I failed in their attempt to remove Ordoño III from the throne of Leon and to put Sancho I in his place, and that the Castilian then had to renew his oath of fealty to the king. The *Sampiro* says of this:

> Fredernandus uero superdictus, qui socer eius fuerat,
> uolens nolens cum magno metu ad servicium properavit.
> The aforesaid Fernando in truth who had been his father-
> in-law, will-nilly, with great fear, hurried to his
> service.

(The "fuerat/had been" shows that Ordoño III had put away his wife Urraca, daughter of FG and Sancha, when FG joined the coalition to unseat him.) Then when Sancho I became king of Leon, he was dependent on Navarre for support, but was dethroned for a time by his uncle FG, replaced by the latter's puppet Ordoño IV, and later restored to the throne. From then on, until his death in 965, Sancho lived in an uneasy truce with FG. He was succeeded by his young son Ramiro III, who was only five years old at the time, and the Castilian continued acting with virtual independence. When FG died in 970, he was succeeded by his son García Fernández: "heredo empos ell el condado et el sennorio de Castiella el cuende Garçi Fernandez so fijo." *(PCG* Chap 729). It is not known whether this succession to the rank of count was made with the authorization of the child king or was brought about by the Castilians and presented to the crown as a *fait accompli* without royal permission. In any case, the succession was established and continued unquestioned, for two more generations, ending with the assassination of the Infante García. By this time, the legends had accepted independence as a fact and had woven it into the poetic traditions of the people, attributing it to the hero of our poem.

It is necessary to resume what had recently occurred in the poem in order to gain an understanding of what the *PCG* gives as the whole of the lost ending of the poem in much the same form as it must have been planned by the Arlantine. A glance back at the beginning of Chapter Eight will show that Sections III A and III C both start with "Cortes in Leon." They are separated by the rest of A and all of B, but they nevertheless form one connected story concerned with the liberation of Castile from Leon. Only part of this account is in the poem itself, but the chronicle reports the whole sequence of events. When read as a single narrative there can be no doubt that the portion found only in the chronicle was taken from the full text of our poem. From the singleness of viewpoint, the flow of events, and from the number of threes completed, it is clear that the whole of Section III is by one writer, the Arlantine. Again one is struck by the human traits portrayed, particularly in the scene of the final "cortes" and by an occasional phrase or sentence with which the poet infuses life into the emotions and actions he sets forth.

A closer look at this part of the *PCG* (Chapters 717-720), makes clear how thoroughly the story of the Leonese-Castilian rivalry has been structured and ordered in the evolving legends about the count. Casalduero correctly said that this last part of the work is almost completely novelesque as compared with the first main section.[1] As such it can and does contain whatever the poet wishes to put in it. We reiterate that the very heart of this portion, liberation, was never achieved in FG's time, but it is the basis of the poem's later course of events. The poet, with the advantage of hindsight, knowing that Castile would become a kingdom, concludes the part just prior to the advent of FG with two stanzas that clearly foretell what is to come, and point out the source of the continuing strength that will make it possible. They are among the most significant of the poem in showing how unquestionably the poet planned the total structure of his work.

>Era toda Castyella solo un alcaldia,
>maguer que era pobre e de poca valia,
>nunca de buenos omnes fue Castyella vacia.
>de quales fueron paresçe oy en dia.

The "oy en dia" is, of course, the poet's day by which time Castile had long been a kingdom, far beyond the "alcaldia" and the "condado.

>Varones castellanos, este fue su cuydado:
>de llegar su sennor al mas alto estado,
>D'un alcaldia pobre fizieron la condado,
>tornaron la despues cabeça de rreynado.   (171-172)

Starting with the efforts of the count, supported by his "varones" and the mass of the "castellanos" of the stanza above, Castile had indeed risen to the "mas alto estado" of kingdom envisioned in the verse. Leon had long been considered the foremost, but that position passed to Castile with power, prestige, and influence it would never relinquish. With the certainty possible only through hindsight, our poet confidently foretells here the coming primacy of his beloved Castyella Vyeja.

As we pick up the story, we begin with Sancho I summoning FG to cortes, which the count attends with ill-grace.

>Ovo ir a las cortes pero con grand pesar,
>era muy fiera cosa la mano le besar;
>"Sennor Dios de los cielos, quieras me ayudar,
>que yo pueda desta premia a Castyella sacar."   (565)

The "la mano le besar" and the "desta premia sacar" must be remembered for they are seeds that will bear fruit at the end of the poet's story. Sancho received him well, he enjoyed honorable treatment from the Leonese nobles, signed a contract for the sale of a horse and hawk. He was then betrayed by Queen Teresa whose family had long been his enemy. Seized, jailed for a year, he escaped from the jail and then from the "arcipreste," won a new wife, and returned to his people. He had to fight this father-in-law/brother-in-law whom he captured and held in jail for a year. He stayed away from "cortes" for two years, and then sent to Sancho asking for payment of the debt. Sancho's tax gatherers were out collecting as the royal treasury was short of funds and the king did not answer.

Another year passed without repayment. García Sánchez overran Castile and in the ensuing battle was beaten for the third time, and the poem ends saying that neither Moors or Christians had ever been able to beat the hero.

There is an important legal matter to consider before taking up the last episode. It is necessary to return to the point in the poem where FG sends to Sancho asking for payment of the debt which is two years overdue. The king is short of funds and sends only part of the money. FG refuses to accept any of it.

> el conde don Fernando non los quiso tomar,
> ovo en este pleito la cosa a delatar. (734cd)

Had he taken any, it would have allowed the debt to continue. The law is clear on this point. The *Fuero Juzgo* says:

> Libro V Titol V Ley antigua Si alguna parte del precio finca por pagar. Si la una parte del precio es pagada y la otra parte finca por pagar, non se deve por ende desfazer la vendicion. E si el comprador non pagare el otra partida del precio al plazo, pague las usuras daquella parte que deve si fuere parado, fueras que la vendicion fuesse desfecha si non pagas el precio al plazo.
> "...except that the sale be undone if the price not be paid on time."

Refusal to accept a partial payment kept the entire debt in force, and FG held the king to paying the whole or canceling the sale and returning the horse and hawk. This would have been an intolerable humiliation for a reigning monarch. There can be no doubt that the poet intended to show that FG knew the law and that by keeping the debt in force he had once again outsmarted his liege lord. Military victories have now been reinforced by an intellectual triumph over Sancho. In the meantime the debt kept on doubling every day.

We take up the last episode as given in the *PCG* (Chap 717). Time passes and FG is again summoned to "cortes" in Leon, under the threat of either attending or of giving up the county. He makes a lengthy statement to his men telling them that he has never seized land from the crown, as the king accused him of doing, because such actions are alien to Castilians. When the count appears in Leon, no one comes out to meet him, contrasting with the joyous reception on his previous appearance, and he "touo lo por mala senna," an understatement which is the last of the few bits of humor in the story of FG.

The dramatic confrontation which now takes place between the king and his haughty subject is striking for it had been carefully developed in the juglaresque tradition that preceeded our poem. One must visualize the scene: King Sancho I, whom an Arab historian has characterized as vain, proud, and quarrelsome,[2] ranged with his court on one side, and the haughty count on the other, alone or accompanied by only a few men. When he goes to kiss the hand of his liege lord, the latter refuses him, rejecting the count as vassal, an act which breaks the bond between the two. Whether he knew it or nor, Sancho had made a grave mistake. (One remembers the words of the unknown poet of the *CMC* "Dios, qué buen vassallo si oviesse buen señore" (v. 20). The ruler's first words to FG are "Tiraduos alla, conde, ca mucho sodes loçano." The nobles of the court are still angry and resentful over not having been allowed to go with the Castilians on the rescue expedition into the Tierra de Campos, so one can understand the apprehension of FG, and know how alone he felt. To this must be added the hatred of Teresa of whom the poem had told us:

> Querya castellanos de grado desonrrar,
> avivo leoneses por con ellos lidiar.   (727)

The *PCG* (Chap 715) said of her: "et punnava de buscarles quanto mal et quanta desonrra podie." When our count and his men returned from Tierra de Campos they found the whole court arrayed against them, including the king who had previously been their ally. One can easily see the hand of Teresa as a "mesturera" and the nobles as her "malsines" working on Sancho to sway him against the Castilian much as a similar group was, a century later, to turn Alfonso VI against the Cid. Both men lost the ruler's favor and suffered: FG was jailed and the Cid was exiled from his native land. Sancho then accuses the count: "alçastes me con el condado," a charge which corresponds to the "tirannidem" of which he had been accused by Ramiro, twenty years and three kings earlier. The charge of the count's "tuerto" against the crown was badly misplaced by the *juglares,* a garbling of history in which the overall result was nevertheless highly effective in the presentation of the scene.

Sancho also accuses FG of numerous other "pesares y tuertos," and demands guarantors to ensure that amends will be made. The count protests his innocence: he hasn't taken over the county, Castilians don't do such things, "ca por lealtad e por mannas tengome por caballero cumplido." He further excuses himself for not having come to "cortes" for two years because of the way he had been dishonored by the Leonese nobles the last time he had been there. Then he adds that even if he had seized the land, he would have been justified in doing so, because for three years the king had failed to pay him, "por fuerça," and in his turn he then boldly asks for

guarantors from the king. Angered at this challenge to his authority from one of his subjects, the king has FG thrown into jail.
When the news reaches Castile, Sancha "cayo amortida." She rallies her Castilians round her, they decide to go to Leon in force to see about freeing their leader. Five hundred men, traveling off the roads and only by night, go with Sancha almost to Leon, then wait in a forest and with only two men she goes on into the city. While her escorts stay outside the palace, she enters into the presence of the king, requests permission to see her husband, and is allowed to do so. Later she asks that FG's shackles be removed, beause "caballo travado nunca bien podie fazer fijos," and Sancho grants her request. She arises, "de muy grand mannana quanto a los maitines" and exchanges clothes with her husband who has been unshackled. She persuades the guard at the door to open for her without waiting for permission from his superior, and then watches from the darkness of the cell while FG, carefully hooded and remaining silent so as not to betray the subterfuge, escapes in her place. He joins the two men waiting outside, and goes with them to their comrades in the forest. (Chap 718). In the meantime the king has learned of the escape and of Sancha's part in it. He is uncertain as to what to do, and "...pesol assi como si ouiesse perdudo el reyno." The audience must have smiled appreciatively at the king's dilemma, knowing that this very loss was soon to occur.

One must now set the scene for another confrontation, this time of a very different nature in which the king will undo precisely what he had done at the meeting with FG. It must be remembered that the king was Sancho I, who had been known as Sancho el Craso for his obesity. Slimmed down now, he is with his aunt Sancha, for whom he had been named, and who had undoubtedly dandled him on her knee in earlier days. In a manner unbefitting to a ruling monarch, he comes to see her, instead of properly summoning her before him, as his father King Ramiro II would have done. The joy of the public, as the *juglar* presents this portion of the entertainment, must have been great. Carefully and knowingly Sancha works on her nephew, with full confidence in her ability to make the scene end as she wishes. Boldly, cannily, and with flattery, she directs the conversation as discussed in the previous chapter. She reminds him of her rank, her relationship to him, the shame to him if he treats her dishonorably, saying that he should act with restraint so others will have nothing for which to reproach him. Convinced, the king acknowledges that she is right and lets her go, ordering an escort to accompany her to join her husband that very day.

"Los leoneses (the same ones who had caused the troubles for FG under the instigation of Teresa) fizieron assi como el rey les mando, et levaron la condessa muy onrradamientre como a duenna de tan alta guisa." (Chap 719)

In this whole scene, Sancho is shown at a disadvantage. One can still feel if not see the Sancho el Craso of former years, slimmed it is true, and wearing the crown to be sure, but still the little nephew before the, to him, imposing figure of his aunt, princess and sister of the king of Navarre, the countess of Castile, wife of the man who has been and still is his nemesis. She keeps him subdued and he can but agree with what she says. How the Castilian public must have loved it!

The last act of this four part drama finds FG in Castile, still having to fight, "ca non le dexaron moros nin cristianos estar en paz." He finally sends to Sancho demanding payment for the horse and hawk, threatening to forcing the issue if the king demurs. When no reply comes, he raids Leonese territory, as a warning, taking much booty and many captives. In alarm the king sends his "mayordomo" with all the "auer" available, but when the two men sit down to figure out just how much is owed after three years of nonpayment, they agree that it cannot be paid by "cuantos omnes avie en Espanna," and the matter is reported that way to the king.

El rey cuando esto sopo, touose por muy embargado por aquel fecho, ca non fallaua quien le diesse y conseio, et si pudiera, repintierase daquella mercadura de grado, ca se temie de perder el regno por y.

Which is exactly what happens. He consults with his nobles, their decision is that the county of Castile should be granted complete independence from Leon. The count accepts:

"et demas touose por guarido por ello porque veye que salie de grand premia, et por que non aurie de besar mano a omne del mundo si non fuesse al Sennor de la Ley; et este es el apostoligo. Et desta guisa es contado que salieron los castellanos de premia et de servidumbre et del poder de Leon et de sus leoneses." (Chap 721)

At the end of this last act of the drama we have FG, the count of Castile, finally achieving his goal of no longer being under the "premia" of Moors, of Navarre, or of Leon. He no longer has to kiss the hand of any king in token of subservience. He is finally his own man in Spain. At last the only one to whom he will owe fealty is the "Sennor de la Ley." One might suppose that this refers to God, but it does not. It is the "apostoligo," the Pope, whom FG will recognize as the only earthly authority above him, whose hand he will willingly kiss, for FG is the "siervo de Dios" (although the poet never uses this term in his work). Inheritor of Gothic legitimacy, Castile through its count took over the leadership of all Christian Spain. Through God's guidance and the common effort of all, Castile fought, struggled, suffered, and persevered until the task was done. FG was no longer under opresion, he no longer had to abase himself by kissing any one's hand in token of submission. His men, his "castellanos," had achieved their goal of raising Castile to "el mas alto estado." Serving his God, FG had freed himself and his Castile from all earthly authorities except that of the Pope, who was, as the representative of God, the only one who could claim his fealty.

Early in the poem just before FG enters, the poet eulogizes his beloved bit of Spain:
Aun Castyella Vieja, al mi entendimiento,
mejor es que lo al por que fue el çimiento,
ca conquirieron mucho, maguer poco convento,
byen lo podedes ver en el acabamiento. (l57)
"They conquered much in spite of little help. You can see it clearly in the ending." And the Arlantine shows us, now at the poem's "acabamiento," his Castyella Vieja which often had to stand alone and at times found itself assailed by those who should have been its allies. Relying only on no earthly power save itself, trusting solely to its own efforts, to its unflagging determination, Castile found itself rewarded for its faithfulness in service to God and to Christian Spain. With the help of the "Cryador," who had shown his approval and had given His support by sending Santiago and the heavenly host, Castile now at the end of the poem reached its goal of liberation. On this note the *PCG* ends its account of FG except for a *post-scriptum* seven chapters later telling of the death and burial in San Pedro de Arlanza of the count of Castile.

It is interesting to consider that when FG was exempted from subservience to Leon, there was no higher earthly authority that he had to obey. According to the political system of that day, he therefore ruled Castyella Vyeja with the powers of a king, just as the Cid really did when he conquered the city of Valencia and replaced its Moorish ruler. The Cid still considered himself to be the ever faithful vassal of King Alfonso, and never assumed the title of king, even though he held and exercised the royal power in Valencia. Neither did FG assume the title of king in Castile. It was enough for him to continue ruling as he had been doing for years, as long as he did not have to "besar la mano" of any man in Spain.

It has often been said that the *PFG* belongs to the "rebellious vassal" cycle of poems. This term originated in France where it designated a series of *chansons de geste* characterized by vassals who rebelled, fought, and humiliated the royal authority. Any struggle against the Sarracens was relegated to a second plane and the war against the king was in the foreground. The poet's sympathies lay. with the rebellious vassal.

In his *De primitiva lírica española y antigua épica*, 1951, Menéndez Pidal said that to Leo Spitzer's two themes for the epic, "venganza por odios de familia" and "destierro," must be added a third, "El tema del vasallo enemistado con su soberano" (FG, Renaud de Montauban, Chevalerie Ogier, etc.).[3] It is clear that in historical fact FG belongs to this group. Among the dubious qualifications of our count for this distinction were his "tirannidem" against Ramiro II, his part in the unsuccessful attempt to unseat Ordoño III, and his successful but short-lived dethroning of Sancho I. Yes, he was a rebellious vassal, possibly not the first in Spain, but certainly the foremost and most successful.[4]

From the time FG appears on the scene, the sympathy of our poet for his hero is unmistakable and unremitting. He is a man who can not permit the repeated offenses of Navarre to go unanswered. He always portrays FG as a man of honor and great military ability against both the Moors and the Navarrese. He keeps his promises, to God and to the woman who frees him from jail. He is generous and humanitarian towards the Christian captives whom he frees from their Moorish captors and to whom he restores the livestock without which they would have had to spend the rest of their lives as serfs or worse. Finally, he is the vassal who obeys his liege lord's summons to "cortes", who comes repeatedly with his men on behalf of his king to drive out the Infidel who again are invading Christian territory.

It is altogether probable that Section III Liberation was originally developed by the *juglares* as a separate story concerned only with the relations of FG and King Sancho I. Into this the poet inserted the last three battles, the treachery of Teresa, and the events which ensued. In the incomplete poem we have today, the material connected with King Sancho I occupies less than thirty stanzas. The *PCG*'s prose account of the missing portion can be roughly estimated at about one hundred stanzas. This makes a total of a little more than five hundred verses, which Menéndez Pidal estimated as the length of the short *cantares* of the juglaresque beginnings of the *epopeya* in Spain. It seems fair therefore to suppose that Section III Liberation was originally a separate, complete, and independent *cantar.* As such, and even though the above supposition may not be acceptable, one sees the poet's consistent portrayal of the obedient vassal who attends "cortes" in answer to his king's summon, who comes with his men to fight the Infidel, and finally appears a third time in Leon in response to the summons to another "cortes" at which he is jailed. There is no rebel here. This passage clearly shows how our poet bent tradition to his needs. There is further illustration of this.

It will be remembered that when FG and his men returned to Leon after defeating the Moors in the Tierra de Campos they found the king's nobles highly incensed against them because they had not been allowed to share in the battle and the spoils. So great was the animosity that:

Leoneses ye castellanos fueron mal denostados,
fyncaron vnos de otros todos desafiados,
fueron los castellanos a sus tierras tornados,
non fueron por dos años a las cortes llamados. (729)

Marden, Victorio Martínez, and Geary accept the MS reading here which is clearly "llamados." Menéndez Pidal, and others following him, changed this to "llegados" because of a coming passage in the *PCG* in which Sancho I accuses FG: " Tiradvos alla, cuende, que mucho sodes loçano. Bien a tres annos que non quisiestes venir a mis cortes." (*PCG* Chap. 717). We can be sure that it was the *juglares* or the *CFG* that provided the arrogant refusal of the count to come to "cortes," and that the *PCG* carried the same "loçanía" which shows the Castilian's refusal to come to Leon, "non quisiestes, venir," intolerable for Sancho I who throws FG into jail. The Arlantine, however, continuing his consistent portrayal of the obedient vassal, changed his verses to show that FG had stayed away from Leon solely because he had not been called. The "llamados" of the MS is correct.

When the summons to "cortes" does come, our count makes the journey to Leon, where he kisses the hand of his liege lord, renewing his fealty, though it is done "mal de su grado." Only after he has been jailed unjustly and suffered the affront to his honor and person does he finally act to restore his *dignidad.* When he gets out of jail, thanks again to his "dulcísima esposa" Sancha, he makes the first overt move against his king. It is essential here to understand that it is Sancho's refusal to let FG kiss his hand that ends the ties of FG as vassal and he therefore no longer owes fealty to the king. When FG overruns Leonese territory taking captives and booty, he is no longer bound to the king. This cannot be called the act of a rebellious vassal. Further, FG considers that he is justified in doing so because the king has for three years failed to pay a legal debt, "por fuerça."

We have nothing here like the magnanimity of the Cid, whose never-failing fealty to Alfonso VI was highlighted throughout that poem by his ever-increasing gifts offered freely to his liege lord. As the Cid's fortunes grew, so also did the marks of his continuing obedience to his sovereign. Our poet reworked the juglaresque material of the *CFG* , telling of the relationship between Sancho I and FG which had been incorporated into the *CFG*, using only what would show FG in a good light. He had, perforce, to omit all the slowly increasing hostility that really marked the relations between the two men. As a result, he had little or no opportunity to gradually develop the story of the "enemiga" between them. We know that he intentionally omitted the whole story of how FG had removed Sancho from the throne and put Ordoño IV in his place, because that would have shown his hero as a real rebellious vassal. He did his best to stretch the inherited material by inserting the last three battles, and the story of Teresa with the capture, jailing and subsequent escape with the help of the Navarrese princess whom he then married. Even so, this interruption to the story did not provide a long enough interval to keep the reversal of FG's attitude towards his king from seeming abrupt, and he had to partially cover the transition by reminding his public that two and three years had passed between episodes.

As a matter of speculation we might suppose that the juglaresque tradition, all the way through the *CFG*, showed a rebellious FG and that the loyal vassal of our poem is due solely to the Arlantine who was intent on portraying the count as we see him in the *PFG*. This would then make the arrogant FG who spattered his king in the river as shown in the *Cl344* and the *romance* "Castellanos y leoneses tienen grandes divisiones" a part of the existing tradition that our poet discarded because it did not conform to his purposes. That he had to make the change was mandated by what for him was the most important consideration of all.

Again we pose the question: was FG a rebellious vassal? In point of fact he was. As presented by the poet, he was not. And this is for the very obvious fact that he was telling the story not only of FG, but also that of the liberation of Castile. He began with the coming of the Goths who were led by God, taking the earliest portion of his account from histories and chronicles, as well as folktales and from already much evolved legends of early heroes such as Wamba, Pelayo, and Bernardo del Carpio. From then on he relied principally on material from the *juglares* to which he added his own contributions taken from a saint's life, the *Bible*, and Trojan War sources, and from Roman and other folklore floating in the popular culture around him. Even bits from the *Chanson de Roland*, the *Cid*, and the Provençal troubador tradition were put to use. All this is presented as seen from his perspective of churchman. The guiding hand of the Lord, who sends Santiago to intervene on behalf of FG and the Castilians, is obvious, from the first verse:

> En el nombre del Padre que fizo toda cosa, (1a)

to the last two verses:

> Quiso Dios al buen conde esta graçia fazer,
> que moros nin cristianos non le podian vençer. (752ab)

It was inevitable, it was God's will that the descendants of his "pueblo escogido" should be free. From this viewpoint it is hard to conclude that the count of our poem was a rebellious vassal, for he had been rejected by his sovereign and, most important of all, he was doing his Maker's will.

The Castilians were first shown with their determination to raise Castile "al mas alto estado." On their way to achieving their goal, led by their indomitable count, they were always doing the will of their God. With FG they considered that they were fulfilling the purpose of their "Cryador." Against Navarre they fought to avenge "tuertos" to prevent further injustices against them, and to put down the "engannos" that the Savior had come to earth to end. From this point of view, which is clearly that of the poet, what FG did can hardly be termed that of a *rebelde*. He was, rather, a "fulfiller" who was carrying on with his Lord's blessing the work of the "Reconquista" to which he had been appointed through the hermit Pelayo.

---

1   Joaquín Casalduero, "Sobre la composición del *PFG*," *Anuario de estuduios medievales*, (Barcelona: 5, 1968), pp.181-206. Casalduero says of his outline that the two main sections: "Contrastan así las dos presentaciones: histórica la primera, novelesca la segunda." p. 188.

2   Dozy, *Histoire, ed. cit.* II.   "Le roi Sanche était vain, orgueilleux, et belliqueux." p. 167.

3   R. Menéndez Pidal, *De primitiva lírica española y antigue épica*. (Buenos Aires: Espasa Calpe, 1951). p. 25.

4   Juan Victorio, "Notas sobre Fernán González," *Revue belge de philologie et d'histoire*, L, (1972), Nos. 3,4. pp.776-792. In order to change FG into a model of

perfections, two things are necessary. One is: "hacer desaparecer el carácter de rebelde impenitente...para ello hay que alejarlo lo más posible de León y hacerle actuar en Navarra..." The other is: "hacer de él un auténtico cruzado."
p.507

Afterword

In the long span of the history of Castile, what FG did could not fail to become the material of legend. With our poet it turned into myth as this heroic figure led his people through a long series of conflicts and suffering, remaining faithful to a goal that they firmly believed was not only theirs but also that of their Maker. If myth is the attempt to explain transcendent matters in the development of a people, involving their God or gods in human affairs, expressing and even creating their "national" consciousness and their ideals through the deeds of their heroes, then this story of FG is truly our poet's contribution to Castilian mythology.

General Bibiography

Amador de los Ríos, José. *Historia crítica de la literatura española.*
    III, Madrid: 1863.

Anglade, Joseph. *Histoire sommaire de la littérature méridionale au
    moyen âge.* Paris: 1921.

Campbell, Joseph. *The Hero with a Thousand Faces.* 2nd. ed.
    Princeton: Princeton Univ. Press, 1968.

Carlos, Príncipe de Viana. *Crónica de los reyes de Navarra.*
    Pamplona: 1843. José Yanguas y Miranda, ed. Valencia: 1971.

Casalduero, Joaquín Gimeno. "Sobre la composición del *Poema de
    Fernán González.*" *Anuario de estudios medievales,* V,
    (1968) 181-206.

Chalon, Louis. "L'histoire de la monarchie asturienne de Pelayo à
    Alphonse II, le Chaste, dans le *Poema de Fernán González.*"
    *Marche Romane, Hommage des romanistes liégeois à la
    mémoire de Ramón Menéndez Pidal.* XX-I (1970), Cahiers de
    'A.R.U.Lg. 61-67.

Cirot, Georges. "Une chronique léonaise inédite." *Bulletin hispanique,*
    XI, No. 3 (1909), 259-282.

----------. "La chronique léonaise." *BH, XIII* , No. 4 (1911). 381-
    439.

----------. "La chronique léonaise et les petites annales de
    Castille." *BH,* No.I (1919). 93-102.

----------. "Fernán González dans la Chronique léonaise." *BH,* XXIII
    No. I (1921) I-14.

----------. "Fernán González dans la *Chronique léonaise, (suite)*. *BH*, No. 4 (1921), 269-84.

----------. "Sur le Fernán González." *BH*, (1928), No. 2, 113-46.

Corominas, Joan. *Diccionario crítico-etimológico de la lengua castellana*. Berna: Edit. Franke, 1954.

Correa Calderón, Evaristo. "Reminiscencias homéricas en el *Poema de Fernán González.*" *Estudios dedicados a D. Ramón Menéndez Pidal*. V, Madrid: CSIC, 1953.

Deyermond, A.D. *Epic poetry and the clergy: Studies on the "Mocedades de Rogrigo."* London: Tamesis, 1969.

----------. "Una nota sobre el *Poema de Fernán González.*" *Hispanófila*, VIII 1960. 35-7.

Dozy, Reinhart. *Histoire des Musulmans d'Espagne (710-1110)*. Nouvelle édition par Lévy-Provençal. Leyde: 1932. V. II.

----------, "Recherches sur l'Histoire et la litterature de l'Espagne

Dutton, Brian. "Gonzalo de Berceo and the Cantares de Gesta." *Bulletin of Hispanic Studies*, XXXVIII 1961. 197-205.

Entwistle, William J. "The Liberation of Castile." *Modern Languge Review*, XIX 1924, 471-2.

Formisano, Luciano. "Cuaderna vía ajuglarada" nel *Poema de Fernán González.*" *La lengua y la literatura en tiempos de Aldonso X*, Murcia: 1985. 181-94.

García Gallo, Alfonso. "El carácter germánico de la épica y del derecho en la edad media española." *Anuario de historia del derecho español*, XXV 1955, 583-680.

Geary, John S. *Historia del Conde Fernán González.* facsimile and paleographic edition, commentary and concordance. Madison: 1987.

----------, *Formulaic Diction in the 'Poema de Fernán González' and the 'Mocedades de Rodrigo,' a computer aided analysis.* Madrid: 1980.

González, Julio. *Historia general de España.* Dirección general de Antonio Canovas del Castillo. Madrid, Boletín de la Real Academia de la Historia, 1891.

Gonzalo de Berceo. *Vida de San Millán* . BAE. LVII, Madrid: 1952. 65-79.

Harvey, L.P. "Fernán González's Horse." *Medieval Hispanic Studies presented to Rita Hamilton.* Ed. A.D.Deyermond, London: Tamesis, 1976. 77-86.

----------, and David Hook. "The Affair of the Horse and Hawk in the *Poema de Fernán González.*" *Modern Language Review.* LXXVII, 1982, 840-7.

Horrent, Jules. *Roncevalles* , Paris: Les Belles Lettres, 1951. Bibliothèque de la Faculté de Philosophie et Lettres de l'Université de Liège. Fascicule CXXII.

----------, "Hernaut de Beaulande et le *Poema de Fernán González.*" *Bulletin Hisppanique,* LXXIX, 1977. 23-52.

Isidore of Seville. *History of the Goths, Vandals, and Suevi.* Trans. by Donini, Guido and Gordon Brace Ford, Jr. 2nd rev. ed. Leiden: E.J.Brill. 1970. "De laude Hispaniae." 1-2

La Chanson de Roland. Jenkins, T.A., ed. Boston: Heath USA, 1924.

Lacarra, José María. "Textos navarros del Códice de Roda." *Estudios de edad media de la corona de Aragón, sección de Zaragoza.* Zaragoza: CSIC, 1945. 193-252.

----------, *Estudios de historia navarra.* Pamplona, 1971.

Lévi-Provençal, E. *España musulmana (711-1031 de J.C.)* Vol. Intro. por Emilio García Gómez. Madrid: Espasa Calpe, 1957. 2nd. ed.

Lihani, John. "Notas sobre la epopeya y la relación entre el *Poema de Fernán González* y el *Libro de buen amor.*" *Homenaje a Fernando Antonio Martínez.* Bogotá: 1979. 474-85.

Lindley-Cintra, Luis. "*O Liber regum*, fonte comum do *Poema de Fernán González* e do *Laberinto* de Juan de Mena.*" Boletim de Filologia.* XIII (1952). 289-315.

López Castellón, Enrique. coord. *Historia de Castilla y León.* Vol.II *Orígenes de León y Castilla.* por Grande Gallego, Cristina, Margarita Cantera Montenegro, and Jesús Cantera Montenegro. Reno: 1983.

Malkiel, Rosa Lida de. "Reseñas del: *Poema de Fernán González.* Luciano Serrano, ed., del *Poema de Fernán González.* Alonso Zamora Vicente, ed., y de *La leyenda de Fernán González.* E. Correa Calderón. *Nueva Revista de Filología Hispánica ,* III (949. 179-89.

----------, "Notas para el texto del *Alexandre* y para las fuentes del *Fernán González."* *Revista de Filología Hispánica,* VII 1945) 47-51.

Marden, C. Carroll. "An Episode in the *Poema de Fernán González."* *Revue hispanique.* VII 1903 22-7.
----------, ed. *Poema de Fernán González.* Crit. ed., notes, glossary. Baltimore: Johns Hopkins Univ. Press, 1904.

Mariana, Juan de. *Historia general de España.* I Madrid: 1608.

Marín, Francisco Marcos. *Poesía narrativa árabe y épica hispánica.* Madrid: Gredos, 1971.

Márquez-Sterling, Manuel, *Fernán González, First Count of Castile, The Man and the Legend.* University, Mississippi: Romance Monographs, 1980.

Menéndez Pidal, Ramón. "Notas para el Romancero del conde Fernán González." *Homenaje a Menéndez y Pelayo,* Ed. Juan Valera, I Madrid: 1899. 429-507.

----------. "Reseña del *Poema de Fernán González.* ed. *C.Carroll Marden."* *Archiv für das studium der Neureren Sprachen.* CXIV 1905 243-57.

----------. *Cantar de Mio Cid.: texto, gramática, vocabulario* . Madrid: Espasa Calpe, 1944. 3 vols.

----------. *Tres poetas primitivos.* Buenos Aires, Espasa Calpe. 1948. See pp. 122-3.

----------. *Reliquias de la poesía épica española.* Madrid: Espasa Calpe, 1951.

----------, *De primitiva lírica española y antigua épica.* Buenos Aires: Espasa Calpe. 1951.

----------. "Fernán González, su juventud y su geneología." *Boletín de la Real Academia de la historia.* CXXXIV (1954). 335-58.

----------. *Primer crónica general de España.* Madrid: 1955. 2vols.

----------. *Poesía juglaresca y juglares.* Madrid, 1956. 4th ed.

----------. *Poesía árabe y poesía europea.* Madrid, 1956.

----------. *Romanceros del Rey Rodrigo y de Bernardo del Carpio.* Edición y estudios a cargo de R. Lapesa, A Galves, D. Catalán y J. Caro. Madrid: 1957.

----------.ed. *Rodrigo el último godo.* Madrid, 1956-8. 3 vols.

----------. *Los godos y la epopeya española.* Madrid: 1969. 2nd. ed.

Montoro, Adrian G. "La épica medieval española y la estructura trifuncional de los indoeuropeos." *Cuadernos hispanoamericanos.* Madrid, 1974. 554-71.

Moret, J. and F. de Aleson, eds. *Anales del reino de Navarra* I Bilbao: 1969.

Nogué, "Bibliografía sobre Fernán González." *Boletín de la Institución Fernán González.* XLIV No. 165 1965, and XLV, No. 166, 1966. (Burgos).

Orlandis, José. *Historia de España: la España visigótica.* Madrid: Gredos, 1977.

Pérez, José Hernando, "Nuevos datos para el estudio del *Poema de Fernán González*. *Boletín de la Real Academia Española.* Madrid: 1986. 135-52.

Pérez de Urbel, Justo (Fray). "Historia y leyenda en el *Poema de Fernán González." Escorial,* 1944. 319-352.

----------,"Las mujeres en la gesta y en la vida de Fernán González." *Investigación y Progreso.* XV, Nos. 7,8. 1944. 193-204.

----------. *Historia del condado de Castilla.* 3 vols. Madrid: CSIC, 1945.

----------. *Sampiro: su crónica y la monarquía leonesa en el siglo X.* Madrid: 1952.

----------. *Fernán González, el héroe que hizo a Castilla.* Buenos Aires: Espasa Calpe, 1952.

----------. "Fernán González: su juventud y su linaje." *Homenaje a Johannes Vincke para el II de mayo,* Madrid: CSIC, (1962). Vol. I.

----------. "Notas histórico-críticas sobre el *Poema de Fernán González." Boletín de la Institución Fernán González.* XLVIII, No. 174, 1970, 2nd sem. 42-75. (Burgos)

----------. "Glosas histórico-críticas al *Poema de Fernán González." Boletín de la Institución Fernán González.* XLVIII, No. 175 1970, 2nd. sem. 231-265. (Burgos)

Polt, John H. "Moral Phraseology in Early Spanish Literature." *Romance Philology.* XV No. 3. (1962). 254-268.

Raglan, Lord. *The Hero, a study in tradition, myth, and drama.* New York: Vintage, 1956.

Rank, Otto. *The Myth of the Birth of the Hero, and other writings.* Ed. Philip Freund. New York: Vintage House, 1964.

Richard, Alfred. *Les comtes de Poitou.* *778-1126.* Vol. I Paris: 1903.

Riquer, Martín de. *Los cantares de gesta franceses.* Madrid: Gredos, 1952.

Rodríguez, Justiniano, *Ramiro II Rey de León.* Madrid: CSIC, 1972.

Sánchez Albornoz, Claudio. *La España musulmana.* Buenos Aires: 1960, 2nd. ed.

----------. "Observaciones a la historia de Castilla de Pérez de Urbel." *Cuadernos de la historia de España*, XI (1949).

Serrano, Luciano. *Cartulario de San Millán de la Cogolla.* Madrid: 1930.

---------- ed. *Poema de Fernán González.* Madrid: 1943.

----------. "Donaciones religiosas del Conde Fernán González." *Patria y altares.*, Burgos Publicaciones de la Institución Fernán González, 1970.

Serrano y Sanz, M. "Cronicón villarense (Liber regum)." *Boletín de la Real Academia Española.* año VI Madrid: (1919). 192-220.

----------. "Cronicón villarense (continuación)." *BRAE.* año VIII Madrid: 1921. 367-82.

Victorio Martínez, Juan J. "Nota sobre la épica medieval española: el motivo de la rebeldía." *Revue belge de philologie hispanique.* L 1972, Nos. 3,4. 777-92.

----------. ed. *Poema de Fernán González.* Madrid: Ed. Cátedra, 1981.

----------. "Notas sobre Fernán González." Festschrift article in *Acta neophilologica,* 80-2-75. 503-8.

West, Beverly. *Epic, Folk, and Christian Tradition in the 'Poema de Fernán González.'* Madrid: Turanzas, 1983.

Zamora Vicente, Alonso, ed. *Poema de Fernán González* (Clásicos castellanos). Madrid: Espasa Calpe, 1946.

Zurita, Jerónimo. *Anales de la corona de Aragón.* Ed. by Angel Canellas López. Zaragoza: CSIC, 1967.

Scripta Humanistica

Directed by
BRUNO M. DAMIANI
The Catholic University of America
COMPREHENSIVE LIST OF PUBLICATIONS*

1. Everett W. Hesse, *The "Comedia" and Points of View*. $24.50
2. Marta Ana Diz, *Patronio y Lucanor: la lectura inteligente "en el tiempo que es turbio."* Prólogo de John Esten Keller. $26.00
3. James F. Jones, Jr., *The Story of a Fair Greek of Yesteryear*. A Translation from the French of Antoine-François Prévost's *L'Histoire d'une Grecque moderne*. With Introduction and Selected Bibliography. $30.00
4. Colette H. Winn, *Jean de Sponde: Les sonnets de la mort ou La Poétique de l'accoutumance*. Préface par Frédéric Deloffre. $22.50
5. Jack Weiner, *"En busca de la justicia social: estudio sobre el teatro español del Siglo de Oro."* $24.50
6. Paul A. Gaeng, *Collapse and Reorganization of the Latin Nominal Flection as Reflected in Epigraphic Sources*. Written with the assistance of Jeffrey T. Chamberlin. $24.00
7. Edna Aizenberg, *The Aleph Weaver: Biblical, Kabbalistic, and Judaic Elements in Borges*. $25.00
8. Michael G. Paulson and Tamara Alvarez-Detrell, *Cervantes, Hardy, and "La fuerza de la sangre."* $25.50
9. Rouben Charles Cholakian, *Deflection/Reflection in the Lyric Poetry of Charles d'Orléans: A Psychosemiotic Reading*. $25.00
10. Kent P. Ljungquist, *The Grand and the Fair: Poe's Landscape Aesthetics and Pictorial Techniques*. $27.50
11. D.W. McPheeters, *Estudios humanísticos sobre la "Celestina."* $20.00
12. Vittorio Felaco, *The Poetry and Selected Prose of Camillo Sbarbaro*. Edited and Translated by Vittorio Felaco. With a Preface by Franco Fido. $25.00
13. María del C. Candau de Cevallos, *Historia de la lengua española*. $33.00
14. *Renaissance and Golden Age Studies in Honor of D.W. McPheeters*. Ed. Bruno M. Damiani. $30.00
15. Bernardo Antonio González, *Parábolas de identidad: Realidad interior y estrategia narrativa en tres novelistas de posguerra*. $28.00
16. Carmelo Gariano, *La Edad Media (Aproximación Alfonsina)*. $30.00
17. Gabriella Ibieta, *Tradition and Renewal in "La gloria de don Ramiro"*. $27.50

18.	*Estudios literarios en honor de Gustavo Correa.* Eds. Charles Faulhaber, Richard Kinkade, T.A. Perry. Preface by Manuel Durán.	$25.00
19.	George Yost, *Pieracci and Shelly: An Italian Ur-Cenci.*	$27.50
20.	Zelda Irene Brooks, *The Poetry of Gabriel Celaya.*	$26.00
21.	*La relación o naufragios de Alvar Núñez Cabeza de Vaca,* eds. Martin A. Favata y José B. Fernández.	$27.50
22.	Pamela S. Brakhage, *The Theology of "La Lozana andaluza."*	$27.50
23.	Jorge Checa, *Gracián y la imaginación arquitectónica.*	$28.00
24.	Gloria Gálvez Lira, *Maria Luisa Bombal: realidad y fantasía.*	$28.50
25.	Susana Hernández Araico, *Ironía y tragedia en Calderón.*	$25.00
26.	Philip J. Spartano, *Giacomo Zanella: Poet, Essayist, and Critic of the "Risorgimento."* Preface by Roberto Severino.	$24.00
27.	E. Kate Stewart, *Arthur Sherburne Hardy: Man of American Letters.* Preface by Louis Budd.	$28.50
28.	Giovanni Boccaccio, *The Decameron.* English Adaptation by Carmelo Gariano.	$30.00
29.	Giacomo A. Striuli, "Alienation in Giuseppe Berto".	$26.50
30.	Barbara Mujica, *Iberian Pastoral Characters.* Preface by Frederick A. de Armas.	$33.00
31.	Susan Niehoff McCrary, *"'El último godo' and the Dynamics of the Urdrama."* Preface by John E. Keller.	$27.50
32.	*En torno al hombre y a sus monstruos: ensayos críticos sobre la novelística de Carlos Rojas,* editados por Cecilia Castro Lee y C. Christopher Soufas, Jr.	$31.50
33.	J. Thomas O'Connell, *Mount Zion Field.*	$24.50
34.	Francisco Delicado, *Portrait of Lozana: The Lusty Andalusian Woman.* Translation, introduction and notes by Bruno M. Damiani.	$45.50
35.	Elizabeth Sullam, *Out of Bounds.* Foreword by Michael G. Cooke.	$23.50
36.	Sergio Corsi, *Il "modus digressivus" nella "Divina Commedia."*	$28.75
37.	Juan Bautista Avalle-Arce, *Lecturas (Del temprano Renacimiento a Valle Inclán).*	$28.50
38.	Rosendo Díaz-Peterson, *Las novelas de Unamuno.* Prólogo de Antonio Carreño.	$30.00
39.	Jeanne Ambrose, *Syntaxe Comparative Français-Anglais.*	$29.50
40.	Nancy Marino, *La serranilla española: notas para su historia e interpretación.*	$28.75.
41.	Carolyn Kreiter-Kurylo, *Contrary Visions.* Preface by Peter Klappert.	$24.50
42.	Giorgio Perissinotto, *Reconquista y literatura medieval: cuatro ensayos.*	$29.50
43.	Rick Wilson, *Between a Rock and a Heart Place.*	$25.00

44. *Feminine Concerns in Contemporary Spanish Fiction by Women.* Edited by Roberto C. Manteiga, Carolyn Galerstein and Kathleen McNerney. $35.00
45. Pierre L. Ullman, *A Contrapuntal Method For Analyzing Spanish Literature.* $41.50
46. Richard D. Woods, *Spanish Grammar and Culture Through Proverbs.* $35.00
47. David G. Burton, *The Legend of Bernardo del Carpio. From Chronicle to Drama.* Preface by John Lihani. $30.00
48. Godwin Okebaram Uwah, *Pirandellism and Samuel Beckett's Plays.* $28.00
49. *Italo-Hispanic Literary Relations,* ed. J. Helí Hernández. $33.00
50. *Studies in Honor of Elias Rivers,* eds. Bruno M. Damiani and Ruth El Saffar. $30.00
51. *Discourse Studies in Honor of James L. Kinneavy,* ed. Rosalind J. Gabin. $45.00
52. John Guzzardo, *Textual History and the "Divine Comedy."* $40.50
53. Cheryl Brown Rush, *Circling Home.* Foreword by Sen. Eugene McCarthy. $24.50
54. Melinda Lehrer, *Classical Myth and the "Polifemo" of Góngora.* $39.50
55. Anne Thompson, *The Generation of '98: Intellectual Politicians.* $41.50
56. Salvatore Paterno, *The Liturgical Context of Early European Drama.* Preface by Lawrence Klibbe. $38.50
57. Maria Cecilia Ruiz, *Literatura y política: el "Libro de los estados" y el "Libro de las armas" de Don Juan Manuel.* Prólogo por Diego Catalán. $37.50
58. James P. Gilroy, *Prévost's Mentors: The Master-Pupil Relationship in the Major Novels of the Abbé Prévost.* $39.95
59. *A Critical Edition of Juan Diamante's "La reina María Estuarda,"* by Michael G. Paulson and Tamara Alvarez-Detrell. $44.50
60. David Craig, *Like Taxes: Marching Through Gaul.* Preface by Howard McCord. $21.50
61. M. Cecilia Colombi, *Los refranes en el "Quijote": texto y contexto.* Prólogo por Juan Bautista Avalle-Arce. $40.50
62. *"La mística ciudad de Dios"* (1670). Edition and Study by Augustine M. Esposito, O.S.A. $36.50
63. Salvatore Calomino, *From Verse to Prose: the Barlaam and Josaphat Legend in 15th Century Germany.* $50.00
64. Gene Fendt, *Works of Love? Reflections on Works of Love.* $37.50
65. Michael Zappala, *Lucian of Samosata in the Two Hesperias: An Essay in Literary and Cultural Translation.* $49.50
66. Oscar Bonifaz, *Remembering Rosario: A Personal Glimpse into the Life and Works of Rosario Castellanos.* Translated and Edited by Myralyn F. Allgood. Prologue by Oscar Bonifaz. Foreword by Edward D. Terry. $27.50

67. *Other Voices: Essays on Italian Regional Culture and Language.* Ed. John Staulo. $35.50
68. Mario Aste, *Grazia Deledda: Ethnic Novelist.* $38.50
69. Edward C. Lynskey, *The Tree Surgeon's Gift.* Foreword by Fred Chappell. $22.50
70. Henry Thurston-Griswold, *El idealismo sintético de Juan Valera.* Prólogo por Lee Fontanella. $44.50
71. Mechthild Cranston, *Laying Ways.* Preface by Germaine Brée. $26.50
72. Roy A. Kerr, *Mario Vargas Llosa: Critical Essays on Characterization.* $43.50
73. Eduardo Urbina, *Principios y fines del "Quijote".* $45.00
74. Pilar Moyano, *Fernando Villalón: El poeta y su obra.* Prólogo por Luis Monguió. $46.50
75. Diane Hartunian, *La Celestina: A Feminist Reading of the "carpe diem" Theme.* $45.50
76. Victoria Urbano, *Sor Juana Inés de la Cruz: amor, poesía, soledumbre.* Edición y prólogo de Adelaida López de Martínez. $43.50
77. Magda Graniela-Rodríguez, *El papel del lector en la novela mexicana contemporánea: José Emilio Pacheco y Salvador Elizondo.* $46.50
78. Robert L. Sims, *El primer García Márquez: un estudio de su periodismo de 1948-1955.* $48.00
79. Zelda Irene Brooks, *Poet, Mystic, Modern Hero: Fernando Rielo Pardal.* $49.50
80. *La Celestina.* Edición, introducción y notas by Bruno M. Damiani. $45.00

BOOK ORDERS

* Clothbound. *All book orders,* except library orders, must be prepaid and addressed to **Scripta Humanistica**, 1383 Kersey Lane, Potomac, Maryland 20854. *Manuscripts* to be considered for publication should be sent to the same address.